Teaching Teachers

The Faculty of Education University of Toronto 1906 – 1996

Edited by

David W. Booth
and
Suzanne M. Stiegelbauer

Published by

Caliburn Enterprises Inc.

Dedication

For Associate Dean Anne Millar
who has supported us
and encouraged us
on so much of the journey

Acknowledgments

We wish to acknowledge the following members of the educational community for their support in this project:

UNITE: for their grant that allowed for the development of this book,

the library staff at the Faculty of Education, University of Toronto, who cheerfully assisted the editors and authors in locating resources and information,

the administrative staff of the Faculty of Education, University of Toronto, who, while working in the background, contributed to and encouraged the writing of this book,

Diane Granato for coordinating the authors and their essays.

Caliburn Enterprises Inc.
86 Auchmar Rd.
Hamilton, ON
L9C 1C5
(905) 575-3122

ISBN 0-9699967-2-1

Contents

Foreword *Michael Fullan* i

Introduction *David W. Booth* *Suzanne M. Stiegelbauer* ix

Part I A Centre for Learning and Teaching

1. A Personal History of the Faculty of Education 2
John MacDonald

2. Towards a Philosophy of Change 26
Suzanne M. Stiegelbauer

3. The Multicultural Experience: Teacher Education, Schools, and Communities 50
Keith McLeod

4. Who Are the New Teachers? 76
Suzanne M. Stiegelbauer
Gary Hunt

Part II The Practice of Teaching

5. Teachers Learning and Growing Together 103
Carol Hennessy

6. Planned Change in Schools: A Focus for Preservice Teacher Education 116
Robert Martin

7. Teacher Education and the Secondary Schools 134
Don Galbraith
Annette Yeager

8. The Role of the Arts in Education 147
Natalie Kuzmich
John Emerson
Chuck Lundy

Part III Communities of Inquiry

9. The Faculty Development Group Initiative — 167
Mary Beattie

10. The Joint Centre for Teacher Development: The Freshness of Transformation — 177
C.T. Patrick Diamond

11. Five Personal Models for Professional Growth — 184
David W. Booth

12. The Role of Research in a Faculty of Education — 202
Nancy Watson

Part IV Partnerships in Teacher Education

13. A Collaborative Partnership with the Field — 222
Ethne Erskine-Cullen

14. Partnership and Program Renewal: Moving Forward — 238
Carol Rolheiser

15. Learning to Teach Inside the Classroom — 258
Jill Lloyd-Jones
Frances Fagan

16. The FEUT-Aga Khan University Partnership — 277
Ian Hundey

Part V A Century of Images

17. The Faculty in Photography, 1906–1996 — 293
Gerald Whyte

References — 304

Foreword

Michael Fullan

Reflections on Changing a College of Education

Michael Fullan is the dean of the newly formed Ontario Institute for Studies in Education, University of Toronto. An innovator and leader in teacher education, he has developed a number of partnerships designed to bring about major school improvement and educational reform. He participates as researcher, consultant, trainer, and policy advisor on a wide range of educational change projects with school systems, teachers' federations, research and development institutes, and government agencies in Canada and internationally. In June 1990, as the first recipient of the Canadian Association of Teacher Educators (CATE) Award of Excellence, he was recognized for "outstanding contribution to his profession and to teacher education" and was seen as a "researcher/scholar/practitioner of the highest calibre" by that organization. He has published widely on the topic of educational reform including Change Forces *and* The New Meaning of Educational Change.

The chapters in this book will provide detail about the nature and processes of reform at the Faculty of Education, University of Toronto (FEUT). I have written elsewhere about the role of the dean in changing colleges of education (Fullan, 1996), and Stiegelbauer's chapter in this book captures some of these perspectives.

On reflection, two basic things are important for transforming colleges of education. One is to make the change in the culture "explicit" as you work on it; related is the matter of developing and deepening ownership to the new way of doing things so that it has a stronger chance of continuing beyond the initial group.

We started the reform period in 1987-88, and quickly became involved in new faculty hiring and pilot program innovations. There was not a great deal of advance planning and development beyond the identification of some guiding principles such as: work on the teacher-education continuum; link teacher development to school improvement; establish field-based programs in partnership with schools; and engage in constant inquiry. Once we became immersed in these early attempts at reform, I wrote a fable, The Best Faculty of Education in the Country. I wrote this to make more explicit what I thought people were and should be working on. The ideas were as much a reflection of some of the new things we were doing as they were a normative guide for the future. The fable, with its ten characteristics, follows.

The Best Faculty of Education in the Country
A Fable

This is a short story about an institution called Central Faculty of Education that set out to be the best it could. Two points of context are crucial. First, despite a long association with a university, Central to this day has not become a vital part of the institution. It became a faculty in 1972, signaling the end of direct funding and governance by the Ministry of Education, but almost immediately entered a period of stagnation from 1974 to 1988. Second, Central has not been seen as a leader by other educational constituencies—school boards, teacher federations, and ministries. The 1990s represents the first full-fledged opportunity for an education faculty in Ontario to become both a leader at a university and in the educational field. But it cannot do so alone; teacher education is a university-wide responsibility. We pick up the story a couple of years after Central began working on this goal.

The staff at Central decided to identify the smallest number of interrelated themes that would make it the best faculty of education. The irony of their situation had become increasingly evident: as teacher educators, they were supposed to be the best teachers of all; as university professors, to be on the leading edge of creating and developing knowledge and good practices; and as advocates of innovation and reform for the school system, to have their own house in order. They decided to see what would happen if they set out to become the best faculty in terms of teaching, inquiry, and innovation. They developed a manifesto that included ten themes that would serve as standards toward which the Faculty would strive. Specifically, it concluded that the best faculty of education in the country should:

Commit itself to producing teachers who are agents of educational and social improvement

As it worked on becoming the best, Central discovered a curious inconsistency. On the one hand, the educational experience of student teachers was essentially conservative and inhibited innovation and risk taking. On the other, society continually introduced and expected restructuring, reform, and innovation. Trying to juxtapose these competing themes, Central realized, was a recipe for failure.

A breakthrough arrived when a group examined why Faculty candidates applied to become teachers. Most hoped to make a difference in the lives of students, a purpose that had changed over the past 100 years when teaching was associated with only passing on the traditions of society. It became clear that faculties of education had to produce teachers who could help to improve society and the lives of students.

Commit itself to continuous improvement

In its first few years of new development, the entire program underwent change, but not uniformly. Central established a series of alternative programs involving groups of student teachers, faculty, and school personnel. Each team designed its own program for the year based on common principles (e.g., inquiry, reflection, and collaboration) and common components. Typically, students worked two days a week in schools and three in seminars designed to integrate theory and practice.

As the graduate studies program grew, the curriculum became more focused on themes: some, such as mathematics and arts education, were subject-related while others, like global education and early childhood, were interdisciplinary. Central considered these studies a continuum to and no more important than its bachelor of education program.

Value and practise exemplary teaching

While it had always been assumed that teaching was important at Central, recent declarations by the president and provost about the university's priority to improve teaching created a vague uneasiness that the Faculty should be leading the way. Central decided to put itself on the line publicly and declare that it would stand for exemplary teaching and develop mechanisms to ensure continuous improvement. Every Faculty member joined a small study group that sought to improve the teaching and support development of those in the group, as well as consult with students to enrich classroom experiences. The best teachers were called upon to conduct workshops on teaching methods.

Engage in constant inquiry

Excellent teaching by itself was not seen as the Faculty's main goal. For teaching to develop, it had to be embedded in a spirit of inquiry and knowledge about teaching. In the past, teaching and scholarship had sometimes been viewed as working at cross purposes, but with its new image, Central was committed to the synergy of both. It conceived "inquiry" as consisting of a dynamic relationship of use, production, and dissemination of knowledge. In so doing, it became committed to the sharing and testing of its work.

Central became aware that if students as teachers were expected to be inquirers, Faculty members had a dual responsibility—to present themselves as models of inquiry for students and to help student teachers become better inquirers.

Model and develop lifelong learning among staff and students

Central became aware that in another area—lifelong learning—students were likely to develop habits and practices similar to Faculty members. It therefore incorporated Faculty development into its policy and practices. When new teaching staff were hired, for example, selection criteria stressed inquiry and collaboration. It established support systems such as Faculty development study groups for teaching, research, field work, service work in the Faculty, and university and career development. Central ensured that certain university policies—merit salary awards, promotion, and tenure, for example—promoted Faculty development.

Model and develop collaboration among staff and students

The ability for teachers to collaborate was increasingly being advocated in the teaching profession. Yet there was nothing in Central's program or in student teachers' past academic experiences that fostered these skills. Thus, when it designed new programs, they were built on the principles of joint planning, team teaching, and collaboration among students and Faculty members.

Be respected and engaged as a vital part of the university as a whole

The university had always valued scholarship and publication, and had seen the Faculty as lacking in that regard. Central's new pursuit of scholarship through innovative field work and research on effective teaching methods clearly met university goals. Since field-based teacher development had increasingly been seen by other institutions as the way to go, the university enjoyed the international recognition that the Faculty received for being in the vanguard of these new developments.

Although the university had frequently talked of the value of teaching, in practice, teaching had not been rewarded. Thus the university watched with interest when the Faculty, in conjunction with professional schools and certain arts and science departments, established a small number of joint projects that worked on the development of innovative teaching practices.

It helped to establish cooperative teacher education projects with arts and science departments, thus increasing both the quality and quantity of teacher candidates.

Form partnerships with schools and other agencies

Since Central realized that teacher education could succeed only if it maintained the teacher education continuum and if schools became places for teachers as well as for students to learn, it realized that both the university and the school system must combine and coordinate their efforts.

New developments occurred with Central's two lab schools. The schools became involved with school boards and other agencies in teacher education and program development experiments and became leading authorities on policy, program, and evaluation issues within their areas of expertise.

Be visible and valued internationally in a way that contributes locally and globally

Central felt it could not develop fully unless it was immersed in the world marketplace of ideas, problems, development, and people. It established projects and exchanges overseas, many of which included Ontario school boards.

Work collaboratively to help develop provincial and national networks.

Central became committed to sharing its ideas and programs with other faculties of education, to learning from others, and to fostering a network of deans and faculties in the province to examine and debate emerging policy issues. It appreciated and valued its provincial and national relationships because it saw its own fate and quality as deeply connected to the quality of the overall system.

As Central reflected on its current and future state, it did become, at least momentarily, self-satisfied. Practicing all ten themes synergistically seemed economical, productive, and deeply meaningful. For once, the future seemed better than the past.

*

Broadening the Base

In our educational reform work, I have come to call the process of changing the culture of the organization "the process of reculturing." So, the fable and other continuous actions and reflections we engaged in the Faculty in the period of 1988 to 1995 were increasingly a matter of making the nature and processes of reculturing explicit.

Part and parcel of these expenditures is the question of whether ownership spreads and becomes deeper. Broadening the ownership base is critical for substance and sustenance. This development was enhanced by several strategies or activities that I have described elsewhere (Fullan, 1996). They include:

- faculty renewal (continuing to hire and support faculty involved in new directions),
- program innovation (the expansion of innovation involving more and more faculty),
- program review and policy making (consolidating new learning by conducting whole-program reviews and forming new policies covering all programs),
- local field-based partnerships (which provide mechanisms, pressure, and support to work on new initiatives),
- international networks and projects (which provide wider opportunities to build on and strengthen new directions),
- internal and external inquiry, communication, and dissemination (engaging in internal inquiry, reflection, and sharing through ongoing groups and periodic presentations; committing to external dissemination through writing, conferences, videos, training, workshops, and so on).

The goal of these interrelated strategies is to foster mobilization and positive contagion. It is only when the majority of faculty are engaged in the new directions that we can consider that the changes have a chance of becoming institutionalized, and that there is a degree of self-generation established.

There are still a number of key issues unresolved at FEUT involving such matters as: consistency of program and curriculum across cohorts; lack of systemic knowledge of the learning outcomes of graduating teacher education students; equity and nature of workload among faculty. At the same time, we are in a better position to address these problems.

In conclusion, faculties of education have generally neglected to turn their reform agendas inward. The internal transformation of faculties of education is a necessary (and neglected) component of the larger issue of educational reform. Making this transformation explicit, engaging in reculturing, and broadening the ownership base are all key ingredients for faculties of education of the future.

Introduction

> Changing the culture of schools—what they do and how they do it—is the real agenda.
>
> (Fullan & Hargreaves, 1992)

Teaching Teachers: The Faculty of Education, University of Toronto tells the story of an institution that spans almost a century of teacher education in Toronto, Canada. The authors of the articles are educators who have been connected with the Faculty of Education during the last thirty years, some who have worked there for most of their teaching careers, others who have recently become involved in teacher education. It is a collection of ideas, essays, stories, perspectives, narratives, histories, and philosophies by deans, professors, lecturers, researchers, associate teachers, and student teachers. These articles represent the complex nature of this centre devoted to educating teachers in both preservice and inservice programs, struggling to prepare them for working in schools amid the changes in culture and society, practice and theory, and curriculum and instruction.

The preparation of teachers has been one of the most debated educational endeavours of the last decade. As the need for teachers has declined, and as the student population has become more diverse, the process of teacher education has been challenged to take on new dimensions. Whether the program is one or two years in length, concurrent or post- B.A., field- or university-based, the dilemmas remain the same—how to provide the kind of education that will support lifelong learners, as well as meet the needs of a changing populace. As yet there are no hard and fast answers.

This book concerns one faculty of education, and its attempts to address those questions. It is really two books: one, an academic case study of change with the theoretical and actual issues that might present; and two, a personal document depicting events in the lives of participants that affected them deeply. In describing this organization's efforts for improvement, it is important to acknowledge what is true of any organization—that it includes many different people, with particular talents and a variety of roles to fulfill. Each has something significant to contribute, both as an individual, and as a member of an organizational system. What you will meet in this book are their individual voices and their emerging collective vision.

Studies of change often remark on the resistance of individuals and the difficulty of creating a shared vision. While this is often true, what might be more important is the process by which individuals come to share their common goals—something this book aims to capture.

There are a number of conceptual themes that cut across all chapters. The first is the theme of what an organizational process related to change is really about. Larry Cuban (1988) makes a distinction between what he calls first-order and second-order changes: first-order changes address the more superficial elements of the system, while second-order changes go deeper—to the very structure of the organization and how people work together. These latter ones can be risky; they are usually multifaceted, involving many different elements at once, slower, and involve changing attitudes, perceptions, behaviours, relationships, and the way people collaborate around issues. They are not about the implementation of new methods, but the required renewal and growth of a system to develop the capacity for change. Many of the chapters we have included comment on how this kind of renewal works, and also on its slowness, and its constantly changing nature.

A second theme concerns the approach taken to change itself. In support of the ideals of experimentation and continuous learning as the foundation for change, organizational guidelines were developed by administration and staff in the form of open-ended "images" rather than specific objectives. How individuals and teams interpreted these images, and how they refined them over time, are again common threads.

Another theme involves the use of what Matt Miles (1992) calls in his review of the phenomena of change "temporary systems or groups," or the power of individuals in collaboration with one another to solve problems and create new modes of working. The Toronto Faculty of Education's "options" are one type of temporary group, where members work together to develop an experimental strategy for a set of teacher candidates in a specific field context. As these chapters reveal, the structural importance of these groups for interaction and support for change cannot be stressed enough. To the individual, they provide support for new ideas; to the system, they provide the structure for experimentation and for the refinement of new strategies.

Finally, an overarching theme is about learning. Throughout these discussions, individuals talk about creating a culture that is responsive to changing needs and situations; that is, they talk about learning to be better educators, better educational partners, becoming flexible in the face of new opportunities, and occasionally, new limitations. In many ways "just doing it" proved to individuals that they were capable of changing; that they can learn and apply something new. It seems simple, but for institutions and their participants, developing the capacity for organizational learning is no small challenge.

The foreword by current Dean Michael Fullan establishes the tone for the book. Dr. Fullan presents his vision for what a faculty of education can become, through what he calls "A Fable." This sets the stage for the five sections that follow, describing the history and background at the Faculty of Education, University of Toronto (FEUT), from its inception in 1906 to the merger with the Ontario Institute for Studies in Education in 1996 (the new OISE/UT). They also present the different elements of work at FEUT—curriculum development, school issues, research and inquiry, and partnerships with the greater educational community.

Part I. A Centre for Learning and Teaching describes the participants, the history and the philosophies guiding the growth of FEUT. Former Dean John MacDonald's chapter presents the history of the Faculty of Education from its beginning in 1906 (just after Alberta and Saskatchewan joined the Confederation) to the current day. Suzanne Stiegelbauer's dialogue with Dean Michael Fullan begins the discussion of the philosophical underpinnings of change at FEUT, interwoven with her personal reflections as a new professor in the Faculty. She presents Dean Fullan's ideas of "ready-fire-aim" as a strategy guiding action toward change. Keith McLeod examines how issues of diversity, multiculturalism, and discrimination shaped his personal and professional life at the Faculty, and set agendas for the Department of Educational Foundations. Gary Hunt and Suzanne Stiegelbauer then describe the teacher candidates at FEUT—who they are and what they want from the teacher education experience. Included in this chapter is a description of life at FEUT from the students' perspective.

Part II. The Practice of Teaching addresses specific areas of curriculum that are part of the instructional life of FEUT. Bob Martin and Carol Hennessy, as coordinators of elementary "options," each with a slightly different focus, depict the emergence of these "options," or program choices, their rationale, and their links to field partners. Don Galbraith and Annette Yeager describe how the secondary education curriculum has changed as a department, from a "secondary school-like" model to one operating from a diverse but cohesive intellectual core. They also discuss the nature of alternative programs at this level and their relationship to models presented in the elementary options. Finally, Natalie Kuzmich, John Emerson, and Chuck Lundy talk about the role and importance of the arts in education, focusing on changes, dilemmas, and responses to social and governmental concerns. As Kuzmich states, "What is yet to come is the full recognition of arts learning and its effectiveness in the education of the mind. These touch on shaping a curriculum to help the new teachers do that, a curriculum that now includes knowledge of using the arts as a teaching tool for all teachers, not just specialists."

Part III. Communities of Inquiry talks about another significant element of university life, that of research and faculty development. Because research is an essential part of work at the university level, and because preservice activities are so time intensive, research activities at FEUT required special supports. Nancy Watson describes some of these supports and how the Faculty addresses research questions given personal and institutional interests. Mary Beattie presents the activities and perspectives of the Faculty Development Group Initiative, a collaborative project designed to survey the needs of FEUT faculty and find cooperative ways to present information, develop support networks, and meet those needs. Patrick Diamond talks about another way of working together, for both teaching and research. Through the Joint Centre for Teacher Development, faculty at FEUT and OISE work within the preservice–inservice continuum to provide a perspective on teacher education that considers it as "continuous learning." David Booth concludes this section with his personal, alternative models for professional growth, through his connections with schools, teachers, and children.

Part IV. Partnerships in Teacher Education illustrates the value of external partnerships in supporting and promoting an educational process. Carol Rolheiser chronicles her experience as professor, program head, and facilitator of FEUT's new two-year collaborative project. In Partnership and Program Renewal: Moving Forward, she describes her developing relationships with school boards and schools, initially through the Learning Consortium, and later through a school-based preservice program.

Ethne Erskine-Cullen focuses on the Learning Consortium itself, outlining its development, progress, and goals. Associate teachers are essential partners in the preservice process and insights about their significance are shared by Jill Lloyd-Jones and Frances Fagan. Ian Hundey concludes this section with a description of the FEUT-Aga Khan University Partnership, a project designed to share information and training at an international level. This partnership has as its goal the training of teachers in Pakistan through the exchange of professors and teacher candidates in three institutions—FEUT, Oxford University in London, and Aga Khan University in Karachi, Pakistan. Each of these chapters presents a different kind of relationship, and describes the possibilities in education, and the variety of ways that preservice, inservice, and ongoing faculty development can be addressed.

Part V. A Century of Images, collected by Gerald Whyte, illustrates how FEUT has altered over the near century of its existence. The book ends with this photo essay revealing how life at the Faculty of Education has changed over the years—in dress, attitude, and activities.

In presenting these authors in this variety of formats, we are trying to encompass all of the dimensions of FEUT, while at the same time acknowledging the value and uniqueness of each of the participants. The Faculty of Education at the University of Toronto will shortly become part of a new organization, OISE/UT, which will include preservice, inservice, graduate studies, research and field development, and a variety of partnerships and collaborations. We wanted to compile these chapters to document an era of teacher education, but we also wanted to provide some insights into the workings of faculties of education, whatever their form, and examine how this one in particular struggled with difficult questions. As this merger moves forward, we do not feel we will loose the ground gained, but rather we will have an energy and a mandate to take on an even more complex agenda—the combination and interrelationship of learning for those engaged in programs both at the undergraduate and graduate levels, preservice and inservice, university and in the field. Joining together is the stepping stone. We are ready to take on the future.

Part I

A Centre for Learning and Teaching

A Personal History of the Faculty of Education

John MacDonald was born and educated in Ottawa. Following his year of teacher training at Ontario College of Education and two years teaching high school in Ottawa and at the University of Toronto Schools, he was appointed to the English Department of the Ontario College of Education in 1959. Over his thirty-five-year professional career at Ontario College of Education/Faculty of Education, University of Toronto, Professor MacDonald has held a variety of administrative positions, including Chair of the English department and Dean of FEUT (1981-87). With graduate degrees in English from University of Toronto and in psycholinguistics from Harvard, Professor MacDonald has exercised his long-standing interest in the theory and practice of second language learning and teaching. Having worked on several projects in China for the World Bank, he taught ESL and linguistics at Beijing Normal University (1991-92). Most recently he was visiting professor of Canadian Studies at Kwansei Gakuin University in Kobe, Japan. Newly retired from University of Toronto and busy with a growing family of grandchildren, Professor MacDonald plans to return to Japan in the near future.

The Faculty of Education was established by a resolution of the Board of Governors, University of Toronto in December 1906 as the university's professional school of education, and having as its major function the training of teachers for the Ontario Department of Education. Its first intake of 215 teacher candidates was in October 1907.

To place this new institution in a broader national context, it might be informative to consider some historical milestones that were contemporaneous with its inception. In 1906, the year of its official incorporation, Roald Amundsen in the schooner Gjoa was the first to find his way through the Northwest Passage to the Pacific. That same year saw the incorporation of the Hydro-Electric Power Commission of Ontario, with Sir Adam Beck as its first chairperson. Ontario Hydro, as it came to be known, was one of the most significant services that led to the rapid development of the whole manufacturing industry in the province. In 1907, the Royal Alexandra Theatre opened in Toronto and Tom Longboat, an Onondaga from the Six Nations Reserve, won the Boston Marathon in record time. In 1905, the provinces of Saskatchewan and Alberta joined Confederation, thus realizing the continental dream of Canada stretching "a mare usque ad marem." Sir Wilfred Laurier was then prime minister of Canada, in which office he would remain until his defeat in the election of 1911 over the issue of "free trade" (reciprocity) with the United States. In Ontario, the Tories under Premier Whitney following their election in 1905 were beginning their relatively uninterrupted dominance of the political landscape for much of the twentieth century. The population of Ontario in 1906-07 was less than 2.5 million, with Toronto as its capital numbering under 300 000 people. The population breakdown between urban and rural dwellers was roughly fifty-fifty. The province was rapidly leaving behind its pioneering history as it began to change from a resource-based economy (lumber, mining) to an industrial and commercial magnet for the rest of the country.

At the turn of the century when our history actually begins, there were 130 secondary schools employing 568 teachers established in Ontario (as opposed to 5 654 public schools staffed by 8 321 elementary teachers). Although only a minority of children could aspire to a secondary school education (and most of those were located in major urban centres), the secondary school system had developed sufficiently to warrant attention from the Department of Education with respect to the training and certification of the teachers working in these secondary schools. For much of the latter nineteenth century, a university degree was considered ample preparation for teaching in the few collegiate institutes then in existence. But the numbers of secondary schools and staff had increased sufficiently that by 1897 the Department of Education felt the need to establish the Ontario Normal College, which it located in Hamilton. The college, which operated between 1897 and 1907, was clearly modelled on the normal school pattern which had already proved its usefulness in the training of elementary school teachers. The Ontario Normal College enrolled two different types of candidates: those who had completed five years of secondary school (honours matriculation); and those who possessed a university degree. Upon graduation, those with five years of secondary school education received a First-Class Certificate, valid for teaching in both elementary and secondary schools; those with a university degree were awarded an Ordinary or

Specialist High School Certificate. When the Faculty of Education was established in 1907 at the University of Toronto to replace the Normal College in Hamilton, the new Faculty maintained the dual role of training teachers for both elementary and secondary schools (alongside the system of normal schools, which continued to train elementary school teachers only).

The principal reason for moving the training of secondary school teachers from Hamilton to Toronto was to locate the enterprise within the context of a university setting. The emerging conventional wisdom of the time, both within the Department of Education and the University of Toronto, favoured the location of formal educational studies inside the academic umbrella of the university. Initially, the feeling seemed to be that cohabitation would somehow elevate, or at least add academic legitimacy to, the fledgling discipline of educational studies. Certainly there was enough widespread support for this move toward university inclusion to prompt the administration at Queen's University in Kingston to lobby the government to establish simultaneously a faculty of education within its university. The rosy rhetoric of the day in support of teacher training within the university milieu while intellectually plausible, even admirable, was never carefully thought through. What happened, of course, was that a normal school model directly funded and largely managed by the Department of Education would never sit comfortably within a university environment, which failed to control, much less set, the standards for its operation. This discomforting lack of "fit" may well have motivated the closing of the Faculty of Education at Queen's in 1920 and the simultaneous transformation of the Faculty at the University of Toronto into what survived for almost five decades as the Ontario College of Education (OCE). It may be symbolic in significance to recall that when the new building for the Faculty of Education in Toronto was built in 1910, it was located at the farthest reaches in the northwest corner of the university campus. History over the succeeding decades would confirm the obvious—that "cohabitation" (however distant) would not necessarily result in the kind of hoped-for intellectual synergy originally envisioned by all parties when the Faculty was first established in 1907.

It is interesting to note the way in which the new Faculty of Education moved in 1907 to accommodate its program of teacher training to a relatively unfamiliar university environment. What the fledgling Faculty did was to rework the curriculum model inherited from the older facility in Hamilton. The Faculty of Education's program of study bristled with content that must have proved daunting to the readers of its inaugural calendar. Schematically arrayed, the preservice course of study looked like the following:

Part I General Course

- history of education and educational systems
- principles of education
- elementary and applied psychology
- school administration and school law
- school management
- general methods
- special methods in all five of:
  English, history, geography, mathematics, Latin
- special methods in one of:
  French and German,
  Greek and French,
  Greek and German,
  biology, physics, chemistry, and mineralogy.

Part II

- professional and academic review of the content of elementary and secondary school curricula:
  nature study, health, reading, English grammar, social studies, and geography.

Part III

- classroom observation for fifty school periods (requiring reports), practice teaching for twenty school periods in different cooperating elementary and secondary schools.

In addition to the above, for university graduates holding specialization in a particular secondary school discipline, there were special provisions for candidates for diplomas as specialists—similar to those seminars held for what later became known as Type A Specialists.

This calendar description is given here for reasons other than mere antiquarian interest. First, it demonstrates the strategy adopted by this new Faculty to cram into a one-year preservice timetable an array of courses that by sheer weight of numbers could not be anything but trivial in content. Quantity might give the appearance of academic credibility, whereas in fact it had the reverse effect by adulterating quality. Stitched together in less than ten months, this brainchild of the Department of Education duly passed by the Governing Council of the University of Toronto without comment, became a pattern which, with minor revision, existed for over half a century. The preservice teacher education program of 1907 looks suspiciously similar to the one I experienced as a teacher candidate in 1956-57.

The Faculty of Education at the University of Toronto survived for only thirteen years between 1907 and 1920. During this first stage in its history, the Faculty trained teachers for both the elementary and secondary schools. Only about one-quarter of the student body held degrees (fewer in fact during World War I), the rest having an honours matriculation from secondary school after five years of study. The fact that three-quarters of these students had only a high school education may explain in some measure the amount of time spent in reviewing the academic content of the elementary and secondary school curricula. The program of course work as previously outlined must have been a brutal wake-up call for many of these eighteen-year-old student candidates. What a faculty of education at the University of Toronto was doing training candidates who themselves had only a secondary school honours matriculation diploma became an increasingly embarrassing question. Thus, in 1920, the Department of Education moved to change admission requirements substantially by restricting enrollment to candidates who possessed a valid university degree, and changed the name from the Faculty of Education to the Ontario College of Education. So, "what's in a name" change? In actual fact quite a lot.

The 1920 agreement between the minister of education and the University of Toronto returned control of OCE to the ministry in all important respects. The ministry retained the "right not only to grant certificates but also to approve the content of courses, approve the appointment of all instructors in certificate courses, inspect the work of the college and approve and control the budget of the college in detail." The Ontario College of Education, from 1920 to 1967, was to remain fully under the control of the Ministry of Education. Its isolation from the rest of the University of Toronto was to be complete—not only in a geographic sense, but also in an intellectual and academic sense. The brave hopes voiced at its inauguration in 1907 were not to be realized until 1973, when it became once again a faculty of education within the University of Toronto and fully subject to the policies and procedures of the university. So, for almost fifty years, teacher training for secondary school teachers in Ontario remained under the de facto control of the Department of Education. Because it held a monopoly in the training of secondary school teachers throughout most of this fifty-year period, OCE became the object of much external criticism that tended to stereotype the institution as an anti-intellectual bastion of conservative mediocrity. OCE was, in all respects, a sitting duck throughout most of its history to this kind of criticism. Perhaps the most forceful voicing of external criticism was made by Stephen Lewis in the Ontario Legislature, April 28, 1964, when he characterized OCE "as the last refuge of the undecided... with a high school atmosphere dominated by regimentation... . The building, he goes on, is a study in depression—it is bleak, overcrowded... cramped and desolate." In practice teaching, "student teachers... are expected to be noncritical... and non-analytical." OCE, he concluded, "breeds an anti-intellectual atmosphere." This catalogue of weaknesses was voiced in the provincial legislature by a then-young politician and social critic, who in later years would go on to serve with distinction as Canada's representative to the United Nations. Leaving aside the political partisanship that partly motivated this speech, how much of this stereotype reflected the reality of life at OCE throughout its almost fifty-year history?

In many ways OCE was the victim of circumstances beyond its internal control. Staff appointments were made by the Ministry of Education and only noted by the Governing Council of the University (no search committee procedures were in effect in those times). The program of studies was mandated by the ministry along lines that became familiar to generations of teachers—practice teaching, foundational studies in the history, philosophy, sociology, psychology, and school management of education, accompanied by courses in the methodology of teaching in two or three secondary school subjects. Many student teachers, freshly graduated from the (sometimes) intellectually challenging environment of university, found the preservice year of teacher training a less than stimulating experience. Some of these student teachers were psychologically unprepared for the reality of classroom teaching and mistook the life of schools for the experience of university. Clearly many were disappointed if they anticipated the preservice year program to rise to the expectations of postgraduate studies in education. Obviously the root of the problem often rested in the clash between student teachers' expectations and the practical reality of teacher training (at least as envisioned by the Ministry of Education). The "normal school" model and its mentality may have served well the training of elementary school teachers without degrees (although that is debatable), but it sat rather uncomfortably on the shoulders of many prospective secondary school teachers freshly graduated from university.

But reality is always more complicated, and hence more interesting, than stereotype, and in one important sense there was nothing stereotypical about OCE between the two world wars—and that was its faculty. The teaching faculty of OCE during this period comprised an array of individuals and characters reminiscent of a Robertson Davies novel. Some were Dickensian in breadth and spirit. They were all males of course (except for the obligatory and quite exceptional women in home economics and women's physical education) loyalist in temperament, politically conservative, but often iconoclastic in matters of education and classroom practice. J.O. ("Jock") Carlisle, professor of Latin, had a withering acerbic tongue, altogether suitable to the boys he had taught at the University of Toronto Schools before joining the staff at OCE. Peter Sandiford, who taught educational psychology, was an engaging and liberal thinker who challenged his students' often narrow views. Professor G.M. Jones and his successor B.C. Diltz in English broadened many beginning teachers' views on English education. Diltz, in particular, placed great emphasis on the Socratic method as a means of opening students' minds to the joy of literary exploration. His more than twenty books on teaching and school anthologies laid down an approach that later assumed the position of orthodoxy in the classrooms of the province. He was a spectacular and original teacher, difficult to imitate, but easily parodied by generations of less gifted teachers. J.T. Crawford, professor of methods in mathematics, was said to have had no equal in his time. A.G. Croal, professor in science, wrote the standard textbook in biology for Ontario schools. Les Bell, in music, gained national renown as the founder of the Bell Singers, popular on radio during the forties and fifties. Helen Bryans joined the college in 1930 as instructor in women's physical education and was internationally known and respected in her field well beyond the confines of Ontario—she was still performing remarkable feats in the gym when she retired in 1965. And then there was Ruth Dean, home economics (1944-64) who could well have served as the model for Lady Bracknell in The Importance of Being Earnest. Then too there were the various deans of OCE—Packenham (1907-34), Althouse (1934-44), Lewis (1944-58), Diltz (1958-63), and Dadson (1963-73)—none of them scholars in the conventional contemporary sense, but all of them sharing the same virtue of having impeccable connections with the ministers of education in their times. If the deans of OCE were never academic leaders, neither were they administrative tyrants; in fact they tended to allow their staffs considerable latitude in the manner in which they delivered their courses. These deans tended to manage the college with relative benign respect for the talents of the teaching faculty. There was indeed much that was altogether patriarchal about this whole period between 1920 and 1963, both at the college and in society itself.

A patriarchal society, as long as one knows one's position in it, is not always oppressive—it is certainly not revolutionary nor risk taking to be sure, but it can be benign, even to the extent it protects a certain amount of limited individualism. From the student teachers' point of view, it could allow a moderate amount of freedom and nonconformity in matters of teaching style and personal experimentation. As a student teacher, coming into this environment near the end of the OCE period in 1956-57, I found much about the institution that was enjoyable and certainly instructive. True it was still rather too "old-school" in certain respects, such as the monthly teas in the library presided over by the dean's wife and her ladies' auxiliary. But there were also other activities, such as the annual Gilbert and Sullivan operetta, the yearly play, and literary magazine—activities that could occupy more than enough of one's spare time from the careful preparation of well-oiled lessons during practice teaching placements in the secondary schools and collegiates of Toronto. The associate or "critic" teachers in the schools were a lively and varied collection of individuals, who were often stuck in their ways—but often sensibly so. There was at the college and in the practice teaching schools a strong emphasis placed upon teaching as a "craft." The orderly presentation of traditionally packaged instructional material and the mastery (within reason) of the art of questioning reinforced a view of education that was teacher-centred and hierarchical, but also investigative. There was little questioning of broader social issues perhaps, but one did learn a considerable amount about the craft of teaching. Craftsmanship and technique are, after all, very useful skills for a beginning teacher to explore. Craft is neither high art nor does it promote revolutionary change. Craftsmanship is associated with tradition, stability, and is often impervious to change. In traditional societies such as Japan, for instance, "craft" is highly valued in the arts. It provides a comforting sense of permanence and even shared values, and can still be seen today in the practice of traditional Japanese crafts such as the tea ceremony, ikibana (flower arrangement), and hiragami (paper folding). True craftsmanship can even achieve the elevated state of real art, but more often than not it tends toward the preservation of the status quo and traditional values and practices. Teaching is a craft to be sure, a repository of long-proven techniques handed down over generations from teachers of skill and integrity. Perhaps in this sense it shares more with homeopathy than modern medicine, more with tribal lore than with scientific investigation. But the real problem with viewing teaching as a collection of home remedies is that it cannot react quickly to the needs of a society that is in a state of rapid change. By the mid-sixties, Ontario was undergoing a whole series of changes that would soon alter the face of society in ways for which teacher education in the province was totally unprepared.

By the mid-sixties, the once monopolistic control of OCE over the preparation of teachers for Ontario secondary schools had been broken with the establishment of two new faculties of education at Queen's University in Kingston and the University of Western Ontario in London. These two new education faculties not only broke the old OCE monopoly, they also forged new models for the manner in which education faculties would reside within their university environments. No longer would the old OCE model be accepted by the host university—a model that for decades had left OCE as an academic orphan outside the normal procedures of university policy relating to appointments, promotion, and budgetary control. In the new agreements established between the Ministry of Education and Althouse College at Western (1963) and McArthur College at Queen's (1965), considerable authority was given over to the host universities. The formal agreement between the ministry and the University of Toronto that replaced the old OCE with a newly constituted College of Education, University of Toronto (CEUT), was not signed until 1966. It is ironic that the senior teacher education institution in the province should be dealt with last, and this indeed may reflect the rapidity with which it appeared to lose its long-standing place of special privilege. But the reason for its rapid fall from grace had less to do with the creation of two new faculties of education at Western and Queen's than it did with the appearance in 1965 of a brand-new educational research powerhouse in the form of the Ontario Institute for Studies in Education (OISE).

The creation of OISE as the premier research institute in education and the major graduate studies facility for the province not only had the effect of eclipsing the transformed OCE (CEUT), it actually had the almost fatal effect of gutting it. The reason for viewing the creation of OISE as resulting in the amputation of CEUT (later FEUT) is quite simple, since OISE was established very largely by the transfer from the old OCE of its department of graduate studies and research to the new semiautonomous provincial institution, OISE. The Ontario Institute for Studies in Education was to become the major research institute for educational research in the province, and for three decades eclipsed all other education faculties in Ontario. Although it retained affiliated status with the University of Toronto for purposes of granting graduate degrees, it was in all other respects—budgetary, appointments and promotion policies, staffing, and hiring—altogether independent and freestanding. The establishment of OISE left CEUT / FEUT in the unenviable position of being unable to pursue graduate work any longer at the University of Toronto and reduced it to a single role of teacher education. CEUT / FEUT, in a matter of two to three years, became (although still the largest) the most junior of teacher education faculties in the province. And for thirty-one years, the University of Toronto would endure the inexplicable embarrassment of having two separate institutions on campus involved in educational studies—OISE, with its mandate in educational research, graduate studies, and field service along with FEUT with its mandate in teacher education. Thirty-one years of "two solitudes" is difficult to explain even to someone passingly familiar with the curious political machinations of the mid-sixties.

The new agreement between the Ministry of Education and the University of Toronto established an advisory board and a college council for the renamed College of Education, University of Toronto (CEUT). The advisory board to which the dean was responsible included representation from boards of education, various teachers' federations, and the ministry, along with Faculty and university representatives. Its purpose was to serve as a sounding board for and an outreach mechanism to the various stakeholders in public education. The Faculty council, on the other hand, was made up of membership from college faculty, staff, students, and university and teachers' federations. The sixties and early seventies was a period of increasing democratization in higher education, and CEUT was not immune to some of the student protests of the age. It is difficult to realize now that as late as 1963, the authority of the dean was paramount and faculty meetings were rare and informational rather than consultative in tone. But during Dean Dadson's tenure (1963-73), very substantial changes occurred both in internal governance mechanisms and in academic programming. The role of the Faculty council in the planning of programs achieved much greater prominence, and the elaborate system of committees and subcommittees that were established began to rival that of the UN. The result of all this experimentation in committee reporting was to moderate the power of the dean and in some instances slow down the decision-making process itself. Some of the debates in Faculty council (e.g. on merit pay mechanisms) came to rival national constitutional conferences in intensity, but this is the price of democratization. And although the strong influence of high-profile department chairpersons often clashed with those of the administration, deliberations in Faculty council were notable for their civility as well as their intensity. In large measure, this tone of participatory debate and cooperation was due to the moderating leadership of a succession of able chairpersons of Faculty council—persons like George Read (business studies) and Vern Gilbert (educational administration). Faculty council and its many active committees (e.g., program committee) worked well and reflected in many ways the archetypal Canadian tendency toward compromise and consensus.

Two principal factors account for the "reconstruction" and survival of the institution (CEUT / FEUT) after the end of the OCE era and the emergence of OISE in 1966. The first of these was history and location—history, in the sense that OCE had long been identified as the single teacher education training facility for the province and was located in the most densely populated area of the province. That location in the heart of the Golden Horseshoe (Oshawa to Hamilton) provided access to a variety and number of secondary schools that the two newer faculties of education at Queen's and Western could not hope to duplicate. But just as important as location was the second factor—size and range of available teaching options. In fact, the expansion of CEUT / FEUT between 1965 and 1975 in terms of faculty and course offerings was so remarkable that it deserves special comment.

It is easy to forget, or perhaps not realize, that the OCE of the late fifties was not a particularly large institution. One reason for overlooking the small size of its permanent staff is that most prospective teachers in Ontario at that time were being trained in two emergency summer programs rather than at the full one-year program at OCE. In 1956-57, there were only 380 students enrolled in the full-year program, but over 1 250 taking the two-summer program. For over fifteen years, from the mid-fifties to the early seventies, by far the vast majority of teacher candidates were trained for the secondary schools not in the full one-year program but rather in a two-summer crash-study emergency expediency, which devalued the whole purpose of teacher education. It has been estimated that within this fifteen-year period upwards of eighty percent of new secondary school teachers were trained in these "special summer" programs. When these programs were finally closed down, long after the protracted emergency situation had passed, it had the effect of forcing teacher candidates into the full-year programs at faculties of education throughout the province. Nowhere was the increase in full-time enrollment felt more dramatically than at the University of Toronto. And to meet that need, full-time faculty had to be hired at a rate that could only be described today as remarkable.

In 1956-57, the faculty teaching in the three theory areas were three (Pitt in psychology, Skinner in history of education, and Lewis/ Dadson in school law and administration). By 1970-71, the membership in each department had mushroomed astonishingly:

Administration & Program Development:
Nease, Greig, Gilbert, Martin, Sheehan, Wood

Educational Psychology:
Barrett, Dent, Brodeur, Kong, Trott, Tan-Willman, Zimmerman

History, Philosophy, Sociology of Education:
Skinner, Paton, Bancroft, MacIver, Goodenough, McLeod, Stott

The same remarkable increase occurred in all of the teaching subjects. In 1956-57 there was, for instance, one person in the English department (B.C. Diltz) and by 1970-71 there were nine faculty teaching English education in the professorial rank. Similar increases occurred in most other teaching subject areas, each of which in 1956-57 had only one or two faculty members, but by 1970-71 had grown to:

Business and Commerce	6
Mathematics	6
Science	6
Geography	4
History	8
Modern Languages	6
Physical & Health Education	7
Technical & Industrial Arts	14

In addition to this very substantial increase in the teaching faculty of traditional courses, new teaching subjects were introduced within this time frame (1956-70), subjects such as:

Computer Studies
Educational Media
Counselor Education
School Librarianship
Theatre Arts

Most of the hiring of this very large faculty intake occurred during the tenure of Dean Dadson (1963-73), and it all came to a screeching halt by 1974. The very rapid infusion of such a large faculty cohort in the late sixties was to create a considerable problem in the early nineties since the appointment of new faculty could not take place until this very large cohort had worked its way through the system. In other words, orderly faculty renewal and replacement were hampered by an intake, which upon reflection, may well have been precipitous and unwise. The consequence of this atypical hiring pattern was that for fifteen years, between 1974 and 1989, there were virtually no new appointments made at FEUT. The situation was exacerbated by the gradual decrease in student enrollment during this same fifteen-year time frame. Thus, the penalty paid by the Faculty for too-rapid expansion in the late sixties was keenly felt by its inability to benefit from the advantages of orderly renewal throughout much of the eighties.

As FEUT struggled to reinvent itself after the loss of its graduate department to OISE in 1966, it flirted with various innovations, some of them successful, others not. Perhaps the most abortive plan was the debate about the whole consecutive/concurrent teacher education model. A committee, jointly chaired by professors Luther and Greig, proposed that the Faculty move from a one-year consecutive teacher-training model to a concurrent model that would integrate teacher training into the undergraduate years. The hope was that by doing so, the Faculty of Education would inevitably become a closer partner with the university in the overall education of its potential clientele. The debate is recorded in the final document titled Focus and Refocus (1972). Objection to the proposal to adopt a concurrent model was strongest from among the teaching subject departments, which feared that such a program would dilute the academic quality of the undergraduate experience. FEUT had long been the faculty of choice for four-year honours graduates from across the province and there was real concern that the Type A Honours Certificate program at the Faculty would be jeopardized by the introduction of a parallel, concurrent teacher education program. Since the proposal was unceremoniously scrapped, the problem never materialized, but the debate reflected a deep division within the Faculty between those who argued in favour of quality academic training as a necessary precursor to teacher education against those who took a more flexible view of the nature of preparation for teaching. While all of this is now history, it does serve to remind us that the Faculty of Education at the University of Toronto was still very much an institution dominated by a "teaching subjects" mentality in which the Honours Specialist Type A Certificate was the most highly valued attainment. FEUT, in those days, prepared secondary school teachers for the province, and paid only passing attention to the training of elementary school teachers. It would require major surgery to alter that mentality and move the emphasis from a teacher-subject model to a more holistic student-centred view.

The major event that shook up the rather elitist attitude toward teacher education came about with the new change in teacher certification introduced by the Ministry of Education in 1974. Prior to this change, FEUT students could elect elementary education as one of their two teaching subjects. However, with the change in certification, Faculty of Education students selected *one* of three possible areas of concentration—primary/junior (K-6), junior/intermediate (grades 4-10), intermediate/senior (grades 7-13/OAC). Primary/junior candidates would teach in the early grades of elementary school; junior/intermediate would look to teaching in the senior grades of elementary school or junior high school, and intermediate/senior students would be targeting the secondary panel. This change in certification had an immediate and profound effect on the nature of the FEUT program. For one thing, it required the teaching faculty, the vast majority of whom had chiefly secondary school teaching experience, to accommodate the different needs of training candidates for elementary schools. Some took to the challenge with relative ease while others never could quite shake off their secondary school subject-centred bias. Since hiring of new staff had ceased by 1974, it was necessary for some faculty who had been hired originally to prepare secondary school teachers to shift suddenly over to a quite different instructional role and philosophy. The transition took time and in the early years of the new program enrollment in primary/junior and junior/intermediate was kept low intentionally, in part to enable faculty to adjust to the new challenge. It is doubtful that the change (which was as much attitudinal as it was programmatic) could have been achieved without the strong leadership provided by professors Jim Fair and Gary Hunt.

Jim Fair had come to the Faculty via the Institute for Child Study, which had been attached to FEUT in 1971, while Gary Hunt had joined FEUT from the Toronto Board of Education in 1971. Both men had a strong vision and experience with elementary schools, and realized that much would be needed to modify the long-standing FEUT tradition, which clearly reflected secondary school biases or proclivities. They were skilful negotiators who could mediate with ingenuity and flair. Although determined and clear-sighted they were not threatening nor dogmatic. Their elementary backgrounds may well have given them special talents that emphasized collaboration and cooperation. Whatever the source of their skill, they gradually built up a solid nucleus of faculty who were willing and able to undertake the new challenge in elementary teacher education—people like Don Fraser (mathematics), Ronald Shephard and Arn Bowers (language arts), Bob Martin (program development), David Booth (drama and language arts), Elgin Wolfe (science), Toni Sheehan (educational administration), Tom Goodenough (history, philosophy, and sociology), and Claude Brodeur (psychology).

A great deal of credit must be given to the members of this nuclear elementary staff since many continued to teach in the secondary teacher education program as well. Those who moved in whole or in part into the elementary panel soon discovered that they had to spend additional time and energy in course preparation and planning. The reason for this substantial increase in commitment was due to the emphasis placed by both Hunt and Fair on collaborative teamwork and integrative teaching and learning. For both men, the preparation of elementary school teachers demanded a quite different approach from that traditionally delivered to secondary school candidates. While secondary school is still viewed as subject-centred, elementary education is far more student-centred in focus, and learning is viewed as an integrative experience. Both Hunt and Fair worked hard to infuse their own cooperating staff with this philosophy, which led them eventually to a novel experiment in program delivery.

A major concern for both Hunt and Fair was the age-old problem of the unnatural divide between "theory and practice" in the delivery of teacher education programs. They and their colleagues had spent some considerable time reflecting on this problem and planning for a possible solution. Their plan was to take the preservice program out of the artificial confines of the university environment and locate it in the real world of children and schools. Hence, in 1979, after much debate in Faculty council, they were given the green light to establish on an experimental basis a teaching centre at Roden Public School in the Toronto Board of Education. Most of the elementary program, therefore, was delivered *in situ* in an environment that reflected the reality of school life. The innovation that began as an experiment remained in place for ten years and was gradually joined by other school-based teacher education programs. Today, there are six such programs in place giving witness to the validity of such a concept. In fact the whole attitude among faculty toward school-based program delivery has changed dramatically from the early eighties when it was viewed with considerable suspicion. Clearly, it is easier to establish school-based programs in an elementary school environment than in that of large multidisciplinary secondary schools, nor was it ever the intention to have such school-based programs wholly replace the normal in-faculty program. Rather, these experiments were intended to serve as alternative choices available to an increasingly varied and experienced student population.

In fact, the word "alternative" serves to remind us that more recently there has been considerable parallel experimentation going on within the intermediate/senior panel for secondary school teacher candidates. In 1994-95, there were four alternate programs offered to intermediate/junior students, each with a different focus:

1. an extensive in-school experience with students of high academic potential (Professor Gutteridge),
2. language education for teachers of French, German, Italian or Spanish (with an ESL intersession offering) (Professor Gagné),
3. teaching development project in conjunction with Dufferin-Peel, Peel County, and Halton boards of education (Professor Eardley),
4. Learning Consortium program in conjunction with the Durham, Halton, North York, and Scarborough boards of education (Professor Hundey).

Each program had limited enrollment and targeted different interests among those candidates applying to it, but they all shared a common feature, which was to extend the student teacher candidates' experience with the schools and the community. The "culture of schools" cannot be fully experienced within the context of university-based lectures; and while practice teaching does provide student teachers with preliminary classroom experience, it may not provide the kind of exposure to systems-wide realities that these alternative programs have been designed to address.

These recent models focusing on increased school-related experience had their precursors in earlier attempts by the secondary education department to reach out to the community of schools. In the late seventies, Dean Ricker had spearheaded an experiment with "teaching centres," which involved both faculty of teaching subjects and theory subjects in collaboration with a selected list of secondary schools in various boards of education within the practice teaching catchment area of the Faculty. Faculty and students were assigned to these secondary schools for the purpose again of investigating the total school experience. In the mid-eighties, professors Dick Baine and Larry Ridge introduced and managed an innovation that was elaborately entitled the Intermediate/ Senior In-School Inservice Practicum, more commonly referred to as IS^3. In essence, this was an extended practicum in selected school locations in which participating students prepared an extended curriculum unit that they taught to targeted classes after the end of the regular practicum in the spring. It was successful in a number of ways, not the least of which was the manner in which it engaged associate teachers in the schools in the whole teacher education process at the Faculty. The list of innovations could be extended further, but must close with brief reference to the MA(T) MSc(T) program jointly sponsored by FEUT and the School of Graduate Studies at the University of Toronto. In its heyday, it involved the following areas of graduate study—English, mathematics, physics, geography, and library science. Although only English still remains operative today, it did illustrate a serious attempt on the part of FEUT to re-establish its presence in the field of graduate studies after the departure of its old graduate studies department to OISE in 1965.

If the history of the elementary department is one of steady growth and enlargement, quite the reverse holds true for what used to be called the technical and industrial arts department. In its heyday, between the mid-fifties and the mid-seventies, "tech studies" was a very large enterprise within (or outside) the old OCE program. The Spadina Wing was opened in 1950 primarily to house the then-modern and well-equipped shops needed to train teachers for the expanding technical schools system of the province. Only a small minority of these tech candidates held degrees, but all were required to have trade papers demonstrating five years of practical experience in industry or the trades. These students were nearly all male and cut from a different cloth compared to the rest of the student body. They required different treatment, and they certainly received it at the hands of "R.D." Phillips, the department's first director, who was characterized by one of his own contemporaries as a person who was "not lighthearted and frivolous." His two successors, A.W. Frizzell and Gordon Luther, maintained the tradition of serious and disciplined leadership well into the seventies. It is sobering to remember that in the mid-seventies the department was staffed by some twenty faculty, only a few of whom also taught in the regular OCE certificate program. That this group constituted a separate culture slightly apart from the mainstream of the college was demonstrated in a variety of ways, including their tendency to lunch together and, as some deans might suspect, plot together. Certainly this group of faculty were fiercely protective, not only of their extremely intricate program, but also of their students in whom they were able to raise a real spirit of group loyalty.

It should be recalled that in the sixties, technical studies was equated with trades such as woodworking and auto mechanics, and was driven quite literally by machinery. One suspects that the noise emanating from the technical shops in the Spadina Wing probably drove away the fainthearted arts graduates who haunted the halls of the rest of the building. This was a pity in a way, since, had they braved the din and the dust, they would have witnessed a kind of vibrant camaraderie not seen elsewhere in the college. The tech students were at once boisterous and vulnerable as were, in a sense, the faculty who taught them. There was Peter Briggs, the bon vivant and Bill Sloan, the disarming storyteller, along with Rudy Sramek, so seriously devoted to industrial arts and the British tradition of tradescrafts. In fact, it is surprising to recall how many of these men were influenced by the English craft tradition, and how they sometimes uncomfortably cohabited among car engines, and the welding and plumbing of the shop floor. Perhaps the person who best characterized this subculture of the arts was Professor Charles Wall, who for decades taught technical students to write well and confidently, to value language as a communicative tool, and to analyze the media with skill. Charles Wall opened the minds and filled the hearts of technical students for over three decades—he was a humanizing and liberating influence in the department. There were others, among them Doug Long, an incessant worrier as an administrator, who happily found relaxation and new life interests after his retirement from the Faculty in the 1980s. Only Gary Burfield and Andy Gaydos remain among this large cohort from the seventies, contributing in a dignified way to a field in which modern technology has so rapidly replaced an older tradition of technical studies. Changing technologies has driven the field into a new direction that has more to do with cyberspace than shops and trades.

In retrospect, the final period of its history, from 1965 to 1995, represents an era of considerable change and challenge for the Faculty. Part roller-coaster ride, part reconstruction, it was a period characterized by rapid expansion followed by equally rapid retrenchment. But the constant that held the sometimes beleaguered and embattled institution together throughout this turbulent era was the faculty and staff who shared a view of the importance of its history, traditions, and achievement. This personal reflection on the history of FEUT closes therefore with some observations of my own on a collectivity of women and men who have contributed with distinction to its storied past.

In a moving poem by Joy Kogawa, titled "What Do I Remember of the Evacuation?" the writer adopts the persona of an innocent young Japanese-Canadian child as she reflects back upon her experiences of the wartime expulsion to the interior of the vast continent. What she recalls are the little things that only a child would observe—a ball rolling down the aisle of the train as it moved haltingly toward an uncertain future.

My own recollection of thirty-five years at OCE / FEUT are filled with memories of faces, occasions, and people. The big issues, many of them hotly debated at the time, dim with the passage of time—but the faces do not. Some of them are ghostly perhaps. Persons like Spence Carlisle who taught me history / geography in 1956-57 at OCE and locked me out of class when I arrived thirty seconds late one wintry morning. This was the same man who delivered one of the most amusing and touching retirement speeches ever in the history of the Faculty. He was the institution's Rumpole (although not in girth), the only person who could refer to his wife as "she who must be obeyed," and probably mean it. There was silver-haired, ebulliently vibrant David Clee whose enthusiasm for media studies and Welsh wit infected all who knew him. David was always in a hurry and would often excuse himself with the phrase, "Excuse me but I'm hellishly late for a meeting." Part imp and part St. Nick, David scampered for years even after having hip replacement surgery in his seventies; he still dances in the memory of his many friends and colleagues. There was B.C. Diltz (Bert to his friends), who served in World War I in the artillery, and became "Mr. English Studies" to generations of English teachers in the province. Also, there was Andrew Skinner, Scotsman extraordinaire, who chose to remain on staff at OCE when most of his colleagues moved to the newly established OISE in 1965. Like Andrew Skinner (although not in accent) there was Walter London, who shared Andrew's stern and uncompromising sense of integrity. "Wally's" hands were callused from years of playing handball at the YMHA—but his heart was soft and his vision clear. He was a fine administrator as associate dean and the most loyal friend and colleague to two deans who remember him always with affection. There was the impeccable and punctilious Helen St. Jean in French, and later her young colleague and student Howard Hainsworth, the former dying old and the latter far too young. No one who has been lucky enough to be invited to the annual Christmas party of the Moderns Department will soon forget Howard Hainsworth's memorable and authentic Québéçois tortière followed by his homemade English trifle—an unintentional but nonetheless lingering testament to gustatory biculturalism.

I have known personally every dean since 1956—Lewis, Diltz, Dadson, Barrett, Ricker, Millar, and Fullan—every dean in the ninety-year history of the Faculty except for the first two, Packenham and Althouse. It gives me pause to realize that I place in that list myself, because many of these men and women, particularly Diltz and Ricker, were figures rather larger than life. I feel more comfortable among the much larger cohort of colleagues, who in one fashion or another, contributed to the teaching life of the Faculty. Among them, certainly because he was a university classmate of mine, was Don Gutteridge, who was for many years a superb principal of UTS. While reference to UTS lies somewhat unfairly outside the narrow confines of this brief history, Don Gutteridge's contribution to its parallel story remains pivotal and recognized as such to all of us at FEUT. And then there is Ron McMaster, the equal and successor to Bert Diltz, who taught most of the students who would later become members of the department of English at FEUT. Ron was a friend to us all, a man of integrity, kindness, and enormous talent. In contrast to Ron's gentlemanliness, there were others too whose fierce public demeanor often belied a gentler side—Don Mumford in mathematics, a giant of a man, and his altogether smaller associate Bruce McLean. When those two were joined later by Don Fraser, only then did I realize that mathematics could have a kinder, gentler, and more creative side. In the field of mathematics education, Dave Alexander remains as one of the best examples of an educator who has contributed at a provincial level to the discipline—both as a professor at FEUT and as a secondee for many years to the curriculum branch of the Ministry of Education.

There are so many others, friends and associates, colleagues all to recall. David Booth is one who taught me (long after I taught him) what it means to be a scholar-teacher. He and his two collaborators, John Emerson (art education) and Natalie Kuzmich (art education) together as a team made a very significant contribution to studies in the arts, both nationally and at OISE. Arn Bowers warned me about the dangers of formal grammar and instructed me in the joys of reading with equal aplomb. And the scamp and scholar among us all, Dick Baine, reminded me that Paris, France, was, and presumably still is, on a parallel on the globe slightly north of North Bay. Dick Baine had the capacity to put things in their proper "perspective," a talent that served the Faculty well in many capacities beyond his own discipline, geography. Upon retirement, Dick was honoured by his fellow geography teachers in Ontario with a lifetime membership in their association.

I have already spoken of the significant contributions made to the development of elementary education at the Faculty by Jim Fair and Gary Hunt. In secondary education, two persons stand out—Annette Yeager and Don Galbraith. With patience, tact, and persistence, they have managed to weld together from among disparate disciplines a real departmental focus and sense of mission. This task was never easy, although Keith McLeod who has done much the same thing in educational policy and foundations, has proved that it can be replicated. Their styles are different, but the outcomes have been similar—in both cases a more unified and focused departmental mission.

And in the broader context of faculty-wide contributions, several persons must be identified. Certainly in terms of endurance, long service to UTS and the Faculty, and capacity to innovate, Don

Fawcett must be singled out; his list of plausible schemes would make an entrepreneur envious. For service to the Faculty and the university, Ronald Shephard stands as a person of stature and integrity. A wonderful teacher and an impressive scholar, Ron has contributed to committees at all levels; a scholar-teacher and the wise conscience of the institution. In the days before the Office of the Registrar became professionalized by the appointment of a full-time staff member, its responsibilities were borne by various Faculty members, among whom Larry LaFave and Charles Lundy should be recognized for their special contribution. During their long tenure throughout the seventies and eighties, the Faculty expanded its continuing education program exponentially. FEUT became the major centre in the province for the delivery of additional qualifications (AQ) courses, the purpose of which was to serve in the upgrading and professionalization of certified teachers across the schools of Ontario. When the history of teacher education in the province comes to be written, the importance of the continuing revitalization of teachers in both the elementary and secondary schools will be acknowledged as one of the cornerstones in teacher development. The stimulus for the rapid expansion in additional qualification courses during this era (1975-95) originated with the productive alliance between Dorothy Dunn, head of the teacher education section of the Ministry of Education and Dean John Ricker and his successor at FEUT. This faculty spearheaded the development of a system of teacher renewal that has no parallel in Canada. And since FEUT had only slight involvement in graduate education, it was, because of its size and large pool of experienced teacher training faculty, able to lead the way in the continuing education of teachers. This initiative not only served as a positive outlet for a highly inventive and creative faculty at FEUT, but also served to professionalize teaching in the province in ways that helped to elevate the standard of classroom practice to a much higher level.

The word "professionalism" has been used throughout this narrative, but never defined. Perhaps it cannot be defined, but certainly it can be illustrated. And no one better exemplifies the qualities of professionalism than Professor Anne Millar, who has served as associate dean and briefly as dean for over a dozen years at the Faculty. Her tireless devotion to the Faculty and the university during a time of great change is recognized by all her colleagues. Grace under pressure, dedication, and selflessness go some distance in defining the word professional. To have known Anne Millar and worked with her as a colleague and a friend is to have experienced what it means to be truly a "professional." The Faculty of Education has been for these past ninety years a collectivity of creative professionals, but none more so than Professor Anne Millar.

To have known so many men and women of dedication and talent over the last thirty-five years has been a great pleasure and an enriching experience. To have worked with them as colleagues has been a privilege.

On July 1, 1996, the Faculty of Education at the University of Toronto will cease to exist as an independent, freestanding institution. On that date, FEUT will finally be reunited with its sister institution, OISE, in the newly integrated complex to be called OISE/UT. For some faculty and staff in both institutions this merger will be regarded with some trepidation. But for the majority at both OISE and FEUT, this significant event has to be viewed as a triumph of rationality, as well as a major opportunity for renewal. From a FEUT perspective, this unification of educational studies marks a return to a vision that was announced in 1905 when education was first established as a discipline at the University of Toronto. In that vision, there was the expressed hope that education would assume its rightful and legitimate place within the university environment. For the thirty-year period between 1965 and 1995, when educational studies were divided between OISE and FEUT, the discipline of education was weakened. A faculty of education with little access to graduate studies could not thrive, any more than a graduate/research institute with no responsibility for teacher education could be expected to reach its full potential. So this merger has to be regarded by both institutions as a rare opportunity to realize the full potential for educational studies at the University of Toronto. To that future FEUT brings a storied ninety-year history. The manner in which the Faculty of Education has begun to prepare itself for that promising future is to be recounted in the pages of this book.

Towards a Philosophy of Change

Suzanne M. Stiegelbauer, an assistant professor at the Faculty of Education, received her doctorate in social anthropology and has studied the process of change in education in such diverse organizations as the United States Federal Office of Education and Improvement, the Texas Research and Development Center in Teacher Education, Toronto region boards of education, and the Toronto Native Canadian Centre. In 1990, she collaborated with Michael Fullan on the writing of The New Meaning of Educational Change (1991). *Suzanne has been a member of an elementary option team, a coordinator of a junior/intermediate option, and currently coordinates and teaches visual arts.*

There is something I don't know
    that I am supposed to know.
I don't know *what* it is I don't know,
    and yet am supposed to know,
and I feel I look stupid
    if I seem both not to know it
        and not know *what* it is I don't know.
Therefore, I pretend I know it.
    This is nerve-wracking
    since I don't know what I must pretend to know.
Therefore I pretend to know everything.
(R.D. Laing, 1970)

It is one characteristic of change that those engaged with the change, whatever it may be, often find themselves in the dilemma of having to do something within the framework of knowing a little, hoping for a lot, and pretending it will all turn out as they planned. In the face of uncertainty, they may resort to at least "pretending they know," especially in situations where the norm is "to know." Accepting the fact that they may not know, and proceeding as if that lack of knowing may even be desired, is a rare act usually common to artists, not academics. Yet, increasingly, meaningful change has come to resemble the artistic process, one, because of the intensity and meaning it has to its participants, and, two, because it is constructed of mixed parts of ambiguity, good ideas, skills, and desire—a desire for something to be different, or to be as good as it can be; the ideas and skills to do it, and a great deal of ambiguity in how to make it happen.

Despite this philosophical beginning, change in faculties of education has, in larger and smaller contexts, gone through many of the same permutations of knowing and not knowing. Given the diversity of needs and influences, deciding what is the right kind of change is a feat in itself—one that each institution has taken to itself as it can and will. With the mandates of the Holmes Reports (1986, 1990) and in Ontario, the Ontario Provincial Report on Teacher Education (Fullan, Connelly & Watson, 1989), among others, it became increasingly clear that the preparation of teachers was not reflective of the changing reality of schools, and that schools and students were changing faster than any response from teacher education institutions could be mustered. If change is needed, the nature and scope of the change itself has become as important an issue as making the change happen.

This chapter describes the strategy of one faculty of education in determining what that change should be and how it should happen. Recognizing that teacher education needed to be more closely aligned with school-based experience, and at the same time, maintain an academic emphasis on lifelong learning and higher education, the Faculty of Education at the University of Toronto (FEUT) began a process of investigating the needs of an improved teacher education curriculum, while at the same time reorganizing itself to be better able to experiment with ways of addressing those needs. To many, this process as it emerged seemed very different from the programmatic changes they had encountered before: it was both ambiguous (or intuitive) and structured. Over the seven years of its current implementation, however, it has laid a foundation for addressing changing program needs and in its own way has created an organizational culture more able to deal with change.

The chapter also describes a more personal process. I met Michael Fullan, the current Dean of the Faculty of Education, when he was involved as a consultant to the Concerns Based Adoption Project at the University of Texas Research and Development Center for Teacher Education. I was working at the time as a research associate investigating the process of change in schools, and, as is often the case with Ph.D. students, developing a research project that would become my dissertation. I didn't know then that change would be the agenda that would drive most of what I would be involved in over the next ten years; nor did I anticipate that I would be involved with change in this particular Faculty. But that early experience and later work with Dean Fullan on The New Meaning of Educational Change (1991) resulted in the perspective on change as learning that permeates this discussion. This chapter is also, at least in part, a dialogue: the first section reflects an interview I conducted with Dean Fullan early in 1995; the second section describes my response as a Faculty member engaged with change at FEUT. Taken together, they help illustrate two pieces of the process: the bigger picture of change and its strategies, and the process as it involved one individual. As the early research on change describes, and as this example may illustrate, change is a process, but not entirely a blind one. To begin with information from the interview:

OPPORTUNITY: 1988-89

In 1986-87, the Provost's Office of the University of Toronto, in conjunction with a Faculty committee, undertook a review of the programs and services of its Faculty of Education (FEUT). Out of that review came the following recommendations (Faculty of Education, 1990):

1. that the Faculty of Education and the Ontario Institute for Studies in Education (OISE) find ways to improve their working relationships such that full integration may be achieved within a ten-year period. This would link preservice and inservice programs and provide an opportunity for teachers and teacher education programs to be developmental in terms of graduate degrees and course evolution.
2. that a process of faculty renewal be engaged in. At the time of this report a large percentage of faculty professors were of retirement age. Faculty renewal included both seeking new faculty and re-examining the kinds of faculty members needed and how they should be placed.
3. that a review of programs be engaged in, current and in potential, for the purpose of program improvement.
4. that the faculty at FEUT be increasingly engaged in educational research; that opportunities for research be developed and supported; and that new faculty be hired with strong research and inquiry backgrounds.
5. that the relationships between FEUT, the Institute of Child Study (ICS), and the University of Toronto Schools (UTS) be strengthened to increase collaboration and sharing. ICS is an

early childhood centre with a two-year training degree; UTS is a private high school located within the Faculty.

6. and that facilities and equipment be improved. As the building itself had been occupied for the purpose of teacher training since 1906, many of the facilities were still in need of updating, despite periodic improvements.

These six recommendations—improved relations between FEUT and OISE, faculty renewal, program review, increased focus on research, strengthened relations between FEUT, ICS, and UTS, and faculty and equipment updating—became the mandate for the then-new Dean of the Faculty, Michael Fullan. A number of these, such as facilities renewal and the hiring of new faculty, could be addressed almost immediately. What was more important to Dean Fullan, however, was the larger strategy (Fullan, in Stiegelbauer interview, 1995).

> These turned out to be watershed themes. From 1974-1988, for example, there were no new appointments. The upcoming period included a lot of retirements. Everyone recognized that change was needed. The kinds of goals in the provostial review were ones you'd expect. But... I don't think anybody knew what it meant to actually act on them.

READY-FIRE-AIM

The broader strategy, as described by Dean Fullan, was what he calls a "ready-fire-aim" approach:

> I cycle back and forth between change theories... and what we're trying to bring about in terms of actual change in the Faculty. I say it that way because I wouldn't say I'm using change theory in direct application, but we're using it all the time in that two-way thinking and reflection about change. I rejected the notion of having a big task force set out the new agenda because our change work was telling us that kind of thing results in a lot of fanfare in the beginning, but it just sits on the shelf. By contrast, I felt an urgency for action to take place.

> The *readiness* was there—there was a feeling that change had to happen. We determined aspects that we thought were important to addressing the provostial review themes. We expressed those aspects at the beginning but didn't say that people had to sign on. We invited them to develop ways to address the themes themselves. They came up with different "pilot" projects of sorts. This is the *firing* part.
>
> *Aim* is where you are as a result of the firing, based on the experiences you are having. You pull out the clarity about what to focus on more intensively for the future... . All of these things were cumulative and provided momentum and the capacity to get more and more focused, but focused in the middle and end of the first sequence (of changes) rather than at the beginning. When people now start talking about the new vision, they know what they are talking about because they're talking about experience.

Ready-fire-aim, then, is a three-stage process. "Ready" is the combination of contextual opportunity and laying the groundwork for a change process to occur. As Fullan says, readiness is a kind of vision in itself, a "rudiment of vision" based on need and certain goals, in this case the provostial review and ideas about teacher education and change. "Fire" is inviting participants to address needs through a number of experimental projects or approaches. "Aim" is the refinement of the vision by reflecting on the experiences of all and consolidating learnings to provide a better focus for the ongoing process.

READY: Change Had to Happen

In the early stages of this strategy, the context facilitated the approach. First, there was the issue of faculty renewal. In the seven years after 1985, forty-five of the eighty then-current Faculty members retired. Between 1986 and 1988 alone, over twenty-two people retired. During this period, approximately thirty new people were hired, at the rate of four or five a year. In hiring new faculty, FEUT was looking for three characteristics: one, that they demonstrated an inquiry orientation in their work; two, that they were committed to research and to working with schools in a field-based way; and three, that they were ready to work in teams as collaboration on all fronts was of increasing importance, especially collaboration with field partners.

Secondly, because of the large number of retirements at one time, what might have become an atmosphere of resistance due to time with the organization and potential territory issues, dissolved in the face of smaller numbers. This provided a unique contextual situation, at least unique to many change efforts. Those that remained, rather than providing conflict, provided support to new faculty. Instead of a "power-related" problem, where a department, an enclave, or a group of hard-core resistors used their power to prevent something from happening, the orientation of the group to the change process became more "culture-related." A "cultural" orientation to the change means that as a part of the change process people become unsure of the new direction because they don't know what it will mean for them. They may be interested in the conception of the change, but feel they don't have the skills or the clarity to define their role in it effectively; that is, they don't know where they and their previous expertise "fit." Providing for an experience where people work together in teams helps with a culture-related problem as it allows individuals to share expertise in developing what they want to do. The pilot projects that emerged later at FEUT helped define a new culture—one that is more interactive, experimental, and collaborative, and where individuals find their "fit" through that experimentation and interaction.

Another aspect of readiness was a response to the provostial review. FEUT administration in combination with a Faculty committee, developed a number of program goals based on the six themes and what they wanted to accomplish in developing a direction and structure for teacher education. One, they decided that they had to focus on the teacher education continuum; that is, they had to link teacher development and school improvement so that the Faculty would be in the business of school improvement and not just teacher education. This meant increasing contact with teachers and school systems or some form of field-based partnerships. Second, they felt they had to infuse the process with good inquiry, ask good questions, do good research, and disseminate those findings. These themes were expressed at the beginning, but with choice:

> I didn't expect everyone to take this agenda because a lot of different people have a lot of different views and I know imposing things doesn't work. But I do think these (goals) are important and I invited people to come forth with developing ideas. This was the beginning of "firing" (Fullan, in Stiegelbauer interview, 1995).

FIRE: Program "Options" and a "Learning Consortium"

The combined effect of the six themes from the provostial review and the goals set by the Faculty for itself was the development of a collaborative field-based project and the beginning of a number of field-based teacher education program "options" or choices, each representing some different inquiry approach or emphasis.

One of the most powerful strategies in the beginning was the structuring of the Learning Consortium, a partnership with four major school boards in the Toronto area. As a consortium, this group planned and implemented development activities that considered the needs of the Faculty and the boards in planning for staff development and research opportunities, provided inservice and consultation support for one another, and created strong links between the developing programs or "options" in teacher education and the real needs of schools. As a start-up phenomenon, the success of the Learning Consortium was powerful and influential. It addressed the two goals expressed by the Faculty—focus on the teacher education continuum and research or inquiry into practice—and sent a strong signal to local boards that the Faculty was serious about working in conjunction with them.

The external collaboration expressed in the Learning Consortium was also developed in two other projects: the Joint Centre for Teacher Development (JCTD) in collaboration with OISE and University of Toronto departments with shared interests, and the Technology for Enhancing Learning Centre (TEL), a partnership between FEUT, the University of Toronto, and TVOntario (TVO), which was designed to enhance teacher education by developing uses of technology (Faculty of Education, 1990).

The other important aspect of "firing" was the "invitation" to faculty or groups of faculty to explore solid ideas about teacher education and field involvement through the implementation of program "options" or "choices," as they were first called. These "pilot projects" were more active initially at the elementary level, as relationships with schools and an emphasis on a more integrated curriculum made programmatic linkages easier. Fullan says:

> You could call them pilot projects, but they were in effect a pressure and support strategy. These projects were saying to the Faculty, we don't expect everyone to take this on. But we do think this approach is important and we invite people to try things (Fullan, in Stiegelbauer interview, 1995).

By 1990, there were nine different "options" at the elementary level and two at the secondary level. While somewhat similar, each emphasized a different aspect of a field-based need or perspective and each had a different approach to their teacher education program. Options included such things as STEP days when teacher candidates would visit their practice teaching school prior to their practice teaching experience—these experiences would then be integrated in some way with the option's curriculum; integrating curriculum and foundation courses; advising strategies; and team teaching by Faculty staff, among others (Kilcher, 1994). The interaction of schools and program staff had the further effect of defining and streamlining the option as needs and effects of strategies became clearer. Over time, option teams were able to compare effects and refine their programs, expressing what Fullan would call "Aim."

AIM: Learning from Experience

> It's obviously a metaphor, but "aim" is where you are as a result of firing. It's what you know from your experience (Fullan, in Stiegelbauer interview, 1995).

The early work on changes at FEUT was largely the work of individuals and small groups in interaction with one another. The more common phenomenon of strategic planning by a large-group task force was avoided to give individuals or small groups more choice and to direct energy to the pilot projects rather than to discussions of strategy. Once a few of the pilots were working well, other groups and individuals began to get excited about some of the new directions and sought to consider ways that they might use some of these ideas, and to look more comprehensively at FEUT's program as a whole.

Four years into the change effort (1991), Faculty administration sponsored a FEUT-wide retreat at the Briars, a resort on Lake Simcoe in central Ontario. The goal of the retreat was to examine the effects of the last few years, to discuss and consolidate learnings, and to see what directions might emerge. This, in one form, was the large-group strategic planning session four years later. This time, however, it was planning based on concrete experience. The strategy-in-waiting for this kind of dialogue is that when people start talking about vision and directions, they are talking from experience—this worked, this excited us, this didn't work, this is a problem: "with this kind of strategy... you are more likely to identify the real directions that are considered to be valuable and more likely to know the real problems" (Fullan, in Stiegelbauer interview, 1995).

A more consolidated focus emerged out of discussions at the Briars, one that involved both faculty and administration in structuring a new direction. This committee, called the B.Ed. Restructuring Committee, took as its mandate the incorporation of ideas from the Briars, experience with ongoing programs, research, and their discussions to develop a set of design principles and key images for teacher education that would guide future programs (Faculty of Education, 1992). The session at the Briars included all faculty whether they had been involved in an "option" or not. The B.Ed. Restructuring Committee also crossed groups and incorporated new information from field programs as it emerged. Further, FEUT departments—elementary, secondary, and foundation studies, did their own reflection and planning, which again was fed to the Restructuring Committee. This culminated in June of 1994 with the unanimous endorsement by the Faculty of the two-year program that reflected the key images and experiences of the pilot programs. Rather than being the vision of the dean or a leadership group, this new vision was a composite of everyone's involvement in one form or another. The "new culture" of the institution, as illustrated in the amount of consensus, sense of accomplishment, and confidence in response to the Restructuring Committee's work, indicated a Faculty that could see itself in a new context and respond to changing needs.

A Strategy for Reinforcement and Synergy

Once focus and some consolidation had emerged from the dialogue at the Briars and the continuing work of the Restructuring Committee, the next step was to investigate other opportunities and resources that would force further growth and develop recognition, dissemination, and interaction with the larger educational community. As faculty saw themselves regarded positively by the educational community, their sense of accomplishment would support them in doing further work and, as they are in interaction with other educational networks, their vision would expand to apply and incorporate ideas as situations required. Support and reinforcement would come from both acknowledgment and new information; situational or financial resources would come available as a result of involvement with other organizations.

FEUT then began to engage in a number of projects with other organizations that would apply and broaden ideas. With the Urban Network for Improving Teacher Education Project (UNITE), they became involved with educational problems in urban settings (Howey, 1992; UNITE, 1992). With the Aga Khan Project, they became a part of the development of a field-based teacher education facility and exchange with Aga Khan University in Karachi, Pakistan, and the University of Oxford, United Kingdom. Faculty were encouraged and supported to attend and present papers at conferences and to apply for research grants. An office of research information and support was initiated to this aim. The Briars also produced "spinoff" subgroups that continue to examine aspects of practice, and that encourage exemplary teachers to give presentations, exchange work, and discuss or develop new ideas.

One such idea has been to look at the application of portfolios to training teachers; another has been to examine strategies for internal staff development.

As FEUT progresses with this agenda, contextual forces continue to change. In 1994-95, the Ontario Institute for Studies in Education (OISE) began active discussions with the University of Toronto to merge OISE and the Faculty of Education. This forced administration and faculty to consider their programs in the light of a larger institution, graduate studies, and the addition of new faculty from OISE. This merger presents another opportunity and dilemma, one that will require new forms, interactions, and relationships to emerge to develop a sense of working community. Fullan comments:

> Growth is something like having ever more complex and variegated relationships with your environment. While this may also mean a kind of loss, or loss of security, it creates possible new opportunities. As an organization we need to go into promising but ever more complex sets of territory. This merger is one of them. And where real growth can occur, there is risk and danger. We could lose a lot, but also gain a lot.... .We may initially lose some of the sense of community this process has given us so far (Fullan, in Stiegelbauer interview, 1995).

Opportunity and an "Option": A Personal Experience

It is one thing to document and observe changes in progress and another to live them. After a number of years working for the Concerns Based Adoption Model (CBAM) at the Texas Research and Development Center (a research project on school improvement issues sponsored by the U. S. Department of Education), I completed my Ph.D. in Social Anthropology and was hired in 1991 as part of the faculty renewal going on at FEUT. I had been a visual arts teacher at a secondary school in Toronto before embarking on a Ph.D., so the Canadian context was familiar to me, and my experiences as part of the CBAM research staff had enlarged this context to include many schools in the United States.

My anthropological research had been in the social context of education and Native Studies. I was hired to teach educational foundation courses that included both social context issues and change theory.

Year One: My first teaching assignment was as a member of an elementary "option" that had been one of the first programs of its kind when FEUT was restructured in 1988. The program included two "STEP" or field-experience days, team teaching, weekly team-planning meetings, and active contacts with schools. I was the only new faculty member on the option team, which included tenured professors, tutors, and seconded staff, most of whom had been with the Faculty for ten years or more. All members of the team acted as willing mentors and the weekly team meeting proved to be an invaluable induction resource. I was encouraged and supported in trying out ideas and strategies they concurred would benefit teacher candidates in the option. I advised students, visited schools, participated in option social activities, and worked with other members of the team to develop curriculum and refine the program. Through this experience, I learned about the kind of students in the program, how an integrated program for teacher education might be run, and what one aspect of professional life at the Faculty might be like.

My first real introduction to the faculty at-large, however, came at the Briars at the end of my first year. The Briars experience presented the longer-term picture of where the Faculty might be going and asked participants to break into small groups to discuss and determine perspectives on various issues. One goal of this professional development workshop was to update everyone on what others were doing and thinking; another was to develop a sense of group cohesion; a third was to refine experiences to more clearly outline directions for the future. As I had not know the "past" at FEUT, this seemed like an open door. I spent much of my time getting to know people and absorbing this new information. It did, however, communicate to me the norms of the new organization and a sense of how to proceed.

Year Two: I got the opportunity to proceed the next year when I was asked to "coordinate" an "option" at the junior/intermediate level. This option program was considered more traditional in that there was no "team" approach to teaching and planning and many of the professors involved overlapped with other programs and were not "dedicated staff." My job was to see to the administrative aspects of the programs, deal with the more than ninety students, oversee student teaching, and decide what program planning was necessary. As a coordinator, I rapidly discovered that, within the confines of courses that needed to be covered and professors that had other responsibilities, I could develop the program according to what I and other professors thought was important, and change structures and directions as we felt necessary. I was also curating a major exhibition of Southwestern Pueblo Pottery at the Royal Ontario Museum and beginning a new project with Anishnawbe Health of Toronto on the teaching and healing approaches of traditional teachers and elders.

Year Three: During the first year in the junior / intermediate option, I was largely involved with learning how to be a coordinator. In the second year, the program began to take a new form. It now included team meetings to plan, portfolio assessment that came out of the research work of one professor, study groups for discussion and practice teaching assignment, micro-teaching to develop strategies for educational problems, two STEP days instead of one (with more direct links between STEP and curriculum), and more interaction across classes and schools. While not perfect, these approaches began to make the option more cohesive internally and more responsive to student and school needs externally. The study groups, in particular, made a significant difference to the practice teaching experience (Stiegelbauer, Woodruff, Meyer, Hall, Cameron & Pireira, 1994; Kilcher, 1994; Stiegelbauer, 1995). A team of staff and students developed a video that described and evaluated program components. This video was part of a student and faculty presentation at the Canadian Educational Research Meetings of the year and has been used as a teaching tool by other programs (Stiegelbauer, Woodruff, Meyer, Hall, Cameron, & Pireira, 1994). My research work with Aboriginal elders and teachers continued with some research also focused on the effects of the strategies used in the junior / intermediate option (Stiegelbauer, 1995).

Year Four: This program, still with over ninety students but now called the Junior / Intermediate Downtown Option given its class location at the downtown University of Toronto campus, continued into the next year with some changes in teaching staff.

These changes meant that those professors continuing from the previous year had to "sell" ideas to new staff as well as attempt to integrate the new ideas, research, or approaches new people were involved in, where possible. One of these new people was a seconded teacher who acted as a "co-coordinator" responsible for practice teaching and field connections. The pairing of an academic and field person as co-coordinators for an option proved to be of great benefit to program planning, field relations, and academic research. It provided a different perspective for the team, and importantly, it provided more time to develop other dimensions of Faculty work. For the most part in year four, however, we continued to develop the approaches of the previous year with some refinements. Portfolios and their evaluation by staff, in particular, was a focus, as was the placement of students in study groups in their practice teaching schools (Stiegelbauer, 1995). This had the effect of greatly reducing the administrative load for the coordinator and the practice teaching office, as well as providing a major support for new teachers in practice teaching schools: they could help one another, and had the foundation for doing so based on their work at FEUT. During this year, I also started a new class in visual arts for non-majors. This allowed me to tap into my personal experience in a different way, but also meant developing a new curriculum. At the same time, I continued work with Aboriginal traditional teachers and elders, and I was asked to be a part of the OISE / FEUT / UT merger committee to develop the academic plan for the new organization.

Year Five: This year provided a new opportunity for me. As the professor responsible for the visual arts curriculum was retiring, this position became available. This meant moving from a coordinator's position teaching foundation and social context classes to over ninety students to, in a programmatic sense, coordinating the art program and teaching between thirty and forty individuals who planned to be visual arts teachers at the intermediate and secondary levels. This opportunity provided me with a way to integrate what I had learned from the previous years with what was a major part of my background and experience. The lower numbers of students was also attractive and allowed me to focus more on their needs and the needs of the curriculum. I developed the curriculum based on ministry guidelines and what I thought was important, and, in line with the norms I had learned as a coordinator, looked for ways to integrate the visual arts with other arts and subjects. I began to coordinate a "team" of arts professors and teachers from UTS to develop ways to integrate an arts approach and to have more real and consistent experience with a secondary arts classroom (at UTS and other schools). I worked to develop an understanding of how the arts are approached in education by visiting schools and inviting teachers into the classroom. I tried to develop the students' understanding of themselves as artists and teachers, as well as their students and classrooms. As this was the first year for this course, the program was still developmental, but my experience as a coordinator and my understanding of the workings of the Faculty at this point made a more dynamic approach to planning possible. Finally, my work with the OISE Merger in year five allowed me to apply many of the understandings from my experience to considering the needs of a new organization, and the needs of faculty and students who would be part of it.

My Experience in Relation to Change at FEUT: A Commentary

What I have described is only one person's experience with change in FEUT. It hardly touches on the real diversity of tasks and time commitment that is part of this kind of applied academic work, nor on the kind of constant communication committees such as the B.Ed. Restructuring Committee. As my experience also reflects the change of a new job and a new context, it is occasionally difficult to say what would have happened in another setting, except in these ways:

1. There was a real emphasis on team work and support, especially at the elementary level, that allowed me to learn and experiment with ideas. This is especially true in year one where senior staff were very helpful. These are the staff mentioned by Fullan as the potential "resistors" who instead greatly contributed their knowledge and expertise to develop a good program. Later, this team emphasis contributed to the development and critiquing of program elements, like study groups, student placements, and portfolios.
2. Fullan describes a strategy of faculty renewal through hiring people who were interested in field connections and in the development of research and program strands based on field experiences—the integration of field and academic work. He also describes in the "ready-fire-aim" discussion placing

individuals in situations or in teams where they had the "opportunity" to fire or develop programs based on their interests, beliefs, and backgrounds, and to refine programmatic and research approaches later. This certainly was a part of my experience and could have been difficult if not for the support offered directly and indirectly by peers and the norms of experimentation that were evident in the context. By the time I was working as a coordinator, the majority of the options were already in operation with different yet similar expressions.

3. As I acquired more experience and learned more about what the Faculty was trying to accomplish through events such as the Briars, as well as through participating in committees related to program planning (committee work is not included here but is a major way of learning about how "things work" and contributing to it) I was asked to apply that learning to further Faculty development, first through the Elementary Department Steering Committee and Coordinators Group, and later through the OISE Academic Planning Group. This is one aspect of "aim," although aim also occurs through the kind of review conducted at personal, group, and departmental levels. The point here is that the opportunity and support was there over time, and the opportunity to contribute to the discussion influencing change was also there.
4. Over the five years I have described, there has been a developing consensus about what the Faculty is doing and a sense of identity in relation to it. More and more of the option programs are finding themselves with similar components as discussion about what works and what doesn't gets generalized. The "pressure" of communicating a direction—the provostial review, the Briars, the B.Ed. Restructuring Committee documents, the development of the two-year program, the OISE merger discussions—supported a dialogue about expectations and vision. That, combined with the support of experienced professors, of opportunity, of teamwork, and of administration, created a context for "firing" and "aiming" to occur in a number of ways.

Finally, I have been involved in options and program development; others in the Faculty have had a stronger focus on research, on more traditional academic classes, and on developing relationships with the field. Each of these experiences, in its own way, has contributed to a developing whole that is constantly changing. If nothing else, my story of the last five years is a story of change. Further, the majority of these changes are not necessarily changes I "knew" about, rather, based on a foundation of personal expertise and experience, I learned as I went. I'm better at it now.

The Best Faculty of Education: Vision, Leadership, and Reculturing

Fullan describes the "Best Faculty of Education" (Fullan, 1991) as having ten components. It should:

1. commit itself to producing teachers who are agents of educational and social improvement,
2. commit itself to continuous improvement through program innovation and evaluation,
3. value and practise exemplary teaching,
4. engage in constant inquiry,
5. model and develop lifelong learning among staff and students,
6. model and develop collaboration among staff and students,
7. be respected and engaged as a vital part of the university as a whole,
8. form partnerships with schools and other agencies,
9. be visible and valued internationally in a way that contributes locally and globally,
10. work collaboratively to help develop provincial and national networks.

While it may be difficult to see all these aspects at play at once, both my personal experience and Fullan's discussion of change illustrate their potential in being. Perhaps the most important elements of developing the "best faculty" lie in modelling some of the key norms through collaboration and dialogue, and through the self-conscious examination of progress, both individually and as a group.

This concept extends to both administration and teaching faculty. As Fullan and Andy Hargreaves from OISE state in What's Worth Fighting For (1991), leaders have to "express what they believe" and "extend" that expression to give the organization the opportunity to be involved and respond to it. They also have to think of the organization in terms of "reculturing" for change and not just for the sake of restructuring (Fullan & Hargreaves, 1991). Richard Wisniewski, Dean of the College of Education at the University of Tennessee, Knoxville, expressed some of the same ideas in his discussion of change at Tennessee:

> An agenda of teacher education reforms was developed by the faculty in the early eighties, partially in response to questions raised by the campus administration. That initial agenda was expanded... the dynamics of how events developed, key decision points... cannot be described here. Suffice to say that as one examines the changes already made and yet to come, my colleagues and I have learned much about the college and about what is possible (and impossible) in a university. None of the changes could have been achieved if they were not supported and shared by a number of key faculty. In respect to my role, I am an advocate of serious reforms, but no dean has the power to change a college unless a significant number of colleagues share those goals (Wisniewski, 1995).

Throughout the sequence of "ready-fire-aim" as discussed earlier, administrative staff have collaborated with Faculty, and in the OISE Merger, Faculty and staff have creatively worked through a reculturing, redefining process. This started as early as the response to the provostial review, and continued through the Briars and the formation of the B.Ed. Restructuring Committee. The feedback and response to the work of those committees set a direction. The experiences of professors and students seeking to interpret that vision, or direction, took the organization even farther. Figure 1 describes the critical incidents related to the period of development from 1987 to 1995. What is important about this figure, however, is the interaction of faculty, administration, and the external realm of schools and education-focused projects, such as UNITE, or the Learning Consortium, to develop an approach to defining the problem, recognizing that the problem is always changing, and reculturing to deal with change as a process.

Figure 1 Critical Incidents in Change at FEUT, 1987 to 1995

1987	Provostial Review sets goals
1988	Dean Fullan appointed
	New administrative plan developed in conjunction with Faculty committee
	Learning Consortium initiated
1989	Administrative reorganization from twenty departments to four academic units: elementary, secondary, foundations, educational psychology
	Faculty renewal hiring begins
	Joint Centre for Teacher Development initiated
	Option programs start up
	TEL Centre initiated
1990	Option development continues
	New hiring continues
1991	Briars conference
	B.Ed. Restructuring Committee established
	Informal discussion groups examine option strategies
1992	Development of B.Ed. Committee key images and themes for teacher education
1994	Faculty endorsement of two-year program
1995	Academic Integration Task Force established for integration with OISE (Ontario Institute for Studies in Education) to become the new OISE/UT in 1996. Integration merges graduate and preservice programs.

Towards a Philosophy of Change

The historical summary of change theory considers it in two aspects: 1) the practical and technological, the "how-to's" of change, and 2) the philosophical, or those principles guiding change processes (Stiegelbauer, 1994, 1995, 1996; Fullan, 1991; Fullan & Miles, 1992; Fullan, 1994). Under the practical aspect, elements of change that are considered important have remained consistent over the more than twenty years of change research. *People* are the major ingredient of change—who they are, how they respond, what they do in the process. *Practices*, or the changes themselves, their definition, clarity, "fit" with the organization, and usefulness are other ingredients. The *process* for putting the change into action involves the strategies undertaken to support it, and the pressure brought to bear by the need and the situation.

Finally, *policies* provide a foundation and the potential of a future in terms of the continuation of developed forms and further growth (Stiegelbauer, 1994, 1996; Loucks & Horsley, 1992). There is a lot of information about these aspects and suggestions for their application.

What is perhaps more difficult is the philosophical aspect of change. As mentioned at the beginning of this chapter, more and more change is looking like an artistic and cultural process, one in which factors and factions are constantly changing in interaction with one another. Philosophy guides the enactment and direction such changes might follow. The dilemma is in the nature of its control. Fullan and Miles describe a number of attributes of a philosophy guiding change: Change is a journey; Problems or opportunities are our friends; You can't mandate what matters; Vision and Strategic Planning Come Later; Every Person is a Change Agent, and the like (Fullan, 1995; Fullan & Miles, 1992). What is clear under the category of philosophy is that there is no formula, a possibility that has worried administrators for a long time. Change requires a kind of structured attitude—making change is part setting the stage for the experience and coaching the actors, part communication about results and part staying on top of opportunity when it arises. All of these factors must be integrated with or on top of older traditions and beliefs:

> Each day is a test of the planning document and its potential. Each committee meeting is a step forward or backward. Old practices have a tenacity difficult to overcome. All of us in the college are trapped by our training, experiences and the university culture to do certain things in certain ways. The remarkable thing about the change at the University of Tennessee, then, is not that we are *doing* everything in our planning document. The remarkable thing is that a faculty socialized to highly traditional practices has publicly committed itself to a new future. As a faculty, we *are* making progress (Wisniewski, 1995).

The Faculty of Education at the University of Toronto is also making progress. As Ann Kilcher (1994, p.23) reported in her survey of "best practices" stemming from the option programs, "several themes are evident in the collection of strategies: collaboration, reflection, inquiry, integration, and experimentation." The original goals of provostial review in 1987, the Briars retreat, the themes from the B.Ed. Restructuring Committee, and the elements of the "best faculty of education" all stress these aspects. Their presence, in different ways and in different contexts, means something is being accomplished (see Kilcher, 1994). They have come to be the hallmarks of an evolving institutional culture.

Change persists. For some it moves too fast, for others not fast enough. Someone said to me recently that change at the Faculty may be a misnomer, and I wondered how close they were to the front lines. In the face of continuing change, only a broad strategic philosophy will guide it—a philosophy that is expressed and communicated becomes part of the emerging culture.

Some aspects of such a strategy are described by Dean Fullan:

> What was happening over the period of seven years is that preconditions were going in a broken front. There was a kind of jagged movement that at some point comes together, which then must be reinforced by additional strategies to go further. At some point those preconditions can really move it quickly. It looked before like it wasn't going to happen. Then overnight there was a convergence. In reality it was a long process.
>
> There is a certain chemistry and luck in this kind of process as well. Some of the norms and ideas were discovered along the way.
>
> The other thing we deliberately did, and I think this is part of the change process, is that we made the key norms very explicit. Once you say, collaboration is important, for example, and we need to model what we teach, then you call upon people to internalize it. Bringing these norms out into the open is almost like everyone talking

about it and saying what kind of culture do we have here, what kind do we want, and how do we get there?

I think it has become clear in all organizational change that you need to have each member of the organization think explicitly about the change process, think about reculturing... once you get it out it's very powerful because peers are talking about it, peers are doing it, and you can see examples.

The paradox of individualism and collectivism, especially in a university culture, means that choice is important.

Invest in the right people, give it time.

Growth is something like having even more complex and variegated relationships with your environment. Non-growth provides more security, but for an organization to grow it needs to go into even more complex sets of territory.

Leadership occurred in the options and the individual faculty, not in departments per se. Leadership, or strategy, or direction, in terms of my role was also conscious. But it required an intellectual forum for debate and interaction about what's happening.

More recently Fullan described his role in part by quoting Senge (Fullan, 1995, p.8):

> In essence, the *leader's task is designing the learning processes* whereby people throughout the organization can deal productively with the critical issues they face, and develop their mastery... this is new work.

Fullan describes the evolution of his own thinking about change as having three aspects that operate in a symbiotic way: one, being involved in the reforming of an institution; two, doing a lot of outside interaction; and three, writing about it. Chaos and new learning theory have made a significant difference in his thinking on change, and altered his approach to change from a more "technique-based" strategy, as in the practical research described at the beginning of this section, to a more developmental, philosophical perspective, evidenced in later work:

> I saw the value of thinking of a learning organization. I saw the value of ready-fire-aim. I could see it alive, working that way. I saw the value of, even the magic, of things coming together. If you invest in the right things and they sort of bubble up and you invest in the right people; if you don't panic too early and you keep going ahead, it's confirming, but also formulating some new perspectives on change. So it's the experience, and the learning.
>
> You can get better at continuous improvement in the same way you get better at anything, which is doing something, reflecting on it, trying to do it better, that's what you would do for change.

Change Is Learning, Just Do It

From a personal perspective, I am a player in this field of change. But a player with an interest in change, growth, and development, my own as well as that of others. I am interested in integrating what I know and giving it new form. That is a creative process, something I consider essential to life, learning, and the evolution of us all. I think being a professor would be much less interesting without the support and dialogue of my peers, though this still happens in many ways in more traditional contexts. One element I would like to comment on from my discussion with fellow faculty members over the five years of my employment is this: they now feel they *can change* and that they have *the active capacity for organizational learning*. They also feel they have choices in this, and that they can, cooperatively and individually, define what they want to work on. They also feel part of a whole, and that whole has accomplished something. Dean Fullan stated in his interview that he was proudest of the fact that ownership of this experience is held by so many people within the organization. It may have been facilitated by administrative and committee thinking, but individuals in groups or otherwise got the organization this far. They did this in part by taking the attitude,"Just do it," as the advertisement says. Do it, and the experience will take you somewhere.

This may then be the theme to communicate. Faculties of education are historically good at "ready-ready-ready" (Fullan in Stiegelbauer interview, 1995); they have to take more initiative at doing something. Goals or directions or themes have to be somewhat explicit, but flexible; there have to be incentives, but the big part is "doing it" and "taking it from there, learning from what you do," and involving as many people as possible in the conception and action—not without structure, not without leadership, not without supports and constraints. Just do it. That's what happened at the Faculty of Education. That's what is continuing to happen.

The Multicultural Experience: Teacher Education, Schools, and Communities

Keith A. McLeod is a professor at the Faculty of Education, University of Toronto. He was the founder and editor of MC Multiculturalism/ Multiculturalisme *from 1977-1993, and is a founding president of the Ontario Multicultural Association and a founder and president (1982-86) of the Canadian Council for Multicultural and Intercultural Education. He is the chair of the Department of Educational Policy and Foundation Studies.*

In the following narrative I give my reflections on my participation, and that of the Faculty of Education and University of Toronto, in formulating policies and practices, not only with reference to cultural diversity in Toronto, Ontario, and Canada, but also in relation to racial, ethnic, and religious discrimination and anti-discrimination, inequities and equity, racism, anti-racism and non-racialism, and the general thrust for pluralism and multiculturalism. This is, in a narrow sense, "my story" as a Faculty member and as a person who has been involved in education in relation to diversity. As the following represents my interpretation of trends, events, policies, and programs, I take sole responsibility for the views and interpretations expressed here.

I came to the Faculty in 1970, having studied ethnic relations, racial and religious discrimination, government policies in education regarding pluralism in Canada, and general minority issues. Therefore, in many ways, it was quite natural that I would participate in this area of teacher education and take an increasingly active role in education for diversity. I was only one of the interested Faculty members; moreover, it should be emphasized that probably contrary to the impressions outside the Faculty and university, the deans of the Faculty generally gave consistent support to education for diversity.

I think that it is appropriate in this introduction to give some explanation of a professor's work in a university. My experience has been that a professor's function is to provide academic and university leadership; this includes contributing to the life of the community at large. In my case, in a professional Faculty, my responsibility included professional leadership. Professors have the freedom and the responsibility, within general and specific criteria of accountability, to create their roles in the academic community and define their contribution to society. I can say frankly that there has never been a single occasion when the university administrators have ever cautioned me against advocacy of pluralism, anti-discrimination, countering racism, or being a proponent of multiculturalism or multicultural education.

When I was hired at the University of Toronto in 1970, the province of Ontario, the city of Toronto, and the country were becoming increasingly diverse, and people were having to come to terms with this. Within two years at the Faculty, it became evident that diversity had to be more fully addressed in education, including teacher education. At the same time, in October 1971, the government of Canada enunciated the policy of multiculturalism. As we had previously adopted the Official Languages Act, it was stated as "multiculturalism within a bilingual framework." The statement by the prime minister outlining the policy included a general commitment to pluralism and a few specifics such as cultural continuity, cultural sharing, and the availability to immigrant persons of one of the official languages. The fundamental point was that Canadians and Canada had moved from a policy of cultural uniformity and homogeneity to a policy of cultural pluralism.

The Policy and Community

To understand the significance of the policy, we have to go over some basic history. School children in many parts of the world were taught about the viability and vitality of the nation-state. The manifest destiny of the United States, the unification of Italy and Germany, and even the strength of Great Britain and France, were ascribed, however inconsistently and incorrectly, to ethnocultural homogeneity. People had been taught that pluriethnic states were doomed to failure. A noted scholar at Oxford, E.A. Freeman, was such a nation-state advocate. The concept was further reinforced after World War II by such concepts as self-determination and liberation. In the nineteenth and early twentieth centuries, the concept of the plural state was held in disrepute, especially in comparison with the nation-state. Every school child was taught, even if they had not learned all the implications, that a nation was based upon the prevalence and predominance of a single nationality. They had equally been taught that a nationality was a group of people bound together by ties of mutual interest such as common history, values, religion, ideas, origin, economic interests, language, and above all, belief that they were one people. Such ideas were common in Canada too, despite our diversity.

There had also been some discussion in Canada in the late nineteenth and early twentieth centuries regarding "race." If I were to summarize what people meant by "race" it would be said in one word—"colour." There had also been "pseudo-scientific" ideas in many quarters about the three major races—Caucasian, Mongoloid, and Negroid. Finally, after World War II, there had been a United Nations commission that had concluded there was only one human race, and if people wished to differentiate among humans, the only way of doing so would be to talk of "genetic pools" or groups of people with similar physical features. The commission made it clear that physical characteristics bore no relation to social characteristics or behaviour—these were learned. What was equally clear, however, was that humans were discriminating against others on the basis of physical characteristics—primarily skin colour, and that this racism needed to be countered.

As the communities in Canada began reflecting upon the new policy of pluralism, the impact began to be felt. In Toronto, as a result, a new organization was formed to support agencies, institutions, and people who were focusing upon working with diverse people and groups. Kay Brown, a social worker, Mae Waese, an emerging community activist, and others formed the Inter-Agency Council for Immigrants and Migrants. At issue were outdated concepts of planning institutional structures and care, values, community involvement and participation, as well as the necessity to face ethnic, racial, religious prejudice and discrimination. In brief, the agencies and institutions, in many instances, were still basing their work and programs upon concepts associated with cultural uniformity, ethnic hierarchies, and assimilation.

The challenge in education was no less—schools and teachers needed to recognize that there was ethnic and racial diversity in

Canada. The policy of multiculturalism recognized this ethnic and racial diversity; at the community level, advocates of multiculturalism said that institutions, including the schools, should serve *all* the diverse people who formed Canadian society. Unicultural concepts and ethnic and racial prejudice and discrimination and religious intolerance were not a suitable basis for the country.[1]

Policy Development

Because of the general nature of the concept of multiculturalism itself and the need to define it more specifically, there was also a need to define and implement multicultural education. This came about slowly.

Many in the province at first interpreted multicultural education in terms of providing English as a second language classes for immigrant children, and other services related to immigrant adjustment. However, in parts of the country where there were older settlements of diverse people, such as the prairies, cultural reinforcement programs and ethnic heritage programs predominated initially. In what might be termed the second phase of multicultural development, group or human relations issues became prominent. Now there was added emphasis on teaching in relation to prejudice, discrimination, racism, stereotypes, and the introduction of ethnic content vis à vis particular groups into the curriculum. Immigrant adjustment and English as a second language and also what was termed English as a second dialect continued to be important.[2]

Another discernible shift, however, took place in the eighties. Those who were succeeding, and to what extent, came to the fore. A parliamentary committee was struck to examine racism and ethnic discrimination. The national report, Equality Now! was released by the federal government. Racism and institutionalized or systemic discrimination became more prominent issues. We had entered the third phase, one of concern over what might be termed life's chances. Equality and equity were the headlines.

In the early eighties, the Canadian Council for Multicultural and Intercultural Education defined multiculturalism[3] in the following way:

> Multiculturalism fosters a society and a Canadian identity in which people and groups of all cultures are accepted. Multiculturalism promotes human and group relations in which ethnic, racial, religious, and linguistic similarities and differences are valued and respected.

The principles or tenets that are inherent in multiculturalism are:

1. equality of status of all cultural and ethnic groups within the framework of our officially bilingual country,
2. freedom of all individuals and groups to the retention and development of their cultures as part of the Canadian identity,
3. equality of access by all individuals and groups to employment and promotion, services and support,
4. commitment to sharing our cultures within the mainstream of Canadian society,
5. undertaking to participate in Canadian citizenship and the democratic process in terms of both rights and responsibilities,
6. belief that individuals have the freedom to choose the particular cultural attributes they prefer within the framework of our democratic principles,
7. respect for, and observance of, human rights and civil liberties as exemplified in the Canadian Charter of Rights and Freedoms, the common law, and human rights codes.

> Multiculturalism includes all Canadians and is for all Canadians (Statement adopted by The Canadian Council for Multicultural and Intercultural Education, May 24, 1984).

The above concepts are similar to those that were legislated into Canadian law in the eighties. The concept of multiculturalism was included in the Canadian constitutional amendments of 1981.

Meanwhile many of the provinces, including Ontario (1975), initiated multicultural policies. The Toronto Board of Education was among the first boards of education to adopt a policy.

Teacher Education: Cross-Cultural Education

Because of the need to target not only ethnic and racial issues but gender and class issues as well, a cross-cultural education course that would encompass a wide range of issues was adopted at the Faculty.[4] We agreed that class and gender were associated issues that should be dealt with as part of a critical approach to educational change. (In the following narrative though, I will concentrate almost exclusively upon the ethnic and racial aspects of the course.) The focus of the course was the cultural context of schooling and education; it was first offered in 1972. Culture was interpreted from the beginning in its full sense of the total way of life of people. I should note here that a second course was added later, in the 1978-79 academic year; however, it played a much smaller role in the overall teacher education program. It focused upon curricula and, to a lesser extent, upon teaching methods and strategies.

In the cross-cultural course, first of all, we designed the priorities. We began by helping the students to develop a sensitivity and understanding of diversity; we then attempted to assist them to see the implications in terms of implementation in such areas as administration, curriculum, and classroom teaching.

Secondly, through the course, we also opted for a philosophical perspective: pluralism was not an adjunct, was not transitory, exotic, or something odd, but a fundamental way of seeing ourselves and relating to one another. In education, we summarized this idea by saying that "multiculturalism must be an ethic underlying the total school program." Being different was not a sign of deprivation, but of cultural difference. Moreover, differences were to be seen in the context of similarities *and* differences.

A third characteristic of the course became increasingly clear as time went on—we had chosen a sociocultural approach. I say this despite the fact that the initial major reference that we asked students to read was Gordon Allport, The Nature of Prejudice (1957). The penchant of psychologists to look at human relations and discrimination in terms of disease and pathology was increasingly abandoned in favour of examining cultural differences and similarities and understanding of what happens when cultures, or people of different cultures, meet. What are the cultural and social processes that become operative? And how can we provide for cultural interaction—and social interaction? Anthropological and sociological analysis increasingly took over from psychology.

A Cultural Approach

The concept of a cultural approach to multicultural or intercultural eduction had some specific advantages in my view. As I stated previously, culture was interpreted as the way of life of a people; I used a simple paradigm to help students analyze and understand culture and the dynamics of culture.

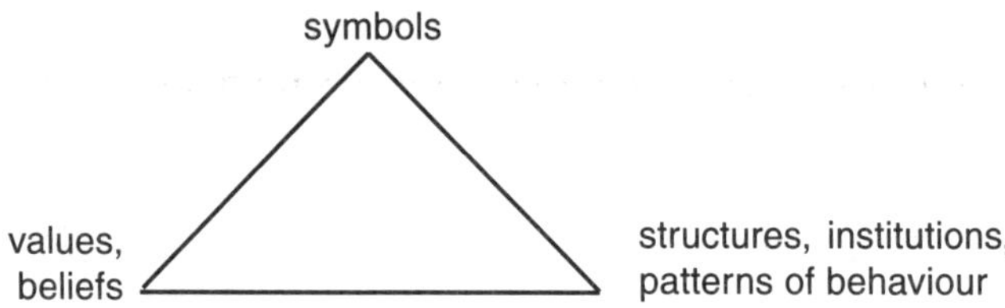

The advantages of the above analytical typology are several, especially in education and teaching. The following is just a brief outline of some of the major assets of this cultural approach:

1. It helps student teachers or teachers to understand and analyze their own perceptions and cultural backgrounds. ("What symbols do you cherish? What values do you uphold? What institutions do you participate in? What is the basis of your cultural behaviour?")
2. It helps teachers to understand components of culture such as languages, institutions, behaviour, values, and symbols, and the interaction of aspects of culture and the effect of teachers' behaviour upon the culture of the school and the learning environment.
3. It helps students to understand that there is a general Canadian culture, as well as ethnic subcultures, and that there is dynamic interaction among them in a plural society.
4. It helps teachers to analyze and understand what cultures the school or education program reflects.
5. It is useful to understand the approaches to multicultural education and how particular ideas and even ethnic and racial discrimination can become institutionalized. It is a comprehensive approach that leads us to look at the institutional and structural aspects of culture, in addition to values and the symbolic dimension. It leads to the key question of

how power and control in a culture operate or function. The typology also enables us to understand and not underestimate or dismiss the symbolic domain in peoples' lives.

The course in cross-cultural education proved to be in high demand among students. Within two or three years, about one-third of the student body was selecting it. While there were some difficulties in responding to the demand, it did have a positive effect. Because of the way students selected and took courses across the Faculty, the content spilled over into the many other courses the students took. However, this could not be taken to mean that the plural perspective was embraced across the Faculty. It wasn't and it could hardly be said to be so today. Change is a slow process.

The Dynamics of Teacher Education and Pluralism

To try to summarize the dynamics of any classroom is risky; to try to summarize the issues and the interchanges that go on in a teacher education course in relation to these "gut" issues (as the students often called them) is doubly risky. Having stated this risk, let me proceed to outline at least some of the major issues that became evident:

1. Especially in the early years of the course, most especially the first decade, a major issue for students was their disinclination to consider pluralism viable. After you have been "schooled" to think uniculturally, after you have been schooled primarily in a single culture, it is difficult to think that diversity is possible, acceptable, or good, and it is sometimes equally difficult to think of how different people have different experiences or cultural attributes. Similarly, if you have lived in a society that simply accepted ethnic and racial, gender, or class hierarchies, it is difficult to consider different ways or even to think of alternative relationships.
2. Secondly, student teachers did understand that the teacher was the one who established the educational environment for learning and the one whose assumptions were not often made explicit, much less debated or challenged by the students, especially young children. Therefore, the student teachers tussled with the question of whether professional teachers had the luxury or even the right to perpetuate uniculturalism when the country's policy was pluralism, or, in particular,

condone prejudice and discrimination in their classrooms or schools. (Similarly they had to face whether sexism and other forms of discrimination that were contrary to human rights codes were to be condoned.) The responsibilities of being a teacher in a compulsory system of education were difficult for students to reconcile with their personal views, for many of them had been brought up to accept institutionalized unicultural concepts and even institutionalized discrimination. Nevertheless, a basic aspect of cross-cultural education is that we all become more sensitive, publicly empathetic, and responsible.

The intersection of class discrimination and racial discrimination came to the forefront quickly. In the press and elsewhere, leaders from the African-Canadian communities pointed out that their children were being treated like working-class kids no matter what their actual status was, and they were also being subjected, for example, to low expectations. What did this mean? The result was a critical examination of how schooling and teaching could be class-biased.

3. The professors working with the student teachers were cautious in responding to requests for ethnic information regarding groups. Student teachers sometimes envisaged themselves as understanding Italian-Canadians or Blacks or Portuguese. The response was cautious in that we attempted to not reinforce stereotypes and to emphasize teacher skills in understanding that there was great diversity within groups and that we should use our analytical and observation skills and not overgeneralize. This point is not unrelated to another phenomenon; some student teachers "expected" that their program should provide them with what might be termed "prescriptions"—prescriptive answers and approaches. Again, the response of the professors was to stress reflective analysis and constructive teaching.
4. An equally important concept for student teachers to understand was the concept of resistance. Why was there individual and group resistance to change, to human rights, to equalizing opportunity, and to rectifying past discrimination? The answers were as varied then as they are twenty-five years later; however, the discussions and analysis had the effect of helping student teachers to understand their own resistance. This issue also naturally led to a discussion of the politics of education.

5. Another aspect of cross-cultural education was to perceive what teachers could do in spite of system insensitivity and systemic discrimination. The roles of individual teachers and their influences upon children and success were explored. Experiences of the student teachers themselves were elicited. What had been their experience in dealing with discrimination and barriers? How had they learned to cope and who had helped them learn to cope? What were good coping skills? While the terminology may not have been the same as today, the point at issue was empowerment—the empowerment of teachers and of students.
6. How did all of this relate to teaching content and curriculum? Who established the content? Who was marginalized or neglected? Student teachers were usually quick to point to history teaching and social studies. They were less likely to think of other subjects and content, such as whose literature and language were being taught.

One vivid recollection: a student said with conviction that she was not going to teach any literature if it was not of the standard of Shakespeare. Another student gave her a withering look and asked, "Have you even heard of Dante?" The issue of language in schooling was bound up in emotional debates regarding Canada, its past, and the future. What assisted a great deal over the years was the research of Canadians who demonstrated that bilingual education was possible, and that the better students knew their mother tongue, the better they were likely to be in learning English.

The issue of language in education was also related to immigration and immigrant students; there was sometimes difficulty in helping student teachers to understand the learning needs of immigrant children: their need to bridge cultures, the demands on them for "rapid" adjustment, the pressure of peers and parents and of the school and community. Student teachers had to develop the ability to observe and understand the varied nature of "settlement" and the processes of acculturation; but most especially student teachers had to learn the importance of language in the lives and educational success of immigrant students.

Inservice Education

The introduction of the concept of multicultural education into the schools and teaching profession did not always come easily. In the decade of the seventies, there was a great deal of resistance. Teachers who had been educated for unicultural teaching were sometimes at a loss when asked to be inclusive in their teaching. There was also stiff reaction, especially at the secondary level to introducing ethnic content; the school curriculum as a legitimator of knowledge was being protected by resistance. On the other hand, a revision of $P^{I}.J^{I}$., the provincial elementary curriculum outline, was more easily accomplished. Of course, the implementation came slowly, but in general, it was more comprehensive and more easily implemented.[5]

One can only reflect upon the hostility that advocates of multicultural education faced in the seventies. School board officials, quite aware of the needs, would invite proponents to speak at inservice education sessions. Sometimes you simply felt the hostility; sometimes it erupted in the form of an angry teacher who denied the need, denied the reason for it and the purpose of it. Even principals sometimes reacted negatively.

Part of the reason for the negative reaction was hostility to change, but underneath that there could be a further hostility—hostility to the challenge of the assumptions these educators had grown up with regarding pluralism: cultural values, institutions, and symbols. The principals were sometimes hostile because, as educational leaders, they were being expected to lead something they knew little or nothing about. In other instances, expectations were heaped upon them to change instantly the nature of the education in their schools.

From the beginning, the implementation of multicultural education has been dependent upon inservice education. Gradually the boards of education and the profession responded. A great deal of inservice time was spent exploring how to implement multicultural education.

Faculty members, including Professors George Bancroft, David Booth, and Vandra Masemann, for example, participated in the inservice work in the seventies and early eighties. By 1979, the

Faculty was also offering a three-part ministry additional qualification; this had limited success or appeal to teachers who at that time were dealing with job loss due to lower enrollments and financial cutbacks.[6] By the mid-1980s, several boards hired their own consultants, and the process of development and implementation became more systematic and comprehensive. However, a great deal of the work of these consultants over the years has been taken up in helping teachers and principals deal with incidents of discrimination. Other areas that occupied a great deal of their attention were school-community relations, teacher sensitivity, and altering the school curriculum.[7]

Racism

Student teachers needed opportunities to deal with issues relating to physical differences, colour, or race. The resistance in coming to terms with racism in the early seventies usually led to the impulse to want to talk about or focus upon the issue in the United States. As the seventies moved into the eighties, there was a marked difference in the realization of "white" students that Toronto, Ontario, and Canada were becoming much more multiracial.

The rapid growth in the number of persons of African and Asian background had several ramifications. Stereotypic discriminatory responses were common. For example, though persons of African and Asian background had been in Canada for generations, the assumption was not uncommon that they were all recently from somewhere else. However, an even more serious issue was to help student teachers understand the subtle and not-so-subtle aspects of institutionalized racism in education and in society. The manner in which discrimination was manifested in school was explored. These analyses ranged from where students were seated in class, to whom was called upon to help the teacher, to teachers' expectations, to who was succeeding in schools. As with other forms of discrimination and bias, the resources, teaching, curriculum, policies, administration, and community and parental participation were explored for barriers and racism.

Anti-Racism

The advent of the concept of anti-racism and anti-racist education both helped and hindered the educational endeavour. The "anti" nature of the movement led to some emphasis of negative approaches. As one member of the African-Canadian community expressed it at a school workshop—"There has to be something more than being against racism." However, the anti-racism perspective did sharpen the focus on discrimination based upon physical characteristics, and it has led to increased awareness that racism must be confronted and dealt with, not only at the personal level but at the systemic level.

Anti-racism became in one sense the response of persons particularly concerned with discrimination based upon physical characteristics or differences. Anti-racists wanted racism to be *the* priority.[8]

Some people or groups saw language as crucial to pluralism and discrimination; they took a linguistic interpretation or approach to multiculturalism. Others saw behavioural factors as key, and they adopted a cultural interpretation or approach. Still others saw values as central, and they adopted a values approach. To members of the African-Canadian communities and others, the issue of discrimination based upon physical characteristics was paramount; they argued therefore that anti-racism was an overriding priority. This was a perfectly understandable position; moreover, countering racism was an aspect of policy that needed emphasis and attention.

One difficulty was that some anti-racists were derisive of, or rejected, the very concept of pluralism that was basic to their cause; forgotten was an understanding that multiculturalism means live and let live and that "there are some things I cannot change and some things I will not change." The anti-racist movement became focused too exclusively on the isolation of discrimination based upon colour and this focus resulted in the breakup of some of the coalitions for change.[9] In fact, the exclusiveness of anti-racism became a problem. Some groups that had encountered generations of severe discrimination on other grounds felt left out. Moreover, the rejection of multiculturalism in favour of anti-racism gave unwitting support to the critics of pluralism, and in other instances it also fractured the community coalitions that had developed.

Unfortunately, the divisiveness that had been fostered showed up when there were attempts to implement affirmative action and equity; there was rapid rejection. Whether there will be a revival of equity in Ontario based upon inclusive multicultural precepts or human rights concepts, or renewed multiculturalism within the concept of citizenship, or some other remodelled version of pluralism, is an open question at this point.[10]

Diversity and Student Enrolment

With the changing demographic makeup of Ontario and the area of metropolitan Toronto, the enrolment of the Faculty changed. By the early 1970s, the Italian-Canadian community had become highly visible within teacher education; males and even more females enrolled to become teachers. Greek-Canadians also became committed to post-secondary education and while they were not as numerous as the Italians, many became teachers.

By the late 1980s, it was clear that students of Asian and African background would be needed in teaching. In fact, there was a serious need for teachers of these backgrounds. There were many schools, especially in urban Ontario, with significant African and Asian populations, but with few or even no teachers of those origins.

This led to a debate. Are students best taught by teachers of their own origin? There is little doubt that the research shows that students need teachers who are role models, including teachers with whom they can identify. The presence in schools of such teachers will help students through emulation, identification, and perceptions of opportunity and participation. There are also issues of cultural understanding that representative teachers can provide the school and other teachers.

However, the positive qualities of teachers of all backgrounds also contribute to education: to intergroup understanding, tolerance and acceptance, and the general willingness and capability to learn from "others." Therefore, it is clear that we need teachers of diverse origins and that all teachers need the knowledge, skills, and dispositions to work in diverse classrooms and schools.

Nevertheless, when it was becoming obvious that students of colour were not applying or securing admission in appropriate numbers, action was necessary. Two ideas emerged. One was to create a mechanism for attracting or recruiting minority students. The second was to re-examine the criteria for admission. The concept of recruiting students from underrepresented groups was proposed to the ministry responsible for "anti-racism." It responded that such a program was the responsibility of the Ministry for Higher Education which was, at that moment, being dissolved and its functions incorporated into the Ministry of Education. It passed the proposal on to the Ministry of Education, which, in turn, responded that faculties of education were responsible! The meaning became clear: no assistance would be forthcoming to help attract or recruit minority students. But, some six years later, under another government, the Ministry of Education was trying to encourage and even demand such programs for recruiting students from underrepresented groups! (Now, with yet another change in government, the efforts will probably cease.)

The process of securing a more diverse and representative student group was underway in any case at our Faculty. The need to attract visible or racial minority students had become part of the discourse. Admission of students was based upon two basic factors, marks or grades in their undergraduate degree and an "Experience Profile" that reflected their experiences or activities, and indicated if they were interested in students, teaching, and learning. Traditional criteria of experience and educationally related activities that would indicate the potential students' interest in teaching were broadened and made more inclusive. Thus on the "Experience Profile," which could constitute as much as half of the students' admission portfolio, minority students now had an equal chance. The academic standards were maintained, but an increasing numbers of students of minority background secured entry because the "playing field" was now inclusive and level. The record speaks for itself. From a point of about five percent of the student body in 1987, the proportion increased to about fifteen percent in 1994-95.

At the same time that admission criteria on the "Experience Profile" were re-examined, other events helped change enrolment patterns. School boards and boards of education had clearly signalled that they were hiring visible minority persons. This was being done for two reasons: one was so that the board could provide role-model teachers in schools, and the second was the board need and responsibility to respond to provincial equity policies. Jobs were now available.

The importance of this signal cannot be overemphasized. Whereas minority students had had difficulty in securing positions (and promotions), there was now an emphasis upon equity. This change helped increase applications at faculties. Another, more local effort, was the establishment of an outreach program (The Future Teachers' Club) where minority students at the Faculty helped to encourage prospective minority candidates, including secondary school students, to think about teaching as a possible career.

MC Multiculturalism/Multiculturalisme

Another activity that the Faculty became involved with was the publication of a journal.

At the same time as I was asked by the University of Manitoba to be a visiting professor in multicultural education for the academic year 1976-77, I was assessing the possibility of establishing a bulletin or journal devoted to multicultural education. About that time, there was a rumour that the Ontario Ministry of Culture and Recreation was planning some kind of in-house publication on multiculturalism. Through Tim Rees, who was at the ministry, I proposed that instead of an in-house publication, a multicultural periodical with community and educational focuses be published by the Faculty with support from the ministry.

The Ontario Ministry approved the venture late in 1976. Betty Wangenheim, who had many years of experience in the field, agreed to be assistant editor. By early spring of 1977, the first issue was in print.

It was not as easy as it sounds. When the idea was initially proposed to my department that they be listed as one of the publishers, they rejected it. Nevertheless, the project went ahead when Dean John Ricker became aware of the project and suggested that it be published simply under the aegis of the Faculty of Education by the Guidance Centre, which at that time was a quasi-publications centre distributing school guidance material.

Thus, Multiculturalism / Multiculturalisme began.[11]

The publication underwent several metamorphoses over the fifteen years that the Faculty was co-publisher. For the initial agreed-upon five years, the Ontario ministry provided funding. However, they then suggested that other support must be found. The University of Toronto stepped into the breech for a year, following which the Canadian Council for Multicultural and Intercultural Education (CCMIE) became the co-publisher. Articles on multicultural issues were published over the years, written by people in all parts of the country. Many of the key advocates and researchers had their work published. From 1981 (Vol.V, #1) to 1993, the associate editor was Dr. Vandra Masemann, who contributed a great deal to multicultural education and community development in Canada. After fifteen years, in May of 1993, with the publication of Vol. XV #2/3, I ceased to be editor, and the involvement of the Faculty in the publication ceased. The Canadian Council for Multicultural and Intercultural Education took over the complete operation of the journal.

For some fifteen years (1977-1993), it fulfilled an important role in helping to develop, broaden, and implement the concept of pluralism or multiculturalism. The focus on education as well as community development, including social work, health, racism, human and group relations, and general ethnic issues, helped people, especially teachers, to understand what pluralism or multiculturalism entailed. As a university-sponsored publication, it gave credibility to multiculturalism at a crucial moment.

Community Participation

Fundamentally, there are two approaches a university can take to involving the community. One is to bring the community into the institution; the other is to go out into the community. Let me take up the latter first.

From 1971, when the Faculty began working with the Inter-Agency Council for Immigrants and Migrants, there was involvement in ethnic and racial or multicultural issues in the community. In 1975, FEUT hosted the first conference on multicultural education ever held in the province. Representatives from community groups, provincial agencies, the federal government, school boards, and schools attended; they explored educational issues and multiculturalism.[12]

By 1979, there was national action. In 1978, a plan to develop a national conference had fallen through. In an attempt to salvage the idea, Abe Peters, from the Manitoba Department of Education, convened a group of interested people in Winnipeg. The result was a national council with one representative per province and territory (Yukon and North West Territories), to plan a national conference on multicultural education in Winnipeg for 1981. To make a long story short, the federal government, by agreeing to fund a national council with broad representation, made multicultural education increasingly part of the discourse in education across the country—in English and in French, as well as many other languages. The conference in November 1981 brought more than 900 people together. Languages, racism, school systems, classrooms, teachers, and students as well as programs, curriculum, and community involvement were focuses. The opening speaker, Dr. Mavis Burke from the Ontario Ministry of Education, set the tone for the need to develop and implement multiculturalism in education. The involvement of Native people was stressed as was overall national involvement.[13] The speakers and workshops at the conference examined a great many issues, from classroom strategies to community involvement in addressing the need to change educational institutions and systems so that pluralism was reflected in education. Stereotypes, racism, and other forms of discrimination were addressed.

Part of the agenda leading up to the conference was the formation of provincial committees to provide input and a more organized base. In Ontario, there was a large committee of educators and community persons. Thirty-five to forty people attended these meetings. At the conference itself, there was time set aside for provincial meetings. There was also time to meet with Roberta Russell, and Kerry Johnson, the Director General of Multiculturalism from Ottawa. They were approached to assist with the continuation of the national council. This ad hoc national council was subsequently transformed into the Canadian Council for Multicultural and Intercultural Education, which still exists and continues to organize national programs and triennial national conferences.

In the case of Ontario, the movement to organize led subsequently to the formation of the Ontario Multicultural Association (OMAMO), which continues to function as an organization supporting educational endeavours with respect to diversity. The founding meeting of this organization was held at FEUT.

A parallel event took place with reference to health and social work. In 1984 in North York, a small group of concerned persons met to discuss "multicultural health." At that meeting, it was agreed to proceed with an organization, the boundaries of which were left indefinite. The result, within one year, was a provincial organization: The Multicultural Health Coalition (MHC), with divisions across the province of Ontario.

At the time of the planning of the first provincial conference on multicultural health (held at FEUT) by this group, it was agreed to invite key participants from the other provinces. These guests agreed to form provincial groups that would become part of a Canadian Council for Multicultural Health (CCMH). This organization has provided leadership in professional education in the fields of health, social work, and allied fields, and also, it has played an instrumental role in educating governments, college and university professors, and community groups regarding what committees and health care needed. The organization itself provided a focus for mutual education and self-help.[14] It also led to my involvement in seniors' issues including ethnicity and aging (1988) and subsequently, two years of work in this field helping with national projects as well as local activities. All of these activities brought many persons from local communities to FEUT and to the university. The university was there to help and participate.

Similarly, there were times when community persons were specifically invited to FEUT. Following the formation of the Urban Alliance on Race Relations in about 1977 by the late Dr. Wilson Head and others, representatives from the alliance were invited to FEUT to discuss mutual concerns with Faculty members. An interesting discussion took place in which Wilson Head made it quite clear that all was not well, and that more needed to be done to promote changes in schools and in teacher education.

Over the years, there have been many occasions when persons meeting at FEUT have continued to express their views on teacher education and public systems of education. The open door in turn led many individuals to seek information and support on a multitude of matters relating to human rights, human relations, and the implementation of multiculturalism. This community orientation also resulted in my being a member for several years of the Ontario Advisory Council on Multiculturalism and Citizenship, and also being called upon to participate in numerous other ethnic and community organizations.[15]

English as a Second Language; Heritage Language Education

In the early seventies, there was no ESL program for teachers at the Faculty; even teachers from the school systems who wanted to develop knowledge and skills in this field attended one of the special courses offered by the Ministry of Community and Social Services. Change finally came in 1977, when the Faculty introduced ESL for students in the teacher education program. It was offered through the English department, not through the department that specialized in second language teaching. In subsequent years, large numbers of teachers secured ESL as an additional qualification. The preservice course was recognized as Part I, and teachers could further develop this area by securing Part II and finally their "Specialist Qualification." In the academic year 1984-85, English as a second language ceased to be part of the preservice offering; teachers could take this teaching subject only after having completed their initial preservice program.

In 1977, Ontario developed the heritage languages program for elementary schools in order to respond to the community demand for mother-tongue support. In order to avoid conflict with intransigent educators and community people who believed that such teaching was deleterious to English language development, the Ministry of Education authorized the new program under continuing education. This had some advantages, however, as teachers for continuing education were not required to have provincial certification. This meant that many educated immigrants, including foreign trained-teachers, could and did teach.

As continuing education courses, the heritage languages could be offered on the weekend, after school, or between parts of a school day, for example, from 10:00 to 10:30 by extending the school day by half an hour. The ministry agreed to provide funds for the payment of the teachers under continuing education costs for up to 2.5 hours per week per course. A disadvantage was that the ministry did not direct, promote, or suggest an appropriate response from the teacher education faculties. The record of FEUT in this area has not been particularly innovative; however, some professors who have taught modern languages have taken a serious interest in this program, even though their first interest was language teaching at the secondary level.

The Faculty has had a long history in language education. We shall simply pick up the story in 1970, when the classics department provided for Latin and Greek and a separate modern languages department provided for French, German, Italian, Spanish, and Russian. There have been some changes over the years with reference to which modern languages are offered. The other change is that the classical languages teacher-education course has ceased to be offered regularly.

Curriculum and Teaching Strategies

In the Faculty, there was some measure of indifference and even resistance to integrating multicultural content in teacher education. Gradually, however, professors in such areas as the English teaching-subject area introduced students to a greater variety of "Canadian" literature. Similarly teacher education professors in history, the social sciences, family studies, and geography gradually took up diversity. Many of these efforts were individual. A more organized approach was developed by the professors of science education; they developed a component on basic classroom and educational issues relating to diversity, which they included in their science education course.

An examination of various school board policy statements and studies have indicated that teachers were addressing many aspects of schooling from resources, classroom activities, co-curricular activities, and the general atmosphere of schools. The Ministry of Education in the period from 1977 to the 1990s published many curriculum support documents.

Being involved much more in policy than methodology, I became increasingly frustrated by the lack of attention to what we might call "strategies that work." Some Faculty members encouraged cooperative learning strategies by bringing into the Faculty persons who were proponents of cooperative learning to introduce the student teachers. One such "guest" was John Myers from the Toronto Board of Education. But more was needed. From the 1950s on, researchers had told us that some strategies and methods were more likely to produce success in schools, classrooms, and societies that were multiethnic or multiracial. We had adopted some of these concepts and techniques in cultural support programs (e.g., cultural reinforcement, language support, and transition). However, in the more general area of teaching for better human and group relations there was a lag in the implementation of research findings. The result was "Putting It All Together," a video that introduced the importance of learning from contact theory, principle testing, and conditioning. These had been current in the research and in some areas of American education. These strategies had also been analyzed by American researchers, who had concluded that the "personal involvement factor" was most important in developing attitudes. Similarly, the research on cooperative learning and other methods had shown positive evidence regarding what was most likely to be effective in teaching for positive human relations. The video explored the need for teachers to implement experiential learning, mixed groupings of students, positive imaging, peer teaching, conflict resolution, parental and community involvement, and several other strategies, methods, or educational principles. In short, the video was a plea that we pay attention to what we teach and how we teach. In a world where process is conceded to be very important, it is quite remarkable there has been so little attention paid to the effects of different teaching strategies and to the learning environment.

As I near the end of this narrative, I cannot help but stop and reflect upon the many persons—local, national, and international—with whom I have had the pleasure of working over the years. I have mentioned Mavis Burke, George Bancroft, and Vandra Masemann. But there are many others, such as Inez Elliston, Jane Gibson, and Karen Mock, and Dr. Ralph Masi, Shanthi Radcliffe, and Maria Herrera from the health field. At the national level, Peter McCreath, Sonia Morris, Jack Kehoe, Kogila Moodley, Walter Temelini. Internationally, friends stretch from Moscow (Mara

Ustinova) to Detroit (Professor Otto Feinstein) to London, England (Professor Jagdish Gundara). All have added interest to my work at FEUT.

To Sum Up

Where does all of this leave teacher education at the Faculty today? There are several points that are evident.

1. There is a continuing need to integrate pluralism even more firmly across the whole institution and program. It is also clear that it takes time for Faculty renewal and for newer teacher educators to become more firmly rooted in concepts of diversity, to incorporate subject matter related to diversity into the teacher education program and into what they are advocating that teachers teach and how they should teach.
2. Another major area that needs greater emphasis is the role of educational psychology in relation to diversity. The lack of integration of diversity into so-called "standard" concepts of child development, parenting, and psychological analysis need to be re-examined; psychology has been culturally bound. Learning theories similarly need re-examination. On the other hand, it is important that over-generalizations regarding particular cultural patterns are avoided. I am thinking here that some educators have made simplistic claims associating learning styles and cultural groups.
3. Teacher educators and educators in general need to be more realistic in their expectations of schooling and teachers. Underlying a great deal of the literature are concepts of liberation and empowerment that need to be tempered. In an increasingly interdependent world, persons and groups are increasingly interdependent. Empowerment is often portrayed only in relation to rights, not responsibilities. Overburdened rhetoric creates unrealistic expectations; there has been ample evidence that schools are not the primary vehicle to reform or reconstruct society. However, there is equally strong evidence that schools should be part of the solution, not part of the problem. It would be more effective if we expected our schools and teachers to be up-to-date, not twenty or thirty years behind society and cultural change and behind in their skills, knowledge, and dispositions.
4. There is a continuing need to strengthen the representative diversity of members of the Faculty. While the visible or racial

minority population in Ontario is about ten percent, and this percentage is reflected in administrators and professors at the Faculty, the Faculty needs to more closely reflect who is in the metropolitan Toronto community (about twenty percent).

5. There should be continuing outreach by the profession and the Faculty in the community that not only supports the university but the schools of Ontario. This should be done not only for the purposes of recruiting teacher education candidates representative of the community and the needs of the students in the schools, but to keep the Faculty up-to-date on matters of community interest and professional and public concern.
6. Lastly, it is crucial that there be a reformulation of the concept of multicultural education. The concept needs to be made more inclusive and overarching. It probably should be based upon fundamental concepts such as citizenship and human rights. Thus the concept could be inclusive of the various aspects that different groups think are crucial or are a priority. The coalitions need to be rebuilt to offset the reactionary views that have become increasingly prevalent not only in education but in Canadian society.

In conclusion, as this century turns into the next, there will continue to be a myriad of issues in the complex communities in which many of the students or new teachers go to find employment. We need to help the beginning teachers secure the knowledge, skills, and dispositions to be successful educators. The encouraging thing is that within this Faculty, in recent years, new, younger faculty members are providing leadership and creative support. It is also encouraging that the students are coming into teacher education better prepared to live and work in a plural society and in classrooms where the students come from diverse origins. They are, in many instances, graduates of schools and universities that have already taken the concept of pluralism seriously. The policy of multiculturalism will be twenty-five years old on October 8, 1996; a generation has been educated during that time. Will the next twenty-five years further improve education and society?

Some forty of the 120 boards in the province had multicultural policies. In 1991, the Ministry of Education, in effect, told the rest of the boards to develop anti-racist and ethnocultural equity policies. That process was just being completed in 1995 when the government went down to a severe election defeat. The status of these policies and the implementation of them under the new government are open questions.

Endnotes

1. An indication of the 1960s background to the policy of 1970 will be found in the Report of the Royal Commission on Bilingualism and Biculturalism and in the work of such academics as Jean Burnet. Unfortunately very little has been written about the early days of multiculturalism and the development of community groups that had to deal with the tension between outdated professional approaches and community solutions that were geared to concepts of assimilation, conformity, and unicultural ideals.
2. One of the first conferences that symbolized the immigrant and ESL focus was held at the Ontario Institute for Studies in Education in the early seventies. See A. Wolfgang (ed.), Toronto, OISE, 1975. For early developments in the seventies see also *Tesl Talk,* Vol. 10, No. 3, Summer 1979. This issue focuses upon reviewing that decade. See also Canadian Society for the Study of Education annual publication, 1981, No.3. Beginning in 1984 this statement was usually printed in French and English on the inside cover of MC Multiculturalism / Multiculturalisme.
4. See calendars of the Faculty of Education, University of Toronto starting with 1972.
5. See P^1J^1 changes in the mid-seventies. Katherine Michalski at the Ministry of Education led this change.
6. Dr. Mavis Burke came to the Ontario Ministry of Education in 1976. Publications from 1979 and 1980 include, *Multiculturalism, Bilingualism and Canadian Institutions,* Toronto Guidance Centre, University of Toronto, 1979; and Intercultural Education and Community Development Toronto, Guidance Centre, University of Toronto, 1980. These, plus articles in Multiculturalism, relate to community involvement.
7. Within the Toronto area an excellent group of consultants were employed, such as Dr. Inez Elliston (Scarborough) Rod McColl (York), Theresa Gonzales, (MSSB).
8. Probably one of the most influential books was that of Enid Lee, Letters to Marcia, Toronto, Cross Cultural Communication Centre, 1985.
9. One of the negative statements came out under the name of the Ontario Ministry of Education. This was quite ironic in that many of us had for years lobbied to get the Ministry of Education to move further along in implementation and addressing discrimination. See Ministry of Education, 1987.
10. See reports #1 & #2 of the Canadian Association of Second Language Teachers—Multicultural Education: The State of the Art—A National Study. There will also be a report from a Commission on Multicultural Education that will attempt to renew the focus of multicultural education.

11. The name at first was simply Multiculturalism. In 1983, we altered the name to MC Multiculturalism / Multiculturalisme.
12. See the reports of this and others of the CCMIE national conferences.
13. The issue of Native people in relation to Aboriginal rights, and in relation to multiculturalism, is very interesting. Many Native people, including leaders of Aboriginal organizations have kept away from involvement in the multicultural policy and program. They insist that Aboriginal rights must be their focus. While this view is very logical and clearly sets out their priority distancing themselves from the concept and supporters of pluralism has also had the negative effect of not encouraging coalitions between Native peoples and others interested in rights and pluralism.
14. My direct involvement with MHC in Ontario lasted some eight years. In the initial years, the major service I assisted with was keeping the organization in line with the rapid growth. Similarly, the rapid growth of the national organization from an Ontario base involved some sensitive negotiations. On the one hand, some Ontarians thought they could maintain control of the national body by keeping the preponderance on the board. Fortunately, the president, Dr. Ralph Masi, had a national view.
15. I was a member of the Ontario Advisory Council on Multiculturalism and Citizenship from 1980 to 1984; it was very interesting to work with representatives from many communities and groups in Ontario. It was an education in itself. I was on the council when it was chaired by Yuri Shymko, and then by Dr. Mavis Burke.

Who Are the New Teachers?

Suzanne M. Stiegelbauer, an assistant professor at the Faculty of Education, received her doctorate in social anthropology and has studied the process of change in education in such diverse organizations as the United States Federal Office of Education and Improvement, the Texas Research and Development Center in Teacher Education, Toronto region boards of education, and the Toronto Native Canadian Centre. In 1990, she collaborated with Michael Fullan on the writing of The New Meaning of Educational Change (1991). *She has been a member of an elementary option team, a coordinator of a junior/intermediate option, and currently coordinates and teaches visual arts.*

Dr. Gary Hunt is the chair of Elementary Education and Student Services at the Faculty of Education, University of Toronto. His department has been creating school board partnerships for the last eighteen years. His work in student services has allowed him to explore advocacy for university students in the areas of academic, financial, and personal concerns. In determining student needs and ways of meeting those needs, he has developed an integrated student services model involving student government, faculty-based student services, and central university services. In 1995, he was given the Meritorious Award for Outstanding Contribution to Education in Ontario.

> Looking back on my application to the faculty, I almost feel embarrassed by what I wrote. This is not to say that what I wrote is not valid. My desire to become a teacher and what I feel I could contribute to the profession are still the same. I am still the same person who wrote that application, but somehow I feel that I have changed. I was definitely not prepared for what I was about to encounter.
>
> (Graduating Teacher, 1992)

Becoming a teacher is as much a process as it is a commitment. Individuals decide that teaching is for them for a number of reasons, from the influence of early role models to the need to change professions. They come from backgrounds that can include a great deal of general experience or very little; many are just out of university and a few are professional hockey players; they have realistic and unrealistic expectations of what the teaching-learning process is; they know something or not much about the social environment of schools. All of this, and more will be part of their eight-month experience at the Faculty of Education. Even if it becomes a two-year program, as proposed (see Stiegelbauer, 1995), "becoming a teacher" is a major endeavour, for teacher candidates and for the Faculty.

This chapter is about people in that process, the new teachers—who they are, why they attend the Faculty, and what they experience while they are here. For that reason, it will feature their voices, interwoven with "facts" about the Faculty, the teacher candidates, and program supports. It is through this subjective voice that the real picture of a teacher education institution emerges, in all its shape and substance. It is through these experiences that individuals start to "become" teachers.

> Teaching is a vocation, a calling. It is difficult to avoid precisely for the sense of responsibility and commitment that it evokes.
>
> (Junior / Intermediate Candidate, 1992)

> I want to make a difference. I would like to be able to help young children discover how to learn and to help build their self-esteem and confidence so that they are able to grow, mature and question things around them. For myself, I could not see any more rewarding and meaningful profession.
>
> (Elementary Candidate, 1992)

The Beginning: Acceptance at FEUT

Each year, the University of Toronto Faculty of Education (FEUT) receives approximately 8000 applicants from across Canada and beyond. From these, 900-1000 candidates are selected for entrance to the post-baccalaureate fifth-year program, which results in certification after one academic year (eight months). The acceptances represent a particularly select group, given the competition. A combination of factors is weighted equally in the admission process—academic grades, an applicant "profile" designed to capture their reasons for entering teaching, their teaching experience to date, and their comments regarding learning from these experiences. Because of the demand for experience in teaching, the average age of applicants is slightly older, around twenty-eight, but includes teacher candidates from the age of twenty-two to fifty. Some form of previous teaching experience is seen by the Faculty as an important element in the application as it illustrates commitment and a knowledge base from which to start with the academic certification year. The minimum academic average required for acceptance is in the "B" range for previous university work (with most acceptances being higher).

> I chose FEUT for a number of reasons. I knew people who had gone through other programs. Some were more theoretical, involved more assignments—written essays, research projects, etc. I wanted more focus on the practical classroom—getting in the classroom and working-up units and doing lesson plans and the things that you are going to have to do every day. I also liked the collaboration and collegiality. I do my best work talking to people, bouncing ideas and working on things together.
>
> (Junior / Intermediate Candidate, 1995)

FEUT has programs in three divisions or panels: primary / junior (JK-grade 6), junior / intermediate (grades 4-10), and intermediate / senior (grades 7-OAC). Applicants select the level they are interested in and are admitted in part on what they say about that interest. Each panel has members of the Faculty and the teaching profession who review applicants to that level. At the elementary level, applicants often write more about their responsibility related to the growth and development of the child; at the secondary level, the relationship between the student, the subject matter, and the teacher is frequently emphasized (Stiegelbauer, 1992). This is considered desirable and natural at this stage of interest. During the teacher candidates' time at FEUT, some of this orientation may change to create overlap—the secondary candidates may think more about adolescent development, and primary candidates may think more about content and its expression in the classroom. For acceptance, however, teacher candidates are specific about a preference, and are considered in terms of what they say about that preference.

> When I didn't get into the Faculty on my earlier application, I appealed. I felt all the work I had done to get into the Faculty was not recognized. I was certain that had anyone from the Faculty known my background, they would have thought that I was a very suitable candidate. However, when I found out that I had been accepted to the TAP (teacher apprenticeship) program, that was a blessing because the opportunity for me to show who I was through the interview was obviously the vehicle for getting into this field. I also felt that getting the experience was just going to make me a better student anyway at the Faculty. I didn't see it as a year wasted. I thought of it more as something that would be better for me in the long run.
>
> (Primary/Junior Candidate, 1995)

Because of the sheer number of candidates, not everyone can be admitted. As a result, the admissions committee has a number of strategies for promising candidates, or those near the cut-off line. Some go on a "next-to-be-admitted" list; some are admitted to a teacher apprenticeship program (TAP), a year-long program that provides experience in classrooms and, upon successful completion, guarantees entrance to the Faculty the following year; some just try again. Most candidates apply to more than one teacher education institution, and some continue to apply for four or five consecutive years until admittance or another interest comes their way.

Teacher Candidates: Who They Are

The statistics collected by the admissions office at FEUT show a cross-section of the Canadian population. A review of the characteristics of candidates by the FEUT registrar (1993, see also Stiegelbauer, 1992) according to age, gender, grades, occupational interests, and country of origin shows the following general characteristics (Figure 1 and text following):

Figure 1 General Characteristics of Accepted Applicants 1992

Gender	*Percent*
Female	65
Male	35
Grade average range upon acceptance	
A	42
B	52
C/Special	6
Other degrees held upon acceptance	
Ph.D	2.5
Master's	14
Baccalaureate	83.5
Age by birth decade	
1930	2.1
1940	8
1950	17
1960	76
1970	7
Acceptance by division	
Primary/Junior	31.4
Junior/Intermediate	21
Intermediate/Senior	47

A closer look at the applicants' characteristics reveals more diversity in age, interest, background, and gender at the secondary level than at the primary/junior or junior/intermediate levels. The number of females and males in the intermediate/senior level is almost equal, whereas at the primary level, females predominate. Elementary candidates are more likely to be female (76%), younger, and have experience in some kind of "helping" field, such as social work or nursing. MAs and Ph.Ds are found in both panels.

Former occupations listed across all applicants include MBAs, MSWs, pastors or priests, CUSO workers, lawyers, nurses, social workers, and applicants who worked in the fields of music production, writing, medical sciences, sales, counseling, engineering, accounting, film production, professional music and acting, business management, journalism, customer relations, computers, insurance, public relations, and graphic design, to name a few (Stiegelbauer, 1992a). Both elementary and secondary candidates cite church or civic experience—Sunday school, church youth camps, girl guides, coaching, and so forth, as important examples of ways that they have worked with children in the past. This presents a picture of a more traditional kind of community involvement than may be the norm for other academic areas.

> I would advise students coming to the Faculty not to be afraid to share their past experience with the people around them, particularly for people in their second career. I think in education there is room for every other experience. Students need to really be aware that the life experience they had before the Faculty will bear some relevance to what they're doing now.
>
> (Primary / Junior Candidate, 1995)

Teacher Candidates: Why We Want to Be Teachers

Teacher candidates apply to a specific panel or division—primary / junior, junior / intermediate, or intermediate / senior, and indicate on their application their reasons for interest in that division. Those reasons are taken into consideration by the admissions committee, along with their academic record, in deciding who will be admitted. A review of these reasons indicated some interesting trends or themes about the people and their perception of teaching at each level (Stiegelbauer, 1992).

Primary/Junior

As a group, these applicants are characterized by a larger number of younger females and by less diversity of background (ethnicity, country of origin) than other program groups. They also include more applicants with specific experience with hospitals, special education, and individuals in special needs populations, as well as more mention of church and community aid experience

(Stiegelbauer, 1992). This emphasis on "helping" professions and statements about "caring" as a needed aspect of working with younger children is a unique feature of this group. Personal statements from primary/junior candidates in their applications also indicate a more traditional home and community life, though these are also mentioned in samples from the other programs to a lesser degree.

Teacher candidates at this level described six themes related to their reason for wanting to work with younger children. All statements following are from elementary candidates.

1. I Want to Make a Difference

By far the most frequent theme in the responses to why applicants wanted to be a teacher was that of "caring" and "wanting to make a difference." Applicants expressed goals related to their sense of responsibility for laying the groundwork for young students so that their later years in school and in society will be more successful. They see working with young students as a way to contribute to the development of a positive future for society and the individuals they teach, and derive satisfaction from working toward that goal.

> Teaching and education is a continuous process of growth and development filled with constant change for both the student and the teacher. Learning is about understanding yourself and the world around you. Through my interaction with the students, I hope to learn and grow to be a more complete person myself. Any experience which helps to enhance this growth is significant.

2. Teaching Allows for Mutual Growth and Continuous Learning for Student and Teacher

The second theme involves the fact that students are active participants in the learning process. They also expressed the view that learning is a reciprocal process where the teacher gains as much as the child, and where both work together to build the educational experience.

> Teachers are the facilitators of classrooms which encourage freedom of thought and independence and allow students to think and act creatively and build healthy attitudes. I believe the essence of the classroom teacher is to provide an environment that is conducive to learning in that it facilitates growth, stimulates and challenges the intellect, and recognizes the gifts and needs of the individual while at the same time promoting within the group a cohesion built on mutual respect and a sense of common purpose.

3. Teachers Must Provide a Safe, Stimulating Learning Environment that Fosters Student Self-Esteem

This theme is followed by others that describe what teachers do: they develop ways to facilitate the self-esteem and flexibility of students within a changing society; they provide students with opportunities to succeed; they guide students; they help students develop respect for diversity through the provision of a safe, positive, stimulating learning environment.

> The role of a teacher goes beyond facilitating learning to disciplinarian, social worker, substitute parent and friend, a model of positive and acceptable behaviors, actions, and attitudes. I have had experience with models of good teachers in my own life. Individuals who showed empathy, emotional support, and respect for development, self-esteem, and communication skills. These people made a difference to me. I would like to make the same impression on my students.

4. Teachers Are Important Models for Students

The next theme, which is common to all applicants, involves the importance of teachers as models of good character in today's society and the influence of their own teachers as models for them. This theme also describes the variety of roles common to the teacher today: "Teaching means providing those around you with a continuous example of leadership, social adroitness, and moral fortitude. Teachers are faced day by day and year after year with an ever-shifting assembly of children to whom they must not only present the fundamentals of the curriculum, but also instill in them cooperation, respect for others and confidence in themselves." A number of applicants mentioned that they came from families where one or both parents were teachers.

5. The Primary Years Are Important to Setting Attitudes to Learning and to Others in the World

Applicants also describe an interest in the primary years due to its importance in developing the aptitudes and conditions needed for learning in the future, especially as it relates to developing skills needed for responsible citizenship. According to these applicants, the primary years are developmentally the most important time in a child's life—a time when children develop a positive attitude to school life and learning; develop base-line knowledge and skills; develop foundational self-esteem, and develop an understanding of responsibility and a respect for differences.

6. I Believe I Have Something to Offer

Finally, applicants described personal motivations for becoming a teacher and what they saw as the necessary qualities of teachers and teaching. This theme also crossed groups. They describe the most important assets of a teacher as experience, communication skills, and sensitivity to other's needs. They see teaching as a creative activity requiring a variety of strategies and organization as teamwork, and as an occupation that is constantly changing: "Teachers must develop and refine teaching methods and techniques that both suit her personality and cater to the diverse needs of students. A teacher must be a creative and critical thinker and flexible enough to meet the needs of students, parents, school, and community alike."

Junior/Intermediate

Applicants to the junior/intermediate program are similar in gender distribution to the primary/junior group, though they tend to be slightly older and more diverse in experience and background. They are more subject-oriented (junior/intermediate students are required to have an intermediate special area), and do not describe the same "helping" theme that primary/junior candidates emphasized. Instead, this group emphasized the importance and challenge of working with adolescents and felt that they had personal qualities or experiences to offer children of this age. Sometimes this involved their expertise in subject areas, but more often stemmed from a personal interest in children of this age, and the feeling that they had something to offer them on a personal level. They emphasized their ability to be role models and also a capacity to involve students in experiences that would broaden their understanding of the world and their role in it. Five themes emerged from the junior / intermediate responses. Again, all comments are from junior / intermediate candidates, and are listed in order of frequency.

> Adolescents require a facilitator, and a friend, to help them through this transitional time. Grades four through ten are important developmental years—where students must gain an interest in learning and applying skills in educational, social and recreational areas.

1. This Is a Challenging Age Group

It is not surprising that the theme most frequently mentioned by junior / intermediate applicants is the uniqueness of this time of life, when students need to be supported in special ways and the development of self-confidence encouraged. Applicants described students in these years as in need of special attention and as a challenge to teachers, in part due to the influence of peer pressure and physical growth.

> I want to help stop the "revolving door syndrome"—through education and preventative care. I want to work with students in the formative years, to help shape their critical thinking skills so that they can become productive and confident adults.

2. I Want to Make a Difference to Children and Future Society

The second theme is that of wanting to make a difference to the youth of tomorrow and the world: or teaching as a social responsibility. Here, applicants expressed the desire to influence the future through "shaping young minds" and "being part of a community where adults and children are working toward a common goal," that of developing skills and attitudes to encourage each child's growth.

> I want to teach because I will obtain a vast amount of satisfaction from witnessing the personal growth and development of each individual student in the classroom. I love seeing students learn and progress. I like being part of that—being able to meet the needs of students is very rewarding. Teaching allows me to use a broad range of skills; to transfer joy and understanding of the subject; finally teaching allows me to actually make a difference in someone's life.

3. I Always Wanted to Be a Teacher; It Allows For Mutual Growth and a Sense of Personal Satisfaction

This theme concerns junior / intermediate applicants' personal reasons for wanting to be a teacher: that it is a vocation; that they enjoy kids; that they have a lot to offer the teaching profession; and that teaching offers them an opportunity for personal growth and development. They also describe teaching as rewarding to both student and teacher, with student success in particular as the impetus for personal satisfaction in teaching.

4. My Ability to Create a Positive Environment, and My Subject Area Knowledge Can Help Students

The next set of comments involves the role of teachers in demonstrating an enthusiasm for learning and in creating an environment conducive to learning. Applicants also mention their commitment to their subject interest and how this subject can contribute to the growth and development of their students: "Art can help with social and personal development. It helps students channel energy productively."

> I am inspired by an outstanding teacher I had. This teacher peaked the class's interest, making us want to learn. She made each student feel important, had a good sense of humor, communication skills, was organized, devoted, and

> patient. She spent time with students. She helped me. This makes me want to repay the system that was so fruitful to myself.

5. Teachers Are Important Models

While specific mention of models, both as a model and the role of former teachers or relatives as models in their lives, comes less frequently in this group than in the primary / junior group, and is less frequently mentioned than other themes, it is still clearly an area of importance. Applicants mention the potential influence of teachers in the lives of students given the breakdown of family systems. They also describe how they want to "give back" what their teachers gave to them.

> Concerning my personal characteristics, I believe I have the patience that is needed to overcome the challenges that teachers come across daily. I also have good communication skills and work well with others. When I find myself in a situation where interests conflict, I use the utmost discretion to resolve it. Finally, I am very approachable, which I think is an important attribute, because students should feel comfortable speaking to their teacher.

> I want to be a teacher to see the gleam of understanding and desire to know more appear in a student's eye.

Intermediate/Senior

Applicants to the intermediate / senior program showed the most diversity of any program group. Females and males are more evenly represented. Applicants tend to be older and have more diverse experience than the other groups. They also cited more diversity in countries of origin, and more variety in professional experiences, including coaching, music, professional writing, self-employment and consulting, medicine, counseling, prison work, acting, engineering, accounting, archeology, biology, religious life, and newspaper work, to name a few (1992 sample, Stiegelbauer 1992). Compared to the primary applicants who have more experience in the "helping" fields, the secondary sample includes more people with business-related experience. In the themes presented, the intermediate / senior group describe their involvement with students as more of a subject-oriented partnership, a sharing that is in part a duty to society and in part a kind of personal fulfillment.

> To me teaching is not just a job. It is a means of passing information from generation to generation. Without this there would be no progress. I am looking for opportunities to refine my own knowledge and skills through working with students and the content of my courses. In my work I want to allow students to find parallels in their own experience.

1. Teaching Is a Partnership with Students; Teachers Are Important Models for Students

By far the strongest theme in the intermediate / senior applicants is that of developing relationships with students and their capacity as positive adult models for students. In this they also mention the role of former models in their lives. They see the learning process at this level as an exchange relationship whereby their own experiences have the capacity to provide inspiration to students when they are matched with students' interests and needs.

> I have a deep love of knowledge, an enthusiasm for the communication of ideas and concepts and a strong wish to serve in some way to foster in our young people a sense of their own worth and dignity and a respect for the dignity of others. We all share the same fragile environment and need to learn to cooperate if we are to survive. Cooperation and interdependence begin "at home" on a personal level and extend through the school to the local, national and international community. I gain great satisfaction from knowing my efforts have improved their lives. As a teacher, I think it is important to be aware of certain problems that exist—like drug use—and try to steer students away by increasing their self-confidence and positive outlook.

2. I Like Sharing Knowledge; Student Success Gives Me a Sense of Accomplishment

The next theme involves sharing knowledge and subject skills, and developing a sense of accomplishment through seeing students succeed. In this success, applicants feel they are contributing to developing the adults of the future: "In order to cope with the rapidity and complexity of changes in the future, students need to be motivated to see learning as a lifelong process and be prepared to meet challenges with well-developed problem solving thinking and analytical skills."

3. Teaching Is My Duty to Society; It Is Hard Work

The final set of themes views teaching as a personal responsibility to society. Applicants commented on the hard work of teaching and the need to provide a positive learning environment for students in the face of other influencing factors: "Teaching is challenging—a profession that requires time and knowledge, but also patience, sensitivity, understanding, and flexibility. Teachers must create an atmosphere and opportunities to enhance learning and allow students to take risks." "It takes a great deal of work to be a successful teacher." "Teaching supplies the necessary building blocks to the betterment of society and I want to share in this essential purpose."

Commonalities and Comparison of Responses by Program

Put simply, the themes emerging from this review (Stiegelbauer, 1992) show applicants to the primary/junior program as emphasizing a sense of caring and recognition of their responsibility for laying the foundation for learning in later years. In this, their comments are more "student-centred." They view the goal of teaching as that of developing student self-esteem and capacity for learning through the provision of a safe, stimulating learning environment. In contrast, the themes from applicants to the junior/intermediate level emphasized the challenge of this age group, and their own capacities to work with children of this age. Intermediate/senior applicants take this further in emphasizing their role as a model and facilitator of student interests, given the subject or life experiences they have to offer students. Comments made by intermediate/senior tend to be more "teacher-centred" in tone—they have a strong desire to communicate about what they know and what they have experienced, but recognize that this must be an exchange with students so that the information becomes relevant to each student's life and experience.

All groups comment on their social responsibility as teachers, and on the fact that teaching is important to the development of productive and healthy adults who can contribute to society and to themselves. In this, all applicants "want to make a difference." All talk about a major goal of teaching as being the facilitation of the development of student self-esteem and capacity to be flexible in the face of a changing society. They see life for students as increasingly diverse and complicated on numerous levels—personal, societal, environmental, and familial. They see their role in part as preparing students to cope with these pressures, even to the point of performing a guidance or parental role as necessary. All groups also mention the influence of former teachers in their lives, though the secondary group places more emphasis on this than other groups, perhaps because they see themselves as role models.

Applicants also mentioned their love of, or personal interest in, the subject they taught, especially at the intermediate / senior level, and talked about their personal aptitude for teaching—they are good communicators; people always told them they should be a teacher; they always wanted to be a teacher; they see teaching as an important profession to making a difference in the world. This discussion of teaching as a "calling" did not occur in the same way at the primary / junior level. Instead, these candidates talked more about the teaching process, and less about themselves. That said, it was a strong theme across all program groups.

Despite differences in emphasis, there are numerous similarities in reasons given for entering the profession when the sample is taken as a whole. As described, all program groups mention the fact that they are involved in teaching because they want to make a difference to society in some way. All talk about teachers playing a major role in the healthy development of students so that they can become productive members of society. All mention the importance of teachers as role models. This is especially true as students increase in age; they frequently mention the influence of one or more of their former teachers as a model for their lives, or as influencing their choice of profession.

> Teaching is a relationship; people relate to other people, not to subjects or rules or institutions. In other words, the key to unlocking the educational potential of any person is a sound human relationship. The students in the classroom today represent the future and how they are taught affects our society. I would like an opportunity to touch the future.
>
> (Intermediate / Senior Candidate, 1992)

The following lists themes of most frequent mention *across* all programs:

1. I want to make a difference to students and society. I want to help develop strong, self-confident, responsible adults who can give something back to society.
2. Teachers are important role models for students, especially with weakening family units and working parents.
3. The teacher-student exchange is one of mutual growth and continuous learning for both. I gain satisfaction from this exchange and from student success.
4. I want to share my personal knowledge and expertise. I feel I can be a good teacher. I have something to offer students. I recognize that teaching is a complicated and taxing profession. I like kids.
5. It is the responsibility of teachers to create positive learning environments and experiences and to lay the foundation for future learning, and a positive attitude about learning.

Teacher Candidates at FEUT: Being Part of a Program

It might be said that the selection of candidates for a program level and the candidate's perception of what that level requires are intimately interwoven; that is, candidates are selected because programs, and perhaps schools, are structured to emphasize those characteristics. The primary / junior level naturally emphasizes helping and caring about the development of young children and chooses people who talk about that; the junior / intermediate level acknowledges the need for models that help deal with the crisis of adolescence; the intermediate/secondary level is a preparation for life and employment, hence the subject emphasis. What is equally interesting are the overlaps in the themes discussed by candidates and the image of the teacher presented through them.

The themes for candidates currently in programs are likely much the same as those from the 1992 review. While the programs themselves have gone through major revisions in the last few years—an emphasis on more school-based experience and linkages with schools, as well as courses that integrate and connect subjects as well as deal with them independently—the qualities of each level remain the same. The elementary level prepares teachers to deal with early childhood and its issues and the secondary level with preparing for later life. What teacher candidates experience is linked to those qualities and structures, as well as to new ideas in education and educational strategies as they emerge from research and practical work with schools.

As an example, there is the question of the stereotypes present in the themes—elementary teachers see themselves as having more of a "parent" role and have more female applicants, and secondary teachers see themselves as "experts" in subject areas. Some ground has been gained in these perceptions in the Faculty's work in alternative programs and in a goal of training teachers as "agents of social change" and people who "make a difference" on numerous levels. Experimenting with different types of delivery systems, especially in subject-centred realms, has broadened candidates' perception that teachers at different levels should have certain characteristics and skill sets.

FEUT Programs

The Faculty of Education is made up of three departments: Educational Policy and Foundation Studies, Elementary Education, and Secondary Education. Courses offered by these departments are grouped into several broad categories, each with various program option choices (FEUT, 1995). The elementary program is made up of the primary/junior (P/J) and junior/intermediate (J/I) divisions. These divisions are again divided into a number of alternative programs, each including a STEP (Student Teaching Experience Program) component, where student teachers observe and teach in an elementary classroom(s) throughout the year. Currently the elementary program has seven option programs, including a two-year pilot program, affiliated with different school boards in the greater Toronto area (FEUT, 1995, Kilcher, 1994). Primary/junior and junior/intermediate candidates are required to take courses in foundations, psychology, and the contemporary classroom, in conjunction with elementary education, as part of the elementary option program.

The secondary program involves preparation for teaching intermediate/senior (I/S) students in a number of subject areas including technological studies. Students in the regular intermediate/senior program are required to successfully complete courses in four areas. They must take two curriculum and instruction courses (qualifying a candidate to teach two different subjects), three foundations and policy studies courses, the contemporary classroom, and practice teaching. As with the elementary program, regular practice teaching consists of three three-week teaching blocks in three schools. The secondary program also has alternative options, where students spend more time in schools. Each alternative program has a specific focus, such as working with gifted students. In addition to the two-year pilot program at the secondary level, there are two alternative programs, as well as a special program for students in music.

> I believe being a teacher is one of the most important professions in our society. We teach students to strive for what they want and for what they believe in. I found myself wishing that I could be in the same school everyday, working with the same children, being a part of a child's whole school experience. This allows me greater use of my expertise to benefit students and furthers my own satisfaction in a sense of accomplishment.
>
> (Elementary Candidate, 1992)

Candidates at the Faculty are now presented with a number of strategies that merge process and content and emphasize the role of teachers as individuals who continue to learn with their students in an environment structured to bring out the best in everyone. While this is an ideal environment, and many candidates describe experiences in schools as different from this ideal, it plants the seed of possibility. Shared vision building, norms and practices of inquiry in the classroom and the professional life of teachers, collaborative work cultures such as those presented in study groups (Stiegelbauer, 1995) and the "best (if experimental) practices" of the option and alternative programs (Kilcher, 1994), are changing the face of teaching for candidates by providing new models and approaches.

> I learned a tremendous amount. All the experiences (at FEUT) were new experiences; they augmented my experiences from the TAP program. I think the best part was knowing that there's so much more for me to learn as well. I have just scratched the surface. There's the whole cooperative learning aspect of a teaching strategy; multiple intelligences; Bloom's Taxonomy; classroom management; assessment and evaluation—the whole portfolio process of not only using it as a document for assessment in classroom, but of being able to document who you are as a learner through the education process and through your experiences as an educator.
>
> (Elementary Candidate, 1995)

> I don't think a faculty of education can make someone a teacher. I think my experience here has certainly made me a better teacher and I've benefited a lot from the background information and the theory that I now have that I can try to reconcile with my personal observations and experiences. I have a lot more ideas, things like that, but I think the basic confidence and the basic skill have to be there to begin with. I don't think that's something that can be taught. Certainly not in an eight-month program. Probably not in a sixteen-month program. They can certainly be refined but in the same way that some people just aren't made to play baseball, there are some people that just aren't made to teach. You can work with what's there but it has to be there in the first place.
>
> (Junior/Intermediate Candidate, 1995)

Teacher candidates at FEUT today are learning more than what they might have thought they would learn, and less. Less in the sense that it requires them to be responsible for their own learning and to use that as a model, even if it is not the same template as what they have experienced as students of other teachers in the past. As one candidate said, "this is not everyone's approach—if you've gone far enough to get accepted into a faculty of education, I hope it's the case that you're interested enough to take ownership of the program and of what you're learning over the years. However, from experience I know that's not always the case." This is both a strength and a weakness, or rather a complaint. For some, the alternative strategies of FEUT do not meet their needs—they want something more practical and directive. For most, however, such strategies begin, or rather continue, the process of learning that is part of being a teacher.

> I was looking for a year that would be a lot of fun because I was hoping I would enjoy what I was doing. Getting into teaching, it was always a worry that if I didn't enjoy the year starting off teaching that I wouldn't like teaching in general. So it was important to me that it was a good year. And it was. I enjoyed the practice teaching and realized I had chosen the right thing to do. Yeah. I think there were times in courses when there were things that we felt were missing or we perhaps could have done something differently but overall it was a strong year. Being involved in the student union as much as we were meant we had practice doing some things like running a conference, organizing groups of people, running the Santa Claus Parade Day, and the like. All of those things helped in developing confidence and skills in dealing with people.
>
> (Secondary Candidate, 1995)

Supports for Candidates: Student Events, Student Services

The year at FEUT is an intensive one for all concerned, but it also includes active support for candidates both as students and social beings. The Student Services Department works with the student union to promote a number of social, athletic, and employment events, including an employment conference, contact with boards, an annual graduation dinner / dance, monthly "pubs," a student lounge, a yearbook, a number of sessions related to educational issues and pre-staff development activities. All of these are geared to supporting students as members of a profession in all its aspects. The level of student engagement with these possibilities varies, but the fact that they are there helps to build the sense of relationship with the institution and with one another that creates good memories of their year. In combination with the academic side of life at FEUT, student services provides an ear and an outlet for many of the frustrations such an intense year brings. A large number of the candidates' comments presented in this chapter are from interviews conducted by student services. As an advocacy group dedicated to promoting the well-being of candidates, such comments are an invaluable indicator of progress and ways to improve.

> The thing I have learned about having a philosophy of education is that *I do have one*, and bring parts of it from many different sources. It is a composite of all my experiences and will continue to be shaped by all my experiences in the future. Some of the beliefs that I had when I started at the Faculty have been completely changed and others altered by the journey of the past year.
>
> (Graduating Teacher, 1993)

Making a Difference to the Future: A Summary

This chapter provides one qualitative snapshot of applicants to the teaching profession. In doing so, it presents a perspective on why individuals enter the teaching profession, at least in terms of what they say about it, and what their experience is like. Brookhart and Freeman's summary of forty-four studies on the characteristics of teacher candidates (1992) supports a number of characteristics described in this chapter: candidates are typically white and female with a higher percentage of males at the secondary level; candidates report a high level of involvement with more traditional community, extracurricular and school activities in their prior experience; diversity increases with subject specialty and the secondary level; and candidates are idealistic in their goals and want to have an impact on society.

These themes describe a consistent pattern for altruistic and service-oriented goals as sources of motivation for candidates. They also describe a difference in motivation according to level: candidates at the elementary level were more child-centred in their motivation, whereas secondary candidates were more likely to cite the influence and modelling of a former teacher (see also Brookhart & Freeman, 1992, p.47). Candidates' statements describe feelings of confidence and optimism, feelings that are replaced with anxiety when faced with the pressures of real classrooms. Brookhart and Freeman conclude (1992, p.51): "Two themes emerge from these studies. Entering teacher candidates view the nurturing and interpersonal aspects of a teacher's role as more important than the academic aspects and entering teacher candidates view teaching as dispensing information. There is contradictory evidence about changes in beliefs about teaching during the course of teacher education."

Stark (1991) also describes teachers' emphasis on caring as the foundation for a pedagogical process: "a way of observing, listening, and relating to children. It is a way of being-in-the-world with children" (1991, p.306). She asks the question of whether teacher education programs help student teachers apply this interest, or whether instead they provide new teachers with experiences oriented to "doing" rather than "being." Abstract as this sounds, in the face of the practical anxiety of new teachers, "how-to recipes" and "doing" become a real pressure, one that needs some resolution, but that also falls prey to the "quick-fix" element of society. Fullan suggests that the emphasis should be on developing the new teacher's capacity for actualizing, understanding, and acting on "self" (1992), within the context of the educational system. As such, this understanding needs to be developed and supported to allow new teachers to have the capacity to act on both. Providing for practical needs while developing the capacity of new teachers to understand the broader context and be proactive in that context continues to be one of the goals of FEUT programs.

> I guess everyone, when they're starting, has this idea of the way things should be and that's the only way it can be. They acknowledge that other people can work in other ways but still for them this is the only way things are going to happen.

> I may not have been that extreme but I certainly did close my eyes to a number of options. And then at the Faculty, being put into groups with other people that had different styles, going and doing three-week practica in classrooms with people that had different styles, being able to see that I can incorporate things that I've seen from other people that normally I wouldn't have thought would work for me, but because they were already set up I had to incorporate them. It was very beneficial.
>
> (Graduating Teacher, 1995)

Moral Imperatives and Making a Difference

Goodlad (1990) aptly describes the dilemma of teaching as an occupation, or a profession, where society, including the society of the school, conspires to alternately value and devalue teachers and what they do. He says: "The primary responsibility of a teacher, technically and morally, is to the students being taught. Teacher education, first and foremost, must prepare teachers to assume this responsibility" and "there has been much talk recently of the need to create a 'true' profession of teaching—talk seemingly based on the premise that creating such a profession will lead to better schools" (1990, pp.12-14). At the same time, "parents and professors advise their children and brightest students not to become teachers. At dances and social gatherings, young teachers often lie about their occupations" (Goodlad, 1990, p.15). In his interviews with students in teacher-education programs, it became clear that, idealistically, students see teaching as a kind of "calling." They said, "Teaching kids is important, somebody has to do it."

Teacher education, as Fullan states, "has the honour of being the best solution and the worst problem in education today. Despite the rhetoric, society has not yet seriously tried to use teacher education as a tool for improvement. Underneath the rhetoric there does not seem to be a real belief or confidence that investing in teacher education will yield results" (1992), or that teaching can make a difference to students, to schools, or to society. Goodlad and his colleagues describe the deeper purposes of education and teaching as related to "moral imperatives":

> Schools are charged specifically with enculturating the young into a political democracy; schools are specifically charged with providing a disciplined encounter with the knowledge necessary to continue society; teaching must combine generalizable principles of teaching, subject-specific instruction, and sensitivity to human qualities and potentials—all going beyond the "mechanics" of teaching—for the lives of teachers and their students intersect; and schools and teachers must be good stewards—purposefully engaged in being responsive and renewing.
>
> (Goodlad, 1990, pp.20-27)

Goodlad's statements reflect the multiple changes affecting today's society. They also reflect the need to develop teachers and teacher education structures that can be responsive to those changes in ways that current conventions and institutions do not. Fullan (1992) and Sirotnik (in Goodlad, 1990) further define the qualities needed in the teaching profession: commitment to inquiry, knowledge, competence, caring, freedom, well-being, and social justice. Fullan narrows these to core capacities that build in teachers and teacher institutions greater change capacity, or "change agentry":

> I define change agentry as being self-conscious about the nature of change and the change process, as being appreciative of its semi-unpredictable and volatile character, and as explicitly being concerned with the pursuit of ideas and competencies for coping with and influencing more and more aspects of the process toward some desired set of ends. (1992, p.25)

Teacher candidates are asking the same questions and have the same goals: they want to make a difference and they want to be valued for the profession they have chosen. Teacher education institutions must go beyond the strictly practical to develop an attitude and experience that supports such goals, as difficult as that might be. And it is difficult, difficult in the face of real practical needs, and difficult in the face of the support given to teaching and learning in conventional society. Individuals are not in teaching for money or vacations. As these new teachers have described, they are in teaching for the kids. The moral imperative is just that, *making a difference for the kids.*

> I still find it hard to believe that this year is over. On the last day of classes, I looked around and saw the same room only it was now filled with excited teachers looking forward to their lives of learning. One final thing I've come to realize this year is that my philosophy of education is not stagnant just because my year is over, but it is an ongoing process of learning. The danger for all of us as teachers is to lose sight of the original commitment that made us choose for ourselves the identity of teacher... . We need to tell our stories to keep them alive. We need to hear the stories of others to enrich our own experience.
>
> (Graduating Teacher, 1994)

Conclusion

The Faculty of Education at the University of Toronto is only one teacher education facility among many. FEUT programs seek to make the connection between the practical realities of teaching and the larger social context; FEUT staff have taken up this goal through the development of program options and alternatives that address both objectives. Many of these are still developmental, but as time passes the effects can be seen (Kilcher; 1994, Stiegelbauer, 1995). This chapter is about teacher candidates, who they are and what they want from the Faculty. The voices of these candidates are loud and clear: they are idealistic, they do recognize that the world is not perfect and that the Faculty is trying, that they have to "walk the talk" and take on the responsibility for learning they would ask of their students. They can make a difference and so can the Faculty, as a "community of learners," candidate and professor alike.

FEUT is not the perfect place for all teacher candidates—it is a short program at present, too short in school experience for some, too abstract in its requirements for others, too much into "process," to use the conventional phrase. Yet, somehow, it makes a difference by the end of the year. If ideas about developmental growth, "concerns of teachers about new ideas" (Hall & Hord, 1987; Fuller,

1976; Fullan, 1991), are any indication, it likely takes that long, and the needs of candidates change from personal concerns to how-to concerns, to big-picture concerns. It might even take another year, as the two-year program anticipates. Still, something is happening.

There are many stimulating and thought-provoking statements made by applicants seeking to enter the profession. What holds true for them also applies to teaching at the Faculty. As a community of learners as well as teachers, approaching the question of "how to make a difference" provides an exciting challenge. As one applicant stated:

> Learning is not a means to oppress or impress others, but instead is a process whereby individuals extend their relatedness, their connectedness to themselves, others and the world. Teaching is a reciprocal process whereby teachers and students create significant educational experiences.

Finally, from a graduating candidate:

> One of my associate teachers, I was her only student teacher this year, and she is phenomenal. I don't think there's a student who couldn't learn from her. I don't think there's a person who couldn't learn from her. I'd like to be that kind of teacher. That's my goal, being that kind of teacher.

Part II

The Practice of Teaching

Teachers Learning and Growing Together

Carol Hennessy holds a doctorate from the University of Toronto. With the university since 1973 as a faculty member in elementary education, she has coordinated university–school board partnerships in Scarborough and Toronto. During her career she has been associated with the University of New Brunswick, the Institute of Child Study, and school boards in Alberta and Ontario.

This is a story about a collaborative experience in teacher education in a university–school board partnership, written from my perspective as the project coordinator. Our partners held tightly to the belief that learning to teach is an ongoing and interactional process best served when all work together for the benefit of the child. Data sources include journal entries by our preservice teachers, teleconferencing entries, project submissions, a mid-phase survey completed by preservice teachers, and their documented feedback.

The collected data is qualitative in nature. Analysis shows the experience encountered by our constituent preservice teachers and mentor teachers as generating strength in changing concepts about teaching resulting from one child connecting with one teacher.

Background

The arrival of Michael Fullan as dean of education provided those of us within the Faculty with an opportunity to "push the envelope" of teacher education with his challenge to us to "ready-fire-aim." During the late 1980s, I became involved in the design and implementation of collaborative ventures between the university and school boards. This story is about teachers learning and growing together throughout one such venture with the Toronto Board of Education.

My background is one of collaborative, team teaching, and multi-age group learning design. I came to the university from the Institute of Child Study. The world of teacher education that I viewed was one that focused on teaching subjects and content delivered by university staff, and providing limited exposure to the school setting for the preservice teacher other than a designated graded practicum or practice teaching.

Within a university–school board partnership, staff from our Faculty of Education and teachers from the Toronto Board of Education began a journey of grass-roots collaboration to provide quality teacher education in what became known as the Toronto program. We blended theory, research, and practice with the promotion of inquiry from a field-based setting in space provided by the board at Wilkinson Junior Public School, and identified as our FEUT–Toronto Teacher Education Centre at Wilkinson Junior Public School. A key feature was the recognition of the need for mutual decision making by the partners. Willingness to trust, share, and support one another on the part of all members of the partnership was essential.

As partners, we collaborated on programs with an aim to:

- developing teacher education within an innovative, integrated field-based university–public school board partnership.
- helping preservice teachers from the program develop knowledge, skills, and attitudes to understand goals and teaching methodologies related to curricula in Ontario public and separate schools.
- helping preservice teachers to become socialized in the role of teacher in the contextual setting of a school system that emphasizes quality elementary education for children.
- enhancing the professional expertise of teachers through stimulating collaborative research about teaching by members of the program community: preservice teachers, classroom teachers, professional teachers, administrators, consultants, and Faculty instructors (Hennessy & Christy, 1995; Hennessy & Booth, 1994; Andrews, Holburn & Wideen, 1988).
- developing effective ways to utilize the expertise of experienced classroom teachers in the program's courses, seminars and workshops.
- providing opportunity through computer-managed conferencing to help preservice teachers put theory into practice (Woodruff, 1995; Brown & Campione, 1994).

Unique Features

A unique combination of planned experiences provided our preservice teachers with opportunities to achieve the role of a reflective practitioner: to learn continually from their own experiences by considering alternatives; interpreting situations; generating and evaluating goals; and examining experiences in the light of alternative goals and hypotheses (Zeichner & Liston, 1987).

Together, as Faculty and board partners, we encouraged our preservice teachers to develop a holistic sense of what it means to be both a teacher and a learner. Our preservice teachers utilized the tools of action research to observe, analyze, reflect upon, and teach about a wide range of educational issues in courses and practica.

Our Toronto Faculty team members fostered supportive actions among one another and preservice teachers, viewing themselves as a community of learners sharing reflections about program design by being receptive and open to feedback. We tried to stimulate reflective practice and connections among the preservice teachers through commitment and role modelling.

Preselected courses offered at our centre provided integrated theory, research, and significant quality practice for the preservice teachers to become immersed in the culture of the school. We recognized preservice teacher preparation as an element of an ongoing process as our teachers progressed through a series of stages where an individual's behaviour and teaching concerns became more mature as insight was gained into teaching (Fuller, 1975). Interacting with one another, our professional teachers from the board of education and Faculty staff provided the preservice teacher with opportunities to gain experience that formulate and change concepts by planning for teaching, and applying developing theories for learning and teaching through practice.

During the academic year, our preservice teachers participated in a linked nongraded STEP (Student Teacher Experience Program) and graded PT (Practice Teaching), and were assigned to an experienced professional teacher in a classroom of the centre school or one of eighteen partner schools closely associated with our teacher education program. Linking STEP and PT enabled our preservice teacher to become progressively involved with a single classroom and school during each trimester, allowing planning; trying out ideas; researching and developing teaching skills. Within a trimester, STEP extended over five to six weeks, one and one-half days per week, and was followed by three weeks of graded PT. An additional, ungraded practical experience consisted of two half-days per week in the same classroom of the centre school over the course of the whole year.

An important feature of our teacher education program was the availability of a release teacher (Martin, Hennessy & Gibson, 1993). The occasional teacher from the board of education was funded as a part-time position by the Faculty and board partners. Responsibility assignments for the program and the centre school performed by the release teacher provided quality substitution coverage and release time for those board of education teachers associated with the program.

The preservice teachers also participated in our Toronto program-identified electronic conferencing for peer-supportive communication.

A Focus on the Child

The Faculty Focus on the Child project began in 1993-94, when Early Literacy Attainment (ELA), a concept of David Booth, became a reality. It was a program designed for the classroom and created to assist literacy growth in children identified as experiencing difficulty in their primary years. Together, David and I from the Faculty of Education, with Una Villiers from the Early Childhood Education Department of the Toronto Board of Education, developed this enhancement strand of teachers teaching teachers. The spotlight centred on the classroom teacher's daily interaction with a child at risk in literacy growth and was supported by our preservice teachers and consultant services.

It was in these classrooms that the ELA mentoring role was fostered and became established between our classroom associate teacher educators and preservice teachers as they jointly designed and implemented strategies to enable a child to progress towards literacy. As volunteers in the project, these classroom teachers made a commitment to work alongside our preservice teachers in implementing the ELA program with a child they considered at risk in emerging literacy. The classroom teachers participated in an inservice professional development credit course, conducted by staff from the Faculty of Education and the Early Childhood Department of the Toronto Board of Education.

During 1993-94, our curriculum focus for the classroom mentors was in the area of mathematics/science. As coordinator of the Toronto program, together with the principal of the centre school, I arranged for the purchase of materials and training for both preservice teachers and mentors in a structures/manipulative project entitled, Mathematics/Science Investigations. One-half of our preservice teachers worked with the whole class to free the mentor to attend the training sessions with the other half of our preservice teachers. The arrangements alternated with the group in attendance and they shared the information with the others.

For the academic years 1994-95 and 1995-96, our team consolidated aspects of major course components into a project known as Focus on the Child. Its aim was to enhance the quality of our preservice teacher education in a context of interaction and reflection.

In 1995-96, sixty-four primary/junior and intermediate level preservice teachers were organized in mentor groups of three to four and assigned to eighteen classrooms ranging from grade one to grade six and located in the centre school where our Toronto teacher education program was delivered. During this practical experience of two half-days per week, each preservice teacher was assigned to a single child selected by the mentor classroom teacher.

The project provided an opportunity for our preservice teachers to focus on one child in the mentor teacher's classroom at Wilkinson Junior Public School. With the mentor's guidance, our preservice teacher provided individual additional support through literacy and mathematics development.

As our preservice teacher worked in the Wilkinson Mentor classroom (WMC), there was opportunity to both assess and assist the child in individual tutoring and in group sessions with the classroom community throughout the year.

Faculty members of our Toronto teacher education program staff offered practical suggestions and techniques for implementing program design, with theory and background that could be applied to understanding the child's wants and needs.

As the preservice teachers collected information about their children, each began to create a portfolio demonstrating the child's intellectual, social, physical, and emotional development by: observing a particular child for the better part of a year; developing a remedial or enrichment program in literacy and numeracy; building a profile on the sociocultural context of the child's life; facilitating the child's well-being in school and in the playground; and considering the child's interpersonal relationships.

The information was reviewed and developed into a report about the child, summarizing his or her progress and development, so that a teacher working with the child during the next year could use the knowledge to build the necessary educational curriculum to maximize the child's development. Our mentor teachers and support staff in the school offered suggestions for specific additional information in the study of the child's background.

The reference readings provided background and suggestions for implementing specific teaching strategies, and for understanding the child.

Through their participation in a mentor group over the academic year, our preservice teachers explored strategies and techniques by collaborative and consultative interaction. Each member of the mentor group had different strengths to share as they completed analyses of their child's contexts, and gained opportunities for inter-child contrasts and comparisons.

The completed portfolio about the child became representative of the preservice teacher's teaching-learning development, and provided the basis for a group interview at the end of the year when each preservice teacher presented relevant findings.

Individually, preservice teachers worked closely with a mentor teacher who provided guidance, support, and encouragement. Our preservice teachers observed, diagnosed, assessed, researched, and designed remediation and/or enrichment to support their focus child. As a volunteer in this collaborative endeavour, the mentor teacher made a commitment to work alongside our preservice teacher with the child the mentor had selected for additional one-to-one attention. Inservice mentor workshops were held with our Faculty staff and board of education consultants in curriculum areas and were scheduled throughout the year. Our intent was to facilitate the role of the mentor, provide two-way communication on the progress in the Focus on the Child project, and give opportunities for professional development. Each preservice teacher met with their focus child for about thirty sessions over seven months. Some met with their child on other occasions. The location of the sessions was arranged on an individual basis.

Typically, the quality of activities by the release teacher during the Focus on the Child project included the teaching of a mentor teacher's class to facilitate review discussions between the mentor and our preservice mentor group members. These sessions sometimes included a parent meeting or a school team meeting to review a child's progress.

Discussion

As I participated with my colleagues on this journey, I recognized that learning to teach is an ongoing and interactive process for each of our preservice teachers and the professional mentor teachers with whom they worked. The ongoing interaction helps the preservice teacher with future teaching. An important role for the mentor is to raise questions that help the preservice teacher grow and develop in teaching practice. A mentor's support is emotional and instructional. Actual classroom experiences help to enhance perspectives of the preservice teacher by viewing the child within the project context.

It appears to me that each preservice teacher approaches the mentor classroom at the beginning of the year filled with enthusiasm, expecting to effect a dramatic change in the life of the child (Fuller, 1975). Each mentor works with our preservice teachers individually and with the mentor group, supported by those of us who are Faculty instructors in class, helping them learn about child development and the rate that children learn. The preservice teacher shares knowledge about the tools of assessment for diagnosis with the mentor. Together, they examine the diagnosis made and logical steps for remediation and / or enrichment. The extent of discussion varies with the individuals involved. The mentor can influence what is learned from the experience with the child and in the mentor classroom (Little, 1990). An important consideration for successful interaction between the mentor and the preservice teacher is the establishment of a mutual liking and respect. There appears to be a need for awareness of one another as individuals.

In supporting the Focus on the Child project with mentors, those of us in the partnership, both from the Faculty and the board of education recognize as Goodlad (1988) suggests, "For a partnership to be successful, each partner must see satisfaction of the self-interests of the other(s) as essential to the satisfaction of its own." We consider it essential that professional development sessions for mentor teachers be scheduled during school time permitting the preservice teachers as mentor groups to work with the entire mentor class and the mentor teacher to attend such sessions as part of the school day. Paper-bag luncheons provide an opportunity to exchange information about the progress of the study and respond to questions.

Members of a mentor group got to know one another through early cooperative learning activities, and for many, the initial practice teaching placement to a school by mentor grouping. The role of peer coaching, although informal at the beginning of the year, took on a stronger function as some mentor group members became both colleague and teacher (Vaiga, 1994). The mentors, preservice teachers, and staff see that the time taken to become acquainted with peers, and the opportunity for choice in grouping, is valuable.

Many participants used the teleconferencing system as a vehicle for communicating with other participants for support and encouragement in the project. The roles assumed by preservice teachers vary according to the individuals involved, with some assuming the role of conference moderators, to those who actively participated in electronic conferencing, to those who took a "read only" position.

During the seven month life-span of the project on the individual child, each preservice teacher and the mentor share experiences beneficial to all. The child is involved in a special one-to-one relationship in which individual interests and needs are recognized.

The preservice student teacher moves through a paradigm shift from the beginning of the year with its specific concepts about teaching to become an individual who realizes what becoming a teacher means. The mentor has the opportunity of helping a beginning teacher, and in return receives assessment and diagnosis about four children in the class and participates in professional development activities.

The perspectives of preservice teachers with respect to the Focus on the Child project appear to cluster within the following areas.

Child Development and Time

There is an increased awareness of the value and importance of child development and the opportunity to witness the growth of a single child over the seven-month period rather than each three-week graded practice teaching session per trimester. One preservice teacher, who worked with a grade 1 child wrote,

> After working through and completing the project, I can honestly say my awareness of child development has been increased. Through investigation and research, I have been made aware of how important an understanding of child development is in the classroom. This comprehension is also frightening as I fear how little I know. What disturbs me is how I have gained some theoretical knowledge, some practical knowledge but only enough to whet my appetite for more and I wonder where and how the two come together. Am I prepared to enter a classroom and feel confident in assessing twenty plus children? I do know now, and I am empowered to investigate further.
>
> I want to make more connections between theory and practice. Questions I ask myself are: How do scribble drawings fit into stages of development? When should one expect changes in math, art and writing? How will these changes manifest themselves? What is a normal range?

> The Focus on the Child was a window to practical and theoretical developments. This simple exposure to one classroom, one child, allowed me to witness a progressive series of small changes over the course of a school year. My project demonstrated a significant development in language acquisition. Although this acquisition was tremendous, my expectations were probably too high as I was not aware of what to expect from an ESL child. What was his range? My expectation for him and the reality of his development were quite different.
>
> So what does this mean? Development is a slow life process. It can be bracketed in short spurts, long arduous changes, enhanced with emotions of physical changes. It means every child is different, every change is significant and every child must have time and space to grow and develop.

Another shares the opinion that the opportunity to put theory into practice is essential. She says,

> While working on the project, I was able to link many things that we were studying in class to things I was observing. I was able to see for myself that you can't teach certain concepts to children and expect them to understand them completely if the child has not reached a stage of development where they are ready to learn the concept. In discussions with my mentor group, we discovered that much of the progress our focus children made could be attributed to a change in their stages of development as well as to our remediation. This was even more evident in the cases of children who were born later in the year as they were sometimes more than six months younger than their classmates.

Experiential Learning

The experiences and behaviour derived from the Focus on the Child project help the preservice teacher to realize what it really means to become a teacher. Another preservice teacher comments,

> The project demonstrates to me what active learning is all about. This is an experience working with a child; interacting with the child; reflecting on what we tried to accomplish as opposed to what we did accomplish; and we had opportunities to communicate our success and failure (portfolio, teleconferencing, phone calls, coffee shops, a sharing fair, and a take-home).

Assessment

The amount of time needed to observe and assess an individual child is more than the preservice teacher initially thinks it will be. When considering doing this for every child in a class, the preservice teacher is awed by the importance of the task. He explains,

> One aim of the project was the opportunity to experience the task of making student assessments. It also provided the opportunity to gain experience in group/cooperative learning. A third was the opportunity to test child-study observations within a particular theme, by looking at theoretical constructs in relation to practical reality. It gave to all the potential of forging a relationship with one child, to observe the child's maturation over a seven-month period, and to test and solidify personal views about how learning happens.

Cooperative Learning

Some mentor groups elect to work together, finding that as the quality of their work improves, they work more quickly and learn from one another. One preservice teacher remarks that it is not until the Focus on the Child project is complete and the individual reflects about the experience that there is a realization of the importance for collegial support and collaboration.

Child as an Individual

One preservice teacher summarizes the experience of the Focus on the Child project.

> The project was a valuable opportunity to both discover and learn many new things as well as to verify and extend upon past understandings and perceptions that I held. The chance to work individually with a child proved how valuable one-to-one interaction and attention can be, but it also highlighted the importance of grander scale interaction in learning and development. It showed me how vital it is to address each child as an individual in order to maximize the help we can offer them.

Conclusions/Implications

An opportunity exists for those of us as university–school board partners to provide mutual benefits, as evidenced by the Focus on the Child project. Annual review by the partners and constituents verify the effective and essential nature of the continuance of the evolving project.

Peer coaching is only beneficial to the extent of the knowledge of the mentor group members and their skills in cooperative enterprise. There is an apparent need to enhance this aspect of the experience through choice and increased awareness of cooperative learning.

Comments from our mentors in 1993-94 for more training, closer involvement, and professional development reflected in the subsequent years of 1994-95 and 1995-96. While in a mentor classroom for a morning and afternoon of each week, each preservice teacher has the opportunity to connect with more aspects of the classroom program, allowing both our Faculty and the board to provide more professional development sessions to support the centre school's priority to provide the richest possible language environment in both English and French classrooms. Training sessions with our mentors on the role of the mentor were implemented earlier in the school year.

The role of teleconferencing as a medium of support and a vehicle for communication is viewed by the preservice teachers and the Faculty instructors as important. At the request of the preservice teachers and mentors, the plan to connect mentor teachers to the teleconferencing system began in the latter part of the 1995-96 school year and will continue into 1996-97, with technological support by the teachers and incoming preservice teachers.

What about the journey we teacher educators began with our ready-fire-aim challenge? We can regroup, review, and redefine, as we hold tightly to our belief that learning to teach is an ongoing, interactive process best served when the professional teacher and the preservice teacher work together for the child; each raising questions of one another, honing skills, and acquiring tools through classroom experiences, just as those of us in the partnership between the Faculty and the board continue to question one another.

Perhaps the reflections of a mentor from the centre school summarizes life in the Focus on the Child project. She wrote:

> Remember the energy, enthusiasm and idealism that you had when you first started teaching? When faced with eager-to-learn student teachers on a daily basis you can't help but catch the disease. While trying to help them you start questioning, analyzing, suggesting, brainstorming, and wondering. As a result of the environment created by having the Faculty of Education at the school, we as teachers, get the chance to learn and grow as well.

Planned Change in Schools: A Focus for Preservice Teacher Education

Robert Martin, associate professor, Elementary Education Department, joined the Educational Administration Department in September 1970 following completion of the Ph.D. (educational administration) program at OISE. He served as chair of both the Educational Administration Department (1988-90) and the Elementary Education Department (1992-94). He established and served as coordinator of the Faculty's first field-based preservice teacher education program, and is coordinator for the PJI: Scarborough program.

Today's preservice teacher candidates are entering the profession at a time when schools are facing multiple demands for change (Fullan, 1991). The demands on a school emanate from a variety of sources: federal and provincial governments; business and community groups; parental organizations; local communities including the group of parents whose children attend that school. Demands for change from any or all of the constituencies do not always point in the same direction. Many demands seem to be at cross-purposes or even in opposition to one another. In addition, demands for change affect a school at different levels. There are calls for change: in what and how children learn; in how to organize the school and its classrooms; in how, when, and under what circumstances teachers should engage in revising and developing curriculum; in how the school and its staff should be accountable to their constituencies. In short, the graduates of today's preservice teacher education programs will teach in schools situated in environments of considerable challenge and complexity.

How can preservice teacher education candidates learn about and prepare for the demanding changes they will soon face? This chapter aims to provide an answer by describing one component of a field-based, preservice teacher education program at the University of Toronto.

The Faculty of Education at the University of Toronto delivers its one-year, consecutive, preservice program for elementary teacher candidates by means of seven different "program groups." Each program group consists of sixty or ninety candidates and a teaching team of instructors. Each group has a "home base" for its classes and a set of associated schools for its practicum.

The preservice program for all seven program groups at the Faculty is eight months, from September to April. There are three blocks of practice teaching of fifteen days each, spaced equally throughout the year. For approximately five weeks before each block of practice teaching, candidates spend up to two days per week working in the classrooms where they will spend the upcoming block. All program groups have these weekly, in-school sessions which, taken together, constitute the Student Teaching Experience Program (STEP). Besides providing ongoing classroom experience to support course projects, STEP enables candidates to become familiar with the classrooms, children, and programs where they will next practice teach.

This chapter focuses on the program group based at Samuel Hearne Senior Public School in the Scarborough Board of Education. The 1995-96 academic year is the seventh year of operation for the group. There are ninety teacher candidates enrolled in the preservice program at Samuel Hearne—sixty candidates at the primary / junior level and thirty at the junior / intermediate level. The candidates in "PJI: Scarborough" have their practicum placements—STEP and practice teaching—in Scarborough board schools or in schools in the Metropolitan Separate School Board. Samuel Hearne provides several practicum placements besides serving as the home base.

The Scarborough program is similar to the other program groups with respect to STEP and practice teaching. However, there is a second field experience in Scarborough that makes the program unique—the "Developmental Unit project," which focuses on change in schools.

The Growth of the Developmental Unit Project

The Developmental Unit project (DU) has been a part of the Scarborough program since the 1992-93 academic year. The project has always focused on change—either in children's learning, school programs, or in both. In the three years since its inception, the project has grown both in the scope of the changes attempted and in the course time allocated to it.

The project grew out of earlier developments in the Scarborough program. In 1989-90, one member of the teaching team organized an "interest" program in which teacher candidates offered their talents to all Hearne students. The intention was that candidates would get to know a small group of children very well as they helped them learn a new skill (e.g., piano playing, juggling, oil painting, recorder playing, story telling, drama, basketball). The interest program took place one and one-half hours per week throughout the year. In the second year (1990-91), candidates again worked with Hearne students, but this time concentrated on enhancing academic skills. Pairs of candidates worked with pairs of children. The candidates completed cognitive assessments of the children, then created a custom-made academic program for each child. On average, candidates devoted three hours per week to the project in the second year. In 1991-92, the project again centred on cognitive assessment, and in addition, candidates shared the children's academic assessment with their homeroom teacher.

The merits of arranging ongoing associations between candidates and small groups of children throughout the preservice year were obvious. The association enabled candidates to observe and perhaps influence the children's growth over an extended time.

In June 1992, the principal of one of the schools connected with the Scarborough program proposed that candidates return to their fall placement classrooms to observe the children's growth. His proposal was the "seed" for the Developmental Unit. The proposal was appealing because it provided confirmation from a school that a longer association between candidates and children than is possible during practice teaching would strengthen the program.

Consequently, in 1992-93, groups of candidates were assigned for a half-day per week to six "developmental unit schools" that agreed to participate.The candidates were to take part in the life of the school as the principal and teachers saw fit. While successful, it became clear that the candidates needed more direction from the schools; school personnel often looked to the Faculty to tell them what the candidates should be doing.

The same six schools wished to continue the developmental unit in 1993-94. There was a meeting in September, during which the principals or their designates came to Samuel Hearne to discuss possible DU activities with the candidates assigned to each school. These discussions seemed to provide candidates with more direction than they had had the previous year. In the spring of 1994, all six schools again indicated a desire to continue the DU.

To prepare for 1994-95, all principals connected with the Scarborough program attended a meeting in June 1994. Those interested in participating in the DU were invited to prepare a proposal outlining a unit plan for their school in the coming year. Thirteen of some thirty principals submitted proposals. The teaching team accepted all of them.

Each year, the Developmental Unit project has improved in clarity of purpose and in effectiveness of operation. The next sections of this chapter describe and analyze the 1994-95 Development Unit project to show how preservice teacher candidates may experience and learn about planned change in schools.

The 1994-95 Developmental Unit Project: A Chronology

Since its inception in 1992, the DU project has focused on change in schools. At the same time, the project itself has undergone continuous change regarding its emphasis and operation. This was particularly true during 1994-95—in part owing to changes in the FEUT teaching team for the Scarborough program group. Of the three instructors responsible for the DU in 1994-95, two were new to the Scarborough program; the third had been connected with it since 1989. The three instructors—the authors of this chapter—decided early in their planning to experiment with the DU concept to a greater extent than had been done previously. The following chronology describes the general direction established at the year's outset, but also outlines the many modifications, adjustments, and new ideas introduced as things progressed.

Early Developments: June-August 1994

A revised statement of purpose for the 1994-95 DU (Faculty of Education, University of Toronto [FEUT], 1994) emphasized a school-level focus on change.

The purpose of the Developmental Unit is twofold.

1. to provide student teachers with a yearlong association with one school—its programs, teachers, and children. The yearlong association with one school will provide opportunities for student teachers to learn about program and curriculum development in schools. While the student teachers work on their unit projects, they also will be able to observe and contribute to the growth and development of individual and small groups of children.
2. to enable schools that are designated "Developmental Unit Schools" to undertake projects in school and / or curriculum development of specific interest to those schools—projects that normally might not be undertaken without the ongoing assistance of student teachers.

Thirty principals attended the June meeting mentioned in the previous section. All had expressed interest in taking candidates for the STEP and practice teaching part of the preservice program. They were given three options: accept candidates for both STEP and practice teaching and the DU project; accept candidates for STEP and practice teaching only; accept candidates for the DU only. Those interested in the DU project received the above statement of purpose to assist them in preparing a DU proposal. As a rule, candidates assigned to a school for the DU would not have STEP and practice teaching placements there. The proposals were to include suggestions for projects that candidates might undertake as well as the number of candidates in the "DU team" assigned to the schools. Thirteen of the thirty schools drew up proposals. Only one chose the "DU only" option.

The proposals prepared by the thirteen schools indicated the nature of the changes that the students would experience in their DU placements. The proposals in terms of the DU's statement of purpose included:

1. Student teachers learn about program and curriculum development in schools.

   All schools mentioned one or more curriculum areas in which a candidate DU team might initiate improvements by developing new teaching strategies and materials (e.g., mathematics or numeracy, science and technology; story publishing using computers, health, music).

Four schools mentioned the integration of computers across all areas of the curriculum as an area for new initiatives.

2. Student teachers observe and contribute to the growth and development of individual and small groups of children.

   Five schools suggested that candidates could learn about children's growth and development over the long term by working with teachers in existing programs (e.g., reading buddies, mathematics remediation, French as a second language). Two schools suggested learning about children's growth and development through involvement in extracurricular activities (e.g., intramural sports, choir).

3. Undertake projects in school and / or curriculum development of specific interest to schools that normally might not be undertaken without the ongoing assistance of student teachers.

   One school suggested that candidates become involved in a pilot project undertaken jointly by the school and a consortium of business and educational agencies (i.e., The Learning Partnership) to foster entrepreneurial skills and attitudes among children.

   One school proposed the creation of an "Ambassador's Club" to "smooth the transition for New Canadians entering the school."

   One school proposed that candidates undertake a number of initiatives in the area of "school spirit" so as to raise children's self-esteem and to develop a sense of the school as a community of learners.

In the main, it seems principals saw the DU as a vehicle for promoting change in the curriculum and the classroom programs in their schools. They saw the policies of their board of education as providing the main pressure for change. The size of the DU teams requested ranged from three to seven candidates.

In August, once the DU instructors had analyzed and accepted the proposals, they divided the roster of candidates into DU teams and assigned them to the thirteen schools. To minimize the candidates' travelling time, the location of the schools with respect to the candidates' homes was the prime consideration in forming and assigning the DU teams.

The Academic Year Begins: September and October 1994

For the first four weeks in the program, candidates spent one morning per week in their DU schools. In the afternoon of those days they returned to the home base to debrief and share their experiences, and to plan for the next session in their schools.

The candidates' first task was to get to know their schools well. Each DU team completed a questionnaire, consisting of some fifty items under the headings: School Architecture; School Goals or Mission Statement; Students, Parents, and Community; Teaching Staff; School Facilities; School Programs (General); School Administration, Routines, and Maintenance. To introduce the survey, the DU instructors first asked candidates to complete it for a "school that you remember." Each candidate described the impact that the remembered school had on him or her. Next, they completed the survey for a school that he or she considered "ideal." Candidates shared their ideal versions with one another, and considered how such schools provided for the five major aims for education found in the Ontario education ministry's document The Common Curriculum. Upon completion of the introductory activities, the candidates set out to learn about their DU schools.

Undertaking the survey gave candidates many opportunities to interact with the entire range of people in the school including the principal, the teaching staff, the children, and the caretaking and secretarial staff. The candidates summarized the results of their survey and prepared a presentation for the school staff. The presentation was to give the staff an opportunity to interact further with the candidates and to tell them about other aspects of the school and its program.

During the survey period when they were in the school, the candidates were able to begin discussions with the principal as to how the school's DU plan might be effected in the coming months. At the same time, most principals assigned candidates to work with individual teachers to get an understanding of the school program at the classroom level. The time spent in individual classrooms was unlike practice teaching sessions because the "mentor" teachers made no assessment of the candidates' teaching performance.

During the afternoon debriefing sessions at the home base in September and October, candidates shared their experiences of conducting the survey, considered how to stage the school's DU plan over the course of the year, and reflected upon how the project was helping them to learn about planned change in schools. The DU instructors introduced a number of ideas and activities to facilitate the process.

1. Ideas about phases in the process of change (Fullan, 1991).
2. The concept of force-field analysis as a tool in analyzing and planning for change in collaboration with the staff of the DU school.
3. The creation by each candidate of a "DU folder" to be a personal record of reflections about and plans for the project. The first entries in the folder included the following:

   a) The survey results for their DU school prepared by the candidate teams including additions or corrections as a result of feedback from the school.
   b) Written reflection to the questions:
   "What are the challenges in conducting a school inventory?"
   "What information is easy (difficult) to obtain?"
   c) Responses to "Describe in detail how you are working in your DU school right now—who are you working/meeting with (school staff/your team). What are you doing—individually and as a team?"

The Middle of the Year: November 1994 to Early February 1995

By the end of October, most DU teams of candidates had developed, in cooperation with school staffs, outlines of what they were to accomplish before the end of April 1995. After reviewing events, the DU instructors formed a set of questions that candidates were to consider every few weeks to assess their progress and to plan their next steps. Under the heading "for ongoing reflection," the questions were as follows:

Purpose of the Project

- What is the purpose of your DU Project as you understand it at present?
- How has the purpose changed or become clearer since the last time?

- If changes or modifications in the purpose have occurred, why did they occur?

Prime Mover

- Who is (are) the key person(s) influencing the direction of the project right now?
- What are they doing?

Forces For and Against

- Which forces are supporting present efforts to achieve the purposes of the project?
- Which forces are hindering present efforts to achieve the purposes of the project?
- What are you doing to manage the forces and move the project along?

Milestones

- What has been achieved to date in the project?
- How effective are the achievements in advancing the purposes of the project?
- How useful to others are the achievements?

Final Accomplishments

- How do you now see the project ending?
- What will have been done?
- What will have been produced?

Functioning of Student Teams

- What are the problems that your DU team is working on right now?
- What strategies, materials, and so forth are you considering as solutions to your problems?
- How is your team working together right now?

Overall

- Overall, how are you doing?

Within each DU team, candidates used the questions to share and consolidate their experiences as they planned together among themselves and later, with their schools. Between November and February, each candidate placed a response to these questions three times in his or her DU folder. The instructors read these entries to monitor each team's progress.

Between November and early February, candidates spent all of each DU day in their schools working on the projects—debriefing sessions were scheduled at other times each week. Devoting more time to the school came about at the requests of some principals who felt that the projects were well underway and that more time was necessary to meet the completion date in April. Also, two practice teaching sessions occurred between November and the end of April. These sessions kept the candidates away from their DU schools for a total of nearly six weeks. Under the circumstances, the instructors thought that instituting full DU days was reasonable and appropriate.

In November, the DU instructors made plans to hold a meeting of representatives from each DU school in early February. The purpose of the meeting was to share and review project events, to consider what needed to be done to bring the projects to a successful conclusion by April, and to look forward to the next year. The February meeting provided an opportunity to share with the schools a model of the DU process that had been evolving in the minds of the DU instructors during the previous few months. The model attempted to clarify and emphasize several key ideas: (1) at the core of the DU is a process of planned change that cycles from "Planning the Project" to "Concluding the Project"; (2) surrounding and supporting the core activities is a second cycle of "Data Collecting, Monitoring, and Reflecting"; (3) by its very form and content, the model establishes the DU project as an experience distinct and different from practice teaching; and (4) central to the DU project is change as defined by the school and its staff.
The DU instructors gave the February meeting as high a profile as possible. It was held at the central office of the board. The director of education made the opening remarks. Each school received a written invitation and agenda before hand. The meeting was very successful with respect to the ideas discussed and the suggestions and recommendations collected—although not all the schools were represented.

Concluding the Year: Late February to April 1995

The third and final phase in the DU project began in mid February, immediately following the second practice teaching session, and finished at the end of April. The DU instructors had decided that the project would conclude with each DU candidate team presenting a final report to their school's staff, in the school, at a time convenient to the school. The decision overcame the problems of trying to assemble all of the DU participants in one place at the same time. In a draft report, the candidates were to summarize and assess the DU experience, and to describe what they had learned from it. School staff would read the draft and make comments that would then be incorporated in the final version of the report. The process of producing a final school report was the central mechanism for joint candidate-school evaluation of the DU project.

As the first step in the concluding phase, the DU instructors provided candidates with the following framework of questions to prepare the final report.

- What has been achieved in the project for both the school and its children?
- How are the achievements like and / or different from the initial plans?
- As a result of the project experience, what have you learned about undertaking program development in a school?
- As a result of the project experience, what have you learned about the factors affecting change in schools.
- What has your DU team left behind in the school that could be extended next year—
  a) if another DU team were assigned to the school next year?
  b) if the school staff were to continue on their own with what you have started?
  c) what recommendations can you make for both (a) and (b)?

In addition, candidates were to plan the assessment strategies they would use to address these framework points:

- What needs to be done between now and the end of the project so that your team will have data to answer the questions above?
- In other words, what assessment strategies will you need to

use to assess the project's impact (e.g., interviews, questionnaires, focused observations)?
- Who should participate in the assessment? How should they participate? When should they participate?
- In a collaborative manner share your assessment plans with the key person in your DU school—and with others as appropriate.
- Incorporate the recommendations of the school in your assessment plans.

Between the middle of February and the end of April, all DU days—a total of six days—were full days in the schools. This was done to ensure the completion of all project work and to compensate for interruptions in DU activities introduced by the school winter break and the third session of practice in March and early April.

Reports to schools took place during the final two weeks in April. The times of the meetings varied from school to school—either during the noon hour or in the afternoon following dismissal. Some DU candidate teams reported to full staff meetings, but most reported to the principal and the group of the teachers most closely associated with the project during the year.

The 1994-95 Developmental Unit Project: What Was Learned?

Two questions that guided the candidates in the preparation of the final school reports were: "What have you learned about undertaking program development in a school?" and "What have you learned about the factors affecting change in schools?"

Following are some excerpts from candidates' statements regarding change:

Leadership and Support for Change

- The principal must be an advocate for change, but also must provide staff the room to experiment.
- Change within the school needs support from the outside, especially a budget for materials. The resource centres in the board are important as well.

- The method of implementing a change is as important as the change itself.
- Ideas should not be imposed from the top, subtlety is the key.
- Support teachers in the new learning they may need.

The Need for a Relevant Vision

- Having a mission statement is crucial.
- Consider the school's existing culture when planning a change.
- It is important to know what you are starting with.
- Each school has an existing timetable—time must be provided for change.
- Agree on the outcome for change.
- Spend time on formulating the objectives for change.
- A change must be relevant.
- It's best to base changes on the academic needs of children in the classroom.

Effecting Change

- Allow time in your plans for reflection.
- Break down the change into manageable steps.
- Change involves taking little steps.
- Have a timetable for change.
- It is important to take risks.
- There must be acceptance of a plan for action—both the why and the how.
- Be willing to modify the goals.
- Be patient—results may not be immediate.
- Research a possible solution—What is its value? How will it be used?
- Ensure you get regular feedback.
- Recognize the importance of not attempting too much.
- Your efforts must be continuous and consistent.

Team Effort and the Process of Change

- Include all staff—teamwork is important.

- Recognize the multiple agendas of different staff members.
- Be open to ideas from others.
- The group initiating change needs to work together cohesively.
- Take time to understand each member's strengths and weakness; it's necessary if the work is to be efficient.
- Everyone needs to work at maintaining a positive, goal-oriented outlook.
- Work collectively—isolation causes uncertainty and impedes progress.

Attitudes about Change

- Recognize that an idea that seems simple at the start becomes more complex as it's adopted.
- Have the courage and the flexibility to face disappointment and the stamina to continue in a more appropriate direction.
- Be flexible.

Virtually all the key factors and themes under the "Initiation" and the "Implementation" phases of the change process are reflected in the candidates' statements regarding change. Their statements indicate that they became aware of the "dual thrust" of outcomes for change (i.e., toward improvement both in student learning and attitudes; and in the skills, satisfactions, and attitudes of teachers). They realized that educational change involves changing the school as an institution—its culture, norms, and traditional way of doing things.

Also revealing of what they learned about change were candidates' periodic entries in their DU folders about the forces acting for and against change. Three major forces appeared regularly in the entries—sometimes as forces hindering change and at other times as forces facilitating change. The forces were: (1) collective understanding of the DU's purpose; (2) teamwork skills; and (3) time for change. Early in the project, clarity of purpose and teamwork skills were "negative "forces hindering the change efforts of many DU teams. Lack of clarity regarding the purpose of the DU project, both for the candidates as learners and for the schools as organizations undergoing change, was evident in early folder entries. At first, some candidates thought their task was to locate new teaching strategies and materials, try them out in the DU classrooms, and report the results. Other candidates—a small minority initially—understood that the object of their learning was the process of change itself. As the teams worked together, understanding of the purpose for many candidates shifted to that of the early minority—the process of change itself. As that shift happened in a DU team, there emerged a clarity of purpose that candidates regarded as a positive force in effecting change.

Limited experience and skills in collaboration were hindering forces for several teams in the project's early stages. Over time, most teams worked together in an increasingly coherent and focused manner. One or two teams did not achieve what they felt to be an adequate degree of internal consensus—members regularly referred to their team's functioning as being problematic or negative. By the conclusion of the DU project, all candidates agreed that the ability to work together in a team can be the single most powerful positive force in facilitating change.

Time, or rather the lack of it, appeared as a negative force for many teams once they began the implementation phase of their change efforts. The complexity of the schedule in many schools (e.g., withdrawals of individual children for special programs, class rotations for French and gym), as well as unexpected or impromptu interruptions at times bedevilled the best-laid plans. Many school principals did sterling service in minimizing the negative force of time by adjusting timetables to accommodate and facilitate the DU's agenda. Coping with time pressures made candidates acutely aware of the truth in the seemingly simple and obvious observation that "Change takes time."

Each candidate wrote a personal reflection on the DU experience as the final entry in their DU folder. The comments from fifty-eight of the sixty candidates were very positive, both about the process itself, and about what they had learned. Typical comments from the final personal reflections were as follows:

> Being involved with the DU project and collaborating with the other team members has been an excellent learning experience, one which has contributed to my personal and professional growth—being at my DU school offered me a

> wonderful opportunity that I may never have again; being able to work at a direct level with an entire school's staff and students toward a meaningful goal. I had the unique opportunity to work with a school to create a meaningful change in its curriculum while still a student teacher.
>
> The project, which was started from scratch, has in the end turned out to be very valuable... each milestone we reached made us feel very proud. One of our milestones was when we had our first kit prepared and ready to be tested with one of the families... our group worked very hard from the beginning to the final accomplishments. The project mostly went as planned, but with some surprising and delightful results.

Two candidates stated that the DU time should have been used in other ways.

The Developmental Unit Project: Prospects.

The Developmental Unit project was an exciting and productive part of the 1994-95 Scarborough preservice program. The DU instructors believed that a valuable new component for preservice teacher education began to emerge from the 1994-95 DU endeavour. Perhaps the strongest impression emerging from the experience was the critical importance of placing at the centre of the project educational issues and challenges, and issues as identified by individual schools themselves. Problems that are relevant to a school provide the essential basis for candidates' participating in and learning about change in schools.

This year's experience provides some instructive insights about the interaction between preservice teacher education programs and change in schools. There are two sets of expectations that warrant consideration by members of both institutions. On the one hand, there is an expectation that school staffs should work together to improve the programs in their schools. One major purpose of the DU project is to gain entry for student teachers into this change-and-improvement oriented aspect of school life. On the other hand, there are expectations associated with the traditional view of the practice teaching placements in preservice teacher education. In the traditional view, candidates are placed in one classroom to observe, model, and learn from the professional practice of the "associate" teacher.

While traditional practice teaching is a potent and necessary part of teacher preparation, the norms associated with it could get in the way of achieving the purpose of the DU. If the merits of the DU justify its continuing presence in the preservice program, it is necessary to foster new and different norms to guide faculty instructors, school staffs, and candidates in the DU teams. Ideally, the new norms should value collaborative group effort—both within the DU candidate teams and between the teams and school staffs. That is: 1) all persons connected with the DU project need to believe that improvement in a school's programs and the children's learning is possible through the combined and collegial efforts of everyone involved; 2) assessment of candidates' DU performance should relate to their ability to work thoughtfully, systematically, and sensitively with others to cause positive change in schools; 3) within the preservice program as a whole, the new and different norms for the DU should complement the norms for practice teaching; 4) and to ensure complementarity: a) the Faculty should organize the DU as a distinct field experience (e.g., it is likely best that candidate do not practice teach in their DU schools), and b) personnel in DU schools should relate to DU candidates as a group of beginning professionals who are joining with them to effect positive change in the school as a whole.

The DU instructors believed the project should continue. While instituting the ideal norms described above will require more time than one year permits, immediate steps should be taken to gather more data regarding:

- the identification of forces for and against effecting change in school-wide reforms;
- the usefulness of preservice candidates in tracking and reflecting on the process of change;
- the potential opportunities for coordinating an individual student teacher performance in one classroom and student teacher teams providing school-wide change;
- the realization by school administration and staff of the forces surrounding the work of the DU team in their school;

- the need for collecting and disseminating data about change and the DU process for larger school and teacher education audiences.

In conclusion, each of the DU instructors would echo the statement of one student teacher:

> I learned many things during the DU project. I do not regret any part of the project and I would encourage all of next year's Faculty students to jump in and hang on for the ride. The "DU ride" can be a fun, challenging, and bumpy ride, all at the same time.

Endnote

The report on the Developmental Unit was prepared by the project instructional staff: Robert Martin (principal investigator); Thomas Goodenough, and Diva Anderson.

Teacher Education and the Secondary Schools

Don Galbraith is chair of the Secondary Education Department at FEUT, with prior teaching experience in East Africa and in Toronto schools. He continues to be interested in development issues and in February of 1995 was part of a World Bank team that visited and examined the secondary education system in Malawi. He is a past president of the Science Teachers' Association of Ontario and is the author and co-author of a number of texts used in Canadian schools including Biology Directions.

Annette Yeager, associate chair of the Secondary Education Department, teaches family studies education and, upon occasion, a course in the Department of Educational Policy and Foundation Studies. She began her career at FEUT in 1968. Her recent teaching interests include a constructivist orientation to teaching and learning, multiple intelligences, portfolios as a tool for assessment, and case method teaching. She is a co-author with Phyllis Meiklejohn and Lenore Kuch of a senior-level text, Today's Family: A Critical Focus.

For many years, there was relatively little change in the organization and delivery of programs at this Faculty. In 1971, all of the traditional colleges of education, charged primarily with preparing secondary teachers for provincial schools, were integrated into neighbouring universities. (Shortly thereafter, the normal schools, the training centres for elementary teachers, were closed and the faculties of education assumed responsibility for preparing both elementary and secondary school teachers.)

During the seventies and indeed, throughout most of the eighties, the Faculty mirrored much of what was typical of a secondary school. Like the schools, there were many small departments, sometimes with only two or three members. Like the schools, there were department chairs responsible for the courses taught within their jurisdictions. And, like the schools, there was often little awareness of what students were learning in other parts of their program. This is not a criticism, but rather an observation of the practice of the day. In short, during this period, the secondary "program" consisted of a number of discrete, independent courses taught by staff in a number of separate, independent departments.

However, this was the period of appointing teacher educators first and foremost, for their strength in teaching.

Slowly but surely FEUT became a faculty that did more than "train" teachers for the schools of Ontario. Under the leadership of Dr. John MacDonald, Dean of the Faculty from 1981 to 1987, Faculty members were encouraged to enter more actively into academic research. Specifically, in 1982, FEUT revised its divisional priorities to include research as a primary activity, and in 1983, re-established the previous Department of Educational Research that had been discontinued with the establishment of the graduate school, Ontario Instutute for Studies in Education in 1965. Understandably, given the backgrounds of the staff, much of this research was field-based. Since new tenure-track academic appointments were not being made during this period, the expectations fell on the shoulders of the existing faculty. Some of the above issues and concerns were addressed by the Provostial Review Committee of the Faculty of Education in their report of March, 1987.

The release of the provostial report and the subsequent appointment of Michael Fullan as Dean of FEUT in February, 1988, marked a watershed in the history of this Faculty. One of Dean Fullan's first acts was to reduce the number of small departments and to create larger, more cohesive academic units. To this end, Dean Fullan struck a committee to recommend the appointment of chairs of the four new, larger departments. The new Secondary Education Department, for example, encompassed all of the former secondary subject teaching departments, such as science, English, and technological studies. Suddenly, some sixteen small departments became one large unit. At the new departmental meetings, no longer could one discuss Ohm's Law, a Shakespearean sonnet, or a Wagnerian opera. These subject-specific conversations were replaced with considerations of much more generic, holistic, educational issues such as the use of portfolios for formative assessment, cooperative small-group learning strategies, and opportunities for research.

Dean Fullan also struck a committee to review both the elementary and secondary programs in the Faculty. The mission statement for the committees reflected the nature of change as follows:

> In its simplest terms, the FEUT mission is to deliver a preservice program that provides both the necessary skills for successful initial teaching experiences and also a foundation for continuing education throughout the teacher's career.

The secondary committee submitted its final report to the dean in June, 1989. It is worthy of note that this was one of the earlier references to the lifelong learning of a teacher. The preservice experience was to be but one of the steps in the continuum of professional growth. The report also focused on images for teacher education and the implications for preservice teachers. These images were built around five themes: reflective practice, inquiry, integration, experience, and collaboration. All of these themes, in one form or another, are now integral components of preservice education at FEUT.

These were not easy times for either the Faculty as a whole or the fledgling Secondary Education Department. Both were struggling to find a new identity in a world that seemed to be changing too quickly after so many years, yes decades, of stability and status quo. Too many of our favourite pedagogical practices were being called into question. We entered into research activities that would validate or give rise to changes in our practice. No longer did the English staff or the mathematics team have control over their own small departments; we were obliged to come together to share, to debate, to discuss, and to grow. It will be left for others to judge whether or not this experiment in change has been a successful one.

During the eighties and more so during the nineties, societal expectations of teachers and schools increased. With the move to free trade, more emphasis was placed on producing graduates with more mathematics, science, technological, and computer skills. In addition, schools were playing the role of surrogate parents, in some cases fulfilling the role of an absent parent. With the increased expectations of teachers and schools came increased admission requirements in faculties of education. A solid academic background was no longer, by itself, a guarantee of admission. Applicants were expected to have acquired "age-appropriate group experiences"—experiences working with adolescents in group settings. Because of this expectation of life experience, the average age of applicants increased markedly. In the early nineties, the average age was 29.5 years. This figure has decreased somewhat in the past two years.

Schools, too, continued to change. Teachers were coping with mixed ability groupings, students with limited language skills, and the mainstreaming of students with disabilities. All these changes added to the complexity of maintaining a positive classroom atmosphere. No longer was the teacher simply the authoritarian figure of the past. New skills had to be used to motivate and manage active, outgoing students. As a result, in 1985-86, the Faculty created a new course, The Contemporary Classroom. This course, modified over time, reflected the changing needs of the teacher and the classroom. Whereas the original components of the course included introductions to computers, special education, guidance, and school law, the current course consists of classroom management, assessment and evaluation, and, once again, school law, a provincial requirement for teacher certification. A careful reader might note and perhaps question the removal of computers from the Contemporary Classroom course. The majority of students now enter the Faculty with at least basic computer skills. These skills are extended while in the Faculty by the inclusion of computers in various courses and the widespread use of the Faculty's internal e-mail system "Tednet." All students now have free access to this system.

The schools in the greater metro Toronto region are marked by cultural and ethnic diversity. Again, the Faculty attempted to prepare itself for these changes by becoming involved in a number of summer institutes, sponsored by the Learning Consortium, a partnership involving four boards, FEUT, and OISE. These week-long courses have been held on the campus of Scarborough College during the month of August each year. One such course, attended by practising teachers, administrators, and faculty staff was entitled, Antiracism and Ethnocultural Equity in the Nineties: Meeting the Challenge of the Diverse Classroom. All students in the Faculty take a course called Teaching: Students, Schools, and Systems, which addresses the sociocultural context of learning and teaching and, in particular, multicultural or ethnic and racial issues that affect people and classrooms. Finally, a course, albeit an optional one, deals with cross-cultural education and is taught by new tenure-track staff members, Tara Goldstein and Carola Conle, who have graduate backgrounds in this field of study.

Today's schools are not without conflict of one kind or another. Once more, the Faculty and area boards banded together to offer another type of summer workshop entitled, Working Together: Managing Conflict. As well, for the past five years, all Faculty students are exposed to many issues not necessarily covered in traditional course. A series of workshops, with a safe schools focus were offered each year. The day included sessions on the Young Offenders Act, conflict management, police and the schools, and health issues.

Alternate Programs

During Michael Fullan's tenure as dean, Faculty members extended the boundaries of the secondary department into a range of different territories. One of the earliest ventures was the establishment of alternate programs, which included all of the elements of the regular program, but which were delivered in different ways. Over the years, a total of four alternates were developed. The first intermediate/senior alternate program, which focused on education of students with high academic potential, represented a major step for the department. For the first time, preservice teachers in the secondary department were grouped together in a program rather than randomly dispersed into separate courses. These students met as a cohort group for their required educational policy and foundation studies course, the prescribed educational psychology course, and the contemporary classroom program. Over the years, this latter course included areas such as special education, guidance, school law, computers, classroom management, and evaluation of student performance. Students received instruction in their chosen curriculum and instruction courses and in an additional self-selected foundations course with students in other programs. In addition to the prescribed weeks of practice teaching, students spent up to two weeks in a school setting working with a mentor teacher. During that time, these students were involved in varied aspects of the total school program, including teaching. Negotiation with mentor teachers over the nature of field-based placements became the norm. For the first time in the department, a team of faculty was designated to one group of students. Such an arrangement opened up the possibility for coordination of assignments. Potentially it became possible to eliminate overlap and to reduce gaps in subject matter or topic coverage. On the down side, however, students often reported that they were experiencing the program as "additional" rather than "alternate."

Other alternate programs followed. The Language Education alternate was designed to respond to a growing need for language teachers with a solid understanding of the processes involved in first and / or second language teaching. In this alternate, the concept of cohort was strengthened. A team-taught core methodology course in the principles of language teaching brought together preservice candidates in the subject areas of Italian, French, German, and Spanish. Students were allocated into separate courses only two hours per week; during that time they focused on their language of specialty. Courses in educational policy and foundation studies, chosen specifically to complement the strong language emphasis of the program, were offered as a package. During almost every in-faculty week, the preservice teachers spent some time in a school setting, visiting four to six different schools and sampling a variety of first and second language programs. Students in the program often enrolled immediately in an additional qualification course exploring teaching English as a second language.

A third alternate program, the Teaching Development project (TDP), had a community focus with an emphasis on career education and transitions to the world of work. This alternate was a joint venture of the Dufferin-Peel Roman Catholic School Board, Peel County Board of Education, Halton Board of Education, Halton Separate School Board, and FEUT. As time permitted, the students participated in school and community events. The preservice teachers supervised extracurricular programs, assisted in school-sponsored student activities, attended professional development programs and school board meetings, participated in visits to local business and industry locations, visited community support agencies, and monitored cooperative education learning activities. For all intents and purposes, students in this alternate came to the faculty site only for their subject-specialty courses.

The fourth option, the FEUT-Learning Consortium Program, was built out of a school-university partnership involving the Faculty of Education, OISE and the boards of education of Durham, Halton, North York, and Scarborough. In addition to regular practice teaching sessions, students spent two days per week and a final practice teaching session in a Learning Consortium secondary school. The focus was on the realities of teaching in a contemporary school. Particular attention was given to life skills, classroom management, and the transition years between elementary and secondary schools. Students were encouraged to become familiar with the full range of school services, including guidance, special education, and student-at-risk programs. Foundations courses were preselected. Instruction in the student's two curriculum and instruction subject courses was situated within the regular faculty program.

Although not in the category of "alternate programs" as described previously, we would be remiss if mention were not made of both business studies and technological education. Because of the nature of their respective programs, wherein students were required to take combinations of subjects, candidates in these areas took classes with peers in the same disciplines. As a result, students in these programs became a very cohesive cohort. Both departments were noted for their excellent programs, cognizant of the fact graduates of these programs often found themselves in schools where they were called upon to draw on their work experience before entering the Faculty. The staff in these departments were practical, creative individuals who applied their years of experience to creating outstanding programs.

Fitting new models into the old structure of policies and timetable organization presented challenges. Open and ongoing consultation among department chairs and with administration was crucial to the launching and day-to-day operation of these secondary alternate programs. Regular meetings of departmental chairs provided an important forum for keeping in touch with developments. The chair of the secondary department routinely consulted with the chairs of elementary and foundations regarding major initiatives. That approach ensured that all parties were involved in decisions that impacted on them. Matters of program, staffing, budget, and routine administrative concerns and dilemmas were all the subject of collaborative dialogue. Associate Dean Anne Millar, the secondary department's liaison to administration, was often a central figure in the interdepartmental negotiations.

Inquiry

Research interests and projects of secondary and other Faculty members expanded over the years. A review of agendas for department meetings reveals the breadth and richness of Faculty involvement in inquiry. Topics included areas such as student misconceptions in science, Shakespearean research in England, anti-racism, reflective practice, and action research. New tenure-stream Faculty members brought specific background in ethnography, reflective practice, and narrative methodology to the department. A joint project in the subject area of history linked seconded Faculty members with students in the University of Toronto Schools. Secondary faculty also conducted or contributed to seminars in a series sponsored by the Faculty Development Group at FEUT. These seminars addressed matters such as the use of portfolios, requirements for tenure and promotion, accessing funding for research, excellence in teaching, and other Faculty development issues. Some secondary faculty served as seminar leaders at the Joint Centre for Teacher Development's noon-hour seminar series. Increasingly, the names of secondary faculty were among those listed in the programs of the Canadian Society for the Study of Education and the American Education Research Association. The number of secondary faculty listed in the CSSE conference program rose dramatically over the period from 1989 to 1996. It was also encouraging to note that a few secondary faculty presented at AERA over the same period. When proposals for UNITE mini-grant funding were invited in 1994 and 1995, the projects of several secondary faculty were successful. The work was subsequently shared in a range of different venues including provincial subject-oriented conferences, CSSE, and a mini-conference offered during a visit by members of UNITE (a collaborative project involving teacher-education institution in sites across Canada and the United States) to Toronto in October, 1995.

Telecommunications

Access to a faculty-wide telecommunications network enhanced the frequency, impact, and character of communication for secondary faculty members. The internal faculty communications network, TedNet, facilitated several subject-based conferences among students, faculty, associates, and others connected to the department. Informal conversations about resources, teaching strategies, AHA's about teaching and learning, projects, practice teaching, notice of meetings, and other information all found a space on TedNet. Several secondary department meetings were held in FEUT's Technology for Enhancing Learning Centre. General networking possibilities and Internet access were addressed in two of these meetings.

Issues

Issues facing secondary education have both long- and short-term standing at FEUT. The maintenance of subject-area integrity and the downsizing of full-time faculty with professorial status represented long-standing concerns. While the workload and teaching-research dilemma touched all faculty, these issues were especially pressing for newly appointed, tenure-stream faculty members. The merger of FEUT and OISE intensified the conversation about the relative status and interplay of theory and practice. The challenge of maintaining the special spirit of collaboration that characterized FEUT was an issue as we moved closer to the realities of a new culture and institution, OISE/UT.

The subject areas at FEUT faced numerous challenges in latter years. Program changes had brought cutbacks in class contact hours. At the same time, the needs of the field had generally expanded and intensified. While increased hiring of secondments enriched the program in countless and significant ways, the policy of a two- or three-year turnover exacted a toll on both curriculum and foundations courses; some of these faculty became heavily committed to research interests or alternate programs, in the latter instance as coordinator or designated team member. At times, secondary faculty also assumed teaching responsibilities in the elementary program. One could not help but observe that the secondary department had become a shadow of its former self. Yet the professional commitment to do everything for everybody lingered.

The issue of workload in the secondary department first surfaced with newly appointed faculty. These individuals struggled valiantly to balance full teaching loads and ambitious research agendas.

For members of the department of curriculum and instruction, supervision of practice teaching was an unwritten expectation. This demand for in-field involvement literally ate up the energy of these individuals. While the field was an important site for the kind of inquiry that new faculty valued, their full-time teaching load restricted their opportunity to gather data. While new faculty often managed to buy off some teaching time, longer-term Faculty members assumed the added role of filling the gap in teaching and at committee meetings.

The perennial teaching-research dilemma for university faculty found expression in several ways in the secondary department. The increased currency of research seemed indirectly to undermine what had been a long-standing regard in the secondary department for "good teaching." Some long-time secondary faculty struggled to get on board the research agenda.

Administrative Support

Over the years, the administrative staff in the secondary education department played a central role in "keeping the ship afloat" and in "calming the waters of change." A large piece of the history of the institutional practices and policies resided in the formal records and informal recollections of the administrative staff. In many instances, these individuals assumed responsibility for managing both the regular winter-day program and continuing education courses in the summer and evenings throughout the year. Such was the regard students held for many of the administrative staff that it was not unusual for students to turn to these individuals for support and advice of both professional and personal nature.

In the late 1980s, the work of the administrative staff changed. In the newly configured secondary department, secretarial staff were assigned primarily to a group of subject-area faculty, but shared office space in small teams. When workload demands were unusually heavy, individuals within that office area provided support to get the job done. The position administrative secretary was established and ably managed by Joanne Lawson, who coordinated secretarial work across the departmental offices and served as the administrative assistant to the chair.

Associate Teachers

A brief history of the department would be incomplete without reference to the contributions made by our associate teachers. The dedication and support of these individuals, in some instances over a great span of years, was remarkable. In most instances, they worked with the preservice teachers within the traditional pattern of the two-week practicum. However, associate teachers also collaborated with a range of Faculty-initiated projects. In the highly successful yet short-lived Intermediate / Senior, In-School, Inservice Practicum. (IS)[3], known as the "Ice Cube" Project, associates served as "host" teachers, welcoming students for one day during each "in-Faculty" week. In the alternate programs, preservice teachers often spent two days per week in schools, a practice that continues with the newly established two-year pilot program. Most importantly, associates modelled strong practices, nurtured new growth, picked up pieces when fledgling attempts floundered, listened, encouraged, and went the extra mile. And it was the associates who assumed the final responsibility for evaluating candidates during practice teaching.

The Two-Year Program

Traditionally, in Ontario, secondary school teacher preparation has been based largely on a consecutive model—the completion of a university degree, followed by a one-year preservice program. This consecutive model is built around the belief that students must first reach a level of proficiency in their chosen discipline before learning how to teach. This model, however, has its limitations. As in any educational endeavour, students require time to think, to reflect, to consider relationships between theory and practice. As well, faculties of education have been expected to add more and more to their program to address the needs of schools in the nineties. The one-year B.Ed. program at FEUT has been modified and improved over time to address these increasing needs, but time still remains our worst enemy.

A comprehensive review of and dialogue about evolving practices in teacher education culminated in a move to a two-year program. After considerable debate and discussion, our faculty in June of 1994, voted to approve the concept of such a program. This move was in keeping with one of the many recommendations of the Royal Commission on Learning. In the eyes of the commissioners, more time was needed to prepare teachers for the complex world of the classroom. Time, however, was not the only concern. It was felt that more attention had to be paid to the integration of theory and practice and to setting the stage for lifelong learning. The new generation of young teachers needed to be more critical and reflective about their work, and needed to develop collaborative and leadership skills for working with their colleagues. So many initiatives and so little time.

Growing out of these Faculty-wide initiatives, in the 1995-96 academic year, two-year pilot programs were launched. One pilot program was in the secondary education department, under the capable leadership of Ian Hundey. In setting out the two-year program, the Faculty identified the following key images for teacher preparation that we feel worthy of inclusion at this time. The rationale and images of the broader Faculty reform were applied to the development of the secondary pilot program:

> We believe that the role played by teachers is vital to the future of society. Initial teacher preparation must provide prospective teachers with the knowledge, skills, and attitudes that will form a strong foundation for effective teaching, and for continuous learning and development throughout their careers. Teachers can make learning exciting and productive for students if their own learning is exciting and productive. Every teacher should become an agent of school and social improvement pursued through the following six goals. Every teacher should be knowledgeable about, committed to, and skilled in:

1. Working with all students in an equitable, effective, and caring manner by respecting diversity in relations, ethnicity, race, gender, and special needs of each learner.
2. Being active learners who continuously seek, assess, apply, and communicate knowledge as reflective practitioners throughout their careers.
3. Developing and applying knowledge of curriculum, instruction, principles of learning, and evaluation needed to implement and monitor effective and evolving programs for learners.

4. Initiating, valuing, and practising collaboration and partnerships with students, colleagues, parents, community, government, and social and business agencies.
5. Appreciating and practising the principles, ethics, and legal responsibilities of teaching as a profession.
6. Developing a personal philosophy of teaching that is informed by contributions to the organizational, community, societal, and global contexts of education.

Subject area courses were now grounded in a vision of teacher education built upon the aforementioned images of the teacher. Courses such as diverse classrooms, diverse learners, teacher development, teacher leadership and school improvement, and the changing context of education shaped perspectives in the subject areas.

With the introduction of the two-year pilot, the field experience in the subject areas evolved as well. Students were located in the field more frequently and for longer periods of time. Student attention was broadened beyond their subject specialty. Field and Faculty links were strengthened. Instruction and reflection on practise occurred in the field as well as in the Faculty, and was shared equally by field and Faculty instructors. Student assignments connected more closely to field practice. Inquiry characterized all aspects of student work. The spirit and character of growth over time was the guiding principle. Finally, not the least of the features of the new program is the period of internship in the second year. Both the internship and its length are unprecedented in the history of the Faculty.

At the time of writing, the "pilots" were still in the first of the two years of the program. As such, it was impossible to evaluate the success of this project. Suffice it to state that teacher education in FEUT has taken a bold step forward into uncharted waters, firm in the belief that we can make a very good teacher preparation program even better.

The Role of the Arts in Education

Music

Natalie Kuzmich

Natalie Kuzmich is a professor at the Faculty of Education, University of Toronto, and is director and conductor of music programs and ensembles at FEUT and the University of Toronto Schools. She has presented papers in music learning, teacher education, and practicum initiatives at Charlottetown and Ottawa, in Austria, and Holland. In 1994, she was invited to Southwest China Normal University in Sichuan to give lectures on topics dealing with curriculum design and integrated arts.

Prior to 1969, music education at FEUT focused on teacher-centred methodologies that emphasized learning through doing, that enabled students to perform in instrumental or choral settings, and that taught the theory associated with reading notation and musical rudiments. Several sessions were devoted to listening (music appreciation). These incorporated studies of musical forms and history—usually the lives of composers. The preservice year also featured a cross-disciplinary cooperative venture: in the fifties, a Gilbert and Sullivan operetta, such as The Gondoliers or H.M.S. Pinafore; in the sixties, a popular musical such as The Boyfriend, or Gypsy.

The majority of Faculty students in music were not specialists, although many had had experiences associated with music, such as taking piano lessons, playing in secondary school ensembles, and singing in choirs. Needless to say, the one-year preparatory program for non-specialists was hardly adequate.

Preferences for child-centred learning and creative problem-solving approaches in the early seventies were evident in primary/junior schools; less so in intermediate/senior settings, where conservative thinking continued to dominate teaching. In music, performance-oriented approaches produced prized instrumental or choral ensembles. Very little, if any, time was devoted to creative problem solving—to improvising, composing, inventing and manipulating musical ideas, shapes, forms, and colours. Many music educators had not had opportunities to make positive use of creative problem solving in class; certainly, they questioned its efficacy.

However, approaches incorporating creative problem solving seemed to enhance music learning (Kuzmich, 1972, 1974, 1986); these were incorporated into pre- and post-service instructional programs at FEUT (Kuzmich, 1987). They became the basis of laboratory programs set up in several elementary- and senior-level schools.

It should be noted that, since the early seventies, the majority of music candidates at FEUT tend to be music education graduates with considerable background in instrumental and/or choral technique, conducting, score reading, harmony, and in teaching children to play the instruments. Few, however, have had the opportunity to implement alternative routes to music learning and expressive music making—to employ strategies that provide direct access to understanding fairly sophisticated musical manipulations, that permit multiple results, and that recognize the different needs, abilities, and interests of school children.

Implementation of alternative approaches (Kuzmich, 1972, 1974) led to expanded practices in non-threatening settings. Student teachers, each working with four or five children at intermediate levels, were encouraged to try different approaches to music learning. Further, they kept journals documenting the activities and strategies they used to implement learning styles, as well as their reflections on what worked or didn't work (Kuzmich, 1975). They also had to meet with their peers to ensure that they were covering the requisite materials for the same grade.

FEUT students also employed creative problem-solving activities in sessions for cognitively handicapped youngsters at senior-public and secondary schools. Music specialists, taking the elementary option (early seventies), also made use of alternative modes to learning in their music-laboratory programs at a local K- grade 6 elementary school.

These instances provided school-based opportunities for FEUT students, although they were not teaching entire classes. They also had to leave their lab students for practice teaching and special faculty functions. They found it difficult to maintain the momentum of learning, particularly in the latter half of the year when even more frequent interruptions tended to destroy lesson continuity. Also they were regarded as outsiders—itinerants—

who were there to teach music to children three times a week. They were not part of the school, nor were their efforts recognized by FEUT.

The musical tended to dominate the Faculty year. In the pre-seventies, it was based on an American or British show. In the post-seventies, it was original and very much in tune with the current philosophy; that is, making creative use of extraordinary talents, untapped capabilities, and specializations of students. In short, the productions were written, composed, arranged, stage designed, costumed, performed, and directed by Faculty students. It was a huge, cooperative venture culminating in successful performances for thousands of primary/junior grade children. For many, it was their first theatrical experience.

Other remarkable happenings in the late seventies were the two integrated arts celebrations—one focusing on the Renaissance; the other, on the contemporary era. The entire Faculty, associate teachers, and friends were invited to take part in numerous superb workshops, for example, making masks, miming, extemporizing in dramatic settings, improvising on percussion instruments, painting or sculpting nudes, recreating an event or era through the media, playing unusual instruments, dancing and moving to the beat of a Renaissance or African drum. The workshops were all geared to making the offerings accessible, and indirectly fostered a greater interest as well as receptivity to the various arts.

The art experience is important. Its transformative effect is truly wonderful, yet how can anyone celebrate or value its meaningful spiritual effect if she or he has never experienced it? The arts should be celebrated for one week in each Faculty year and specialized workshops, presentations, performances, and lectures should be open to all.

Currently, timetabling and alternative programming tend to discourage the musical production—not enough people are available for the requisite time commitment to the mounting of a production. However, music-education students have been and are involved in retirement or nursing home projects—that is, they plan and perform activities that encourage the participation of people in these homes. Indeed, the residents have proved to be wonderfully receptive. They enjoy activities that acknowledge their needs, interests, and capabilities at the same time that they exercise both mind and body. They reach out to those who show they care.

Although projects related to nursing homes are different from those related to the musical, they are, for the most part, wonderfully satisfying.

Changes in Faculty offerings and timetabling in the late eighties encouraged other kinds of initiatives in teacher training, particularly those involving collaboration with practitioners in the field. In 1991, after considerable planning with the department head of a very successful music program, a different kind of extended practice—five consecutive weeks in one school—was made available to FEUT music students. It was a research project directed to people who had had teaching experience prior to the Faculty year, who knew the materials of music and music making, and who could then concentrate on differing approaches leading to musical growth. Each candidate would work with a peer who would supply guidance, assistance, planning, and feedback, and the host teacher would be on hand to respond to any calls for assistance, and would become immersed in the programs and activities of a school. Each candidate would assume responsibility for the work missed at the Faculty.

Qualified candidates were expected to:

1. help the host in all aspects of his or her program,
2. establish a rapport with students,
3. implement a unit incorporating creativity, performance, critical listening, and different learning styles,
4. meet the expectations of the associate school,
5. keep a detailed journal that, among other things, was to indicate the effectiveness of peer coaching; different teaching and learning styles; and ideas and experiences that had been internalized or had brought about growth, change, and consolidation in thoughts related to music learning and education; and the advantages or disadvantages of a five-week placement over the traditional two-week placement.

There was great enthusiasm for this proposal, which recognized that teacher candidates posted in strong programs had to have considerable musical expertise (specialized skills as well as broad musical backgrounds), teaching experience, and good teaching skills. Each candidate had to have a strong work ethic in order to be able to cope with the challenges of early- to late-evening teaching demands, and each candidate had to be willing to take risks, be creative, and be open to constructive criticism and self-discovery.

The hosts, as mentors or role models, were expected to be exemplars in teaching and creative problem solving; to be in touch with current scholarship in music education; and to have a strong liaison with FEUT.

The extended practice exists—in modified form—as a kind of alternate program for all music-education students. Indeed, Faculty music students wish it. Throughout the preservice year, students, in pairs, spend one day a week at a host school, and are posted there for one or two sessions of their practice teaching. They view it as a wonderful opportunity to become versed in the internal workings of a department and school, and believe it helps them to become more effective and competent music educators.

Features of this program include:

1. collaboration between hosts and Faculty,
2. contributions of host practitioners to the Faculty—as models, mentors, and workshop leaders,
3. opportunities for research based on practices in the classroom,
4. greater involvement of hosts in critical, reflective, and active implementation of philosophies and theories of learning.

While there are few incentives for hosts to remain committed to this program, their centrality to teacher education is crucial and should be recognized by way of certain privileges—release time from classes to attend and/or give professional development sessions at FEUT; access to university libraries; and courses free of charge.

Hosts who become committed to research, learning, and their role as joint participants in teacher preparation will be invaluable to education, particularly when research and professional training have had little effect on what the teacher does in the classroom (Kagan, 1992). Educators might look to the field to probe into belief systems and classroom practices for some direction, as well as to come to a consensus regarding what and how learning occurs (Kuzmich, 1995). Remarkably, even in differing societies, there appears to be considerable agreement regarding the goals of music education. Good teachers heed students' needs by setting attainable goals, yet stretch their music potential to the highest level possible; they enable students to make connections to the manipulations in the music of differing styles and cultures; and they enable students to become lifelong learners. Methods of implementing the preceding goals are many and varied (Kuzmich, 1995).

The responses to a questionnaire regarding beliefs and practices of music teachers point to research that attempts to provide answers to the following:

1. Given the same content, teacher, number of students, and time frame, which instructional style—teacher-centred or student-centred—is more effective to learning?
2. What can and should music communicate? What music knowledge is of most value? How do you determine the answers to these questions?
3. What musical skills are portable throughout life? What can be taught and learned in one or two periods per week? Should portability determine the music content in school offerings?
4. What kinds of music learning can or should be evaluated?
5. What are the criteria for admired music programs?

Some changes in pre- and post-service training show great promise—joint ventures in teacher education, in learning, in research. What is yet to come is a full recognition of the importance of arts learning and its effectiveness in the education of mind.

Visual Arts

John Emerson

Professor John Emerson's connection with the Faculty of Education dates from 1944 when he entered University of Toronto Schools as a grade 9 student. He earned an Honours B.A. in art and archaeology from Toronto in 1954, then an M.A. in 1955. After a brief career in institutional interior design, he returned to OCE and acquired his specialist's certificate in art, teaching art and English in Etobicoke secondary schools. He worked as inspector, program consultant and inservice instructor in art with the Ontario Ministry of Education. In August 1971, he was appointed associate professor and chairman of art education at the Faculty, and continued these duties until retirement in June 1995.

Fragments from the past occasionally turn up: an oak art desk from the original east third-floor studio, a collection of geometric solids for drawing lessons, a few teaching texts on design, art history, and curriculum from the century's—and the Faculty's—first decade, and a kit of 1930s design exercise sheets, testimony to the structured approach of Annette Marsh.

Then followed the quarter-century (1945-1970) of Percy Tacon, a painter-thinker whose ground-breaking non-objective experiments were featured this winter in a belated retrospective at the Mississauga Art Gallery. Under Tacon, students followed a set program of school-oriented exercises in design and art media, along with a freewheeling seminar on modern art history, aesthetics and pedagogy. As the Faculty expanded, including an elementary option, other instructors joined the team, mainly from the industrial arts group of Rudy Sramek, Bill Sloan, Peter Briggs, and Ed Emerson. Outreach occurred through Percy's addresses to community and professional groups, and events such as George Tait's panel presentation to the 1952 landmark conference of the Canadian Education Association, which spawned the Canadian Society for Education through Art.

Michael McCarthy came from Kingston on Tacon's retirement, found the old art room converted for science, and compensated by supplementing his own scholarly lectures with studio sessions under artists across the campus. He fleshed out the artistic presence by inaugurating or expanding annual art exhibitions, purchasing of works by students and instructors, and subsidized field trips to centres such as Rochester's Eastman House and Buffalo's Albright-Knox Gallery.

When I took over the chairmanship in 1971, I brought with me perspectives shaped by Hall-Dennis, and the experience of his ministry work across the province. The place of art in education was—and still is—governed by educators' and the public's attitudes to art in life. Ontario seems unable to accept that art doesn't fit neatly into a structure that divides the academic from the vocational, and the evolution of the Faculty's program has been coloured by attempts to deal with competing views and dichotomies: art for art's sake vs. art for education's sake; specialist vs. generalist; elementary vs. secondary. Typical of the challenges were the university's 1982 threatened devaluation of art as an arts and science admission credit, and the continuing struggle for equivalency of non-degree art credentials for specialist teaching qualification.

Through the 1970s, we carried on the secondary school specialist program—a calculated balance of studio, history, and curriculum theory—mainly in the subterranean gloom of the Ontario Institute for Studies in Education concourse level. The studio ceiling was barely high enough for the students' ambitious paintings, but support in photography and material arts from our colleagues over at the Faculty of Education building helped maintain our solidarity. Our 1979 repatriation to the remodelled wood shop in the Spadina wing raised our profile, but it was only the first of several space-modification ventures, which might even have meant a return to the original third-floor studio if amalgamation priorities had not intervened.

Though content was often flavoured by the staff's special expertise, we recognized the wide range of student background, and sought to exercise these resources in shared in-faculty workshops, while filling gaps through presentations by guest instructors and artists such as Gordon Rayner, Colette Whiten, Vera Frenkel, Richard Nevitt, David Rifat; urban experts such as Ken Greenberg and Mike Filey; and a liberal assortment of ministry and school board consultants and department heads. Other Faculty departments were invited to attend where feasible. The additional two hours timetabled for "studio" seemed well justified in terms of rounding out essential hands-on experience and meeting needs of students who lacked accessible home-studio space. Individual skills found further outlets in a range of Faculty enterprises: a 1972 logo design, settings for the annual children's musical, arts festivals of 1978 and 1979, and recently beginnings of cross-disciplinary integrated studies for intermediate division and "broad-based" interaction with technology classes.

Enrichment through field trips continued, though reduced funding forced us to rediscover local potential: the charm of the Annex neighbourhood, the engineering and symbolism of St. Michael's Cathedral. Until changing Faculty objectives discontinued the complementary studies component in 1993, we enjoyed offering art experiences to B.Ed. candidates in other disciplines—a regrettable loss, since they helped enlighten future educational leaders about the distinctive contribution of the arts.

We saw the practicum as an essential vehicle of our partnership with schools. Beyond the important contributions of regular associates, we valued the exceptional opportunities developed for selected candidates in major galleries and museums, and were grateful for the extended practicum offered in the seventies, during which, for instance, some students produced teaching kits for the Art Gallery of Ontario. Our visual arts newsletter, begun in 1976, provided a convenient pipeline to colleagues throughout the system.

Elementary art, formerly an option given by industrial arts staff to classes crammed into a basement classroom, expanded with the closing of the Ontario teachers' colleges and divisional reorganization. With retirement of key instructors during the eighties, the slack was taken up valiantly by Bob Martin and Al Downs. Proliferation of off-campus elementary sections presented serious concern, however, since these groups often received only superficial, disconnected introductions to art education by board personnel co-opted on short notice. Interaction with our on-campus lab schools became increasingly important. At the University of Toronto Schools, art instruction under Tacon's son Peter and J. Spence Carlisle, succeeded by the long tenure of Don Boutros and Ann Unger, gave opportunities for professional dialogue, formal and informal practicum, and sharing of facilities in ceramics, photography, and printmaking—nowhere more gratifying than in those evening life-drawing sessions, and the hiring of students as summer-course assistants. Dorothy Medhurst (originally an Arthur Lismer protégé) and Paola Cohen of the Institute of Child Study were respected colleagues, for whom we gave occasional workshops. We take pride in finding our recent graduates on the art staff of both schools.

At least from McCarthy's time, we sponsored a yearly exhibition of student art—occasionally augmented by a few staff submissions. Held in OISE during the seventies, the event gained wider popularity when it moved to the common room at 371 Bloor Street in 1980, and eventually to the refurbished second-floor conference room. Opened by celebrities such as Dr. C.D. Gaitskell and sculptor Mark Prent, and enriched by music, poetry, and refreshment, the project gave curatorial experience to our students and heightened profile for our program. For a few artists, it meant purchase of a work for the permanent collection, selected by a staff/student committee, and funded since 1984 by our trade fair exhibitors and the student union. Previous acquisitions had come through the Fowler Memorial Awards and contributions from the dean and various retirees. An Ontario Arts Council grant enabled a student team to assemble our original catalogue.

Visual arts public lectures have long been an extracurricular feature, with a distinguished roster in the seventies including the Victoria & Albert Museum's Sir John Pope-Hennessy, historian Horst Janson, psychologist Lorna Selfe, and Inuit culture authority George Swinton. In 1984, this program was regularized through the generosity of Mrs. Mary Tacon, who established an annual bursary for an art-education student and a companion lecture, in memory of her late husband, Percy. Tacon speakers from all fields of arts and education have ranged from Robert Ott of Penn State to wildlife painter (and FEUT grad) Robert Bateman. The series is given broader circulation through publication in the Journal of the Ontario Society for Education through Art.

Inservice courses have formed a vital link in our teacher education continuum. Following the summer courses of the 1970s, we were a major campus to assume the full Ministry of Education program—summer days and winter evenings—in 1980. We were now offering all parts of specialist, honour specialist, intermediate and senior qualifications, both in-faculty and in partnership with school boards, our reputation maintained by long-term leaders such as Dan Tomlinson of Durham, Maureen Birrell of Halton, and Bill Stadnyk of Scarborough.

From my arrival in 1971, visual arts enjoyed a special connection with OISE: we were *in* it physically but not *of* it. However, the 1970s saw our personal contact with the institute nurtured by Richard Courtney, and teamed with our Faculty arts colleagues, we experienced two decades of a rich montage of research, publications, seminars, and tutorials, initiatives of the Canadian Conference of the Arts (including the submission to the 1975 OECD review of Canadian education, and the 1977 National Inquiry into the Arts and Education), briefs to the 1982 Applebert-Hebert Federal Cultural Policy Review, and planning for The Arts Work—the 1991 international conference on the arts in education. Such collaborative ventures caused the U of T/OISE Joint Council on Education to highlight the efforts of the Forum for Arts and Media Education as exemplary of liaison between the two institutions.

We have always valued our links with the larger arts-and-education community. Opportunities for service and influence have been possible through executive, advisory, and writing connections with voluntary professional groups, such as The Ontario and Canadian Societies for Education through Art and Visual Arts Education Administrators (Ontario consultants). In 1975, we initiated an intervarsity body—The Ontario Society for Art in Teacher-Education—and Visual Arts Ontario was founded with McCarthy as first president.

Increasingly, advocacy groups have been multidisciplinary in composition. Membership in the Arts Education Council of Ontario—a school-board-oriented body initiated by our forum—enabled us to advise on publication of The Artspaper and a 1992 survey of preservice arts teacher education in Ontario. We contributed to formation of the artist-oriented Coalition for the Arts and Education—an initiative of the Ontario Arts Council, and to the 1993 Ontario Arts Education Accord—a joint statement by several groups to the Royal Commission on Learning. When the Regional Arts Advisory Committees (RAAC) grew out of the ministry's 1985 community survey, The Arts in Ontario Schools, we represented the teacher education constituency in their development.

We have played collaborative and liaison roles with a wide range of institutions and agencies. For the Ontario government, we introduced several contingents of "Anglicistes" (French teachers of English) to Canadian art—on screen at the Faculty and at the McMichael Gallery. We hosted meetings on arts content for the Canada Studies Foundation, funded by the Council of Ministers. We advised TVOntario on the 1983 Visions series on Canadian artists, and the Ontario Arts Council on its 1990s workshops for artists in education. Institutional contacts included information sessions at university fine-art departments, teacher education representation in program reviews of the Art Gallery of Ontario and the Ontario College of Art, and advice to the College of Applied Arts & Technology on their offerings for teachers. Involvements of this sort were mutually beneficial: in sharing our expertise, we kept in tune with those populations that supply our candidates and those that employ them.

Today, Suzanne Stiegelbauer brings fresh areas of expertise and interest to the B.Ed. program, and Bob Phillips is shepherding the summer courses. We await news of vital initiatives in the preservice inservice-graduate continuum, expansion of useful research and application of new technologies, the cross-fertilizing effect of integrated studies, progress in breaking the arbitrary and counterproductive barriers between elementary and secondary levels, and between academic and vocational programs, and further links with the museum community and others beyond our walls. If the visual arts team continues to address such objectives, while preserving the distinctive identity of the art experience, visual arts will be ready to help lead the new institution into the next century.

Charles (Chuck) Lundy has taught drama and language arts at FEUT since 1974. He was chair of continuing education from 1979 to 1983 and Faculty registrar from 1983 to 1988. He has co-authored several texts for drama students and has produced and directed a number of professional development videotapes on drama in education. Since 1988, he has been principal of the additional qualification courses in drama offered in Toronto, Stratford, Ontario, and Stratford, England. He has also served as chair of the council of the Faculty of Education for several years.

Drama as a curriculum and instruction subject in the preservice program was a late arrival in relation to the other arts subjects—music and visual arts. I was a student of theatre arts, as it was called then, in 1963-64 as a teaching option taught by John Dodd, and it is my understanding that it had been in the program for a few years before that. As you can see from the other articles in this chapter, music and visual arts had been in the secondary school teacher's preparation program long before that.

Drama, of course, had been part of the extra-curricular program of elementary and secondary schools for decades, mainly in the form of the school play or musical. In addition, the study of plays, usually Shakespeare's, have formed part of the English curriculum for as long as anyone can remember. However, the concept of examining and experiencing the creation and presentation of dramatic art forms as a discrete art for credit on a secondary school graduation certificate was to occur a number of years after my preservice year. Indeed, if I remember correctly, there was no practicum session in theatre arts that year since there were no classes in the subject in Toronto schools. It should be noted that candidates at the College of Education, as it was then called, took three teaching subjects; my other two were English and history. The content of theatre arts at the Faculty was the study, preparation and presentation of scenes and one-act plays. I recall being on the stage of the theatre arts room (now room 237) rehearsing Jean Paul Sartre's play No Exit for presentation to the class when someone burst into the room to announce that President John Kennedy had been shot in Dallas. It was November 22, 1963. The rehearsal was cancelled but, eventually, we did perform the play.

That was the nature of the subject in those early days: we performed, we directed, we organized the technical aspects of lighting, sound, costumes, and props, and we studied acting techniques, movement, and mime. In collaboration with the music department, the theatre arts students presented Guys and Dolls in the auditorium that year. In all, it was highly enjoyable, and we graduated in the firm belief that we would impart all we had learned to our students, if any courses were to be offered. Certainly, we would all be involved in the school play or musical.

As it turned out, some far-sighted principals began to obtain permission from the Ministry of Education to offer theatre arts courses in grades 11 and 12. From 1966 to 1968, I was fortunate to participate in the pilot program that established theatre arts as a recognized credit course for those grades. The curriculum roughly corresponded to the program we had followed at the Faculty and most teachers continued to prepare their students in acting techniques and play production. At the Faculty, Esme Crampton had become the instructor and had added the element of voice development, which was one of her particular strengths.

However, the rumbling of change was heard in the distance. The writings of teacher-educators in England, such as Peter Slade (1954) and Brian Way (1967), began to appear in Canada and were having a profound impact. They advocated a move away from the theatre training focus to more emphasis on the personal development of students through the use of what they called creative drama. At FEUT, John Saxton, Juliana Saxton, Gary Wagner, and later, Tony Gifford, had been hired in the theatre arts department. They all had studied these writers, had had workshops with them, and had adopted their philosophy. The program changed to incorporate these new ideas. Theatre production and actor training were de-emphasized. In their place, candidates learned how to use drama games and exercises to help students develop self-confidence, communication skills, and positive interaction with others. While there were some dramatic presentations, they tended to be student-created collaborative efforts. I was able to participate in these new techniques when the Faculty obtained permission to offer the first additional qualification courses in the summer of 1970. It is fair to say that most of the teachers who participated in those courses changed their school programs in significant ways by using the approaches of creative drama. The impact of these new techniques was sufficient to cause the Ministry of Education to change the official designation of the courses in secondary schools from theatre arts to dramatic arts.

However, every change brings a reaction. In order to emphasize the importance of the new techniques, some advocates of creative drama suggested that actor training and play production should not be part of a secondary school program. Of course, many teachers who still favoured the theatrical training approach, felt that their programs were being diminished, and they mounted strong opposition. Thus arose a dichotomy between process and product, creative drama and theatre, that still persists in some quarters today.

In the 1970s, the pace of change in both the theory and practice of drama in education accelerated. In England, Dorothy Heathcote (Wagner, 1976) and Gavin Bolton (1979) were breaking new ground and adding to the concepts of Way and Slade. Both added a focus on the collective nature of drama and provided a deeper understanding of improvisational drama and roleplaying. They added the important technique of the teacher taking a role in the drama with the students, rather than standing outside it and critiquing the work. In Canada, Richard Courtney (1980) added scholarship to the study of the place of drama in the curriculum, and David Booth (1994) was sharing his use of storybooks in the creation of improvisational dramas in the classroom.

The expansion of enrollment of teachers in the summer drama programs demonstrated the increasing interest of the profession in the use of drama in the classroom at all grades. While drama courses in secondary schools continued to flourish, the most interesting development was the increasing use of drama as a powerful teaching methodology in elementary school classrooms. Many of the teachers using this methodology had the opportunity to work with Bolton, Heathcote, Booth and others in these summer programs, and drama was recognized by the Ministry of Education as a component of the program from grades 1 to 8 in its curriculum guidelines.

David Booth came to the Faculty in 1973, and I joined the following year. At this time, the elementary education part of the program was expanding because of the closure of the province's teachers' colleges and this provided David with the opportunity to teach a course on the use of drama in the elementary classroom. The enrollment in the secondary dramatic arts teaching option was large enough and the contact time of nine hours sufficient to occupy three instructors on a full-time basis at the beginning of this period but, as the Faculty was restructured and enrollment dropped, we found we had to adapt to new teaching assignments. David had more responsibility for language arts in the elementary program, and I taught secondary school drama and had administrative responsibilities for continuing education.

During the seventies and into the eighties, both the elementary and secondary drama programs were infused with the techniques developed by educators in England, but adapted to Canadian students and Canadian schools. There was a recognition that secondary schools were not the most appropriate place to train actors and theatre technicians, but rather that drama programs could and should provide a wide range of students with skills, attributes, and experiences which would be useful to them regardless of what they did after secondary school. To that end, the goals of drama in secondary school became defined as: the development of personal resources, the development of communication skills, the ability to work positively with others, and an understanding of and experience in the art of drama. In elementary schools, in addition to the above goals, drama became an effective means of providing experiences to help children develop skills in listening and speaking.

During the eighties, I stopped teaching while serving for five years as Faculty registrar, and David had full-time responsibilities in the elementary language arts program. Several superb teachers taught the secondary dramatic arts option. Since this was a period during which the Faculty could not hire permanent staff, we are thankful to Wayne Fairhead, Gary Schallenberg, and Ellen Messing for maintaining and enhancing this program. During this time, the additional qualifications program in drama continued to flourish. Summer courses were full and a new program was added in England, where Ontario teachers could work with a new generation of English theorists and practitioners such as Jonathan Neelands (1990), Tony Goode, and Warwick Dobson. Winter evening courses in drama expanded to include off-site courses with boards such as North York, Simcoe, Scarborough, MSSB, Peel, and Durham. At times the, combined annual enrollment in drama courses exceeded 400 teachers.

It was during the 1980s that David Booth (1985) and I (Lundy, 1983) published two textbooks for intermediate/senior drama. David published numerous books on drama and language arts, and we collaborated on professional development videos for drama and assessment in language arts. It was clear that drama had a legitimate voice in Ontario education as evidenced in curriculum guidelines, published resources, and professional development opportunities in both inservice courses offered by a number of faculties of education, and workshops offered by the growing number of drama consultants and coordinators at boards of education. In addition, the Ontario Council of Drama in Education (CODE) provided an annual conference for elementary and secondary drama teachers, and there was a growing international network of drama educators in the United States, Great Britain, Australia, and Europe, with the result that international conferences were becoming regular occurrences.

As we entered the nineties, it appeared that the infrastructure necessary for vital drama programs was in place and those programs should continue to grow and prosper. That, as we know now, is not the case. In times of severe fiscal restraint, the arts, including drama, become marginalized in society and education. There is ample evidence that this is happening now. Secondary school students who are concerned with acquiring skills deemed necessary for employment in the future are choosing science and technology options over arts. In elementary schools, teachers attempting to cope with an overfull curriculum tend to set aside arts teaching for other areas deemed to be more important. Also, the specialist teacher is disappearing from elementary schools so the opportunity for children to work with someone skilled in the practice of drama is diminishing. Perhaps even more insidious is the need for teachers to be more accountable in terms of testing and reporting, with the result that some drama teachers are reverting to teaching observable theatre skills and techniques, rather than incorporating authentic assessment strategies.

The Faculty staff responsible for drama are aware of these trends, and feel the need to adjust the preparation of teachers to reflect these new realities. At the heart of our programs is the knowledge that learning through drama is too powerful a teaching / learning tool to be lost. In the elementary program, we feel that all teachers should learn to use this tool in effective ways to provide a context for children's learning, regardless of the subject area. The power of drama is its ability to ground abstract concepts in concrete experiences. Any field of study that examines human dilemmas that are not capable of easy solution is the stuff of drama. Thus, when characters in a story are faced with a difficult decision, the students can take on the roles of those characters to negotiate and argue which decision is to be taken, or they can examine situations in history by being the people who have to make the best decision.

Preservice and inservice courses are the best means to give teachers experience in using drama and to help them understand the following points:

- roleplaying is the heart of the dramatic experience in the classroom,
- roleplaying is not acting in front of an audience, but rather thinking and talking as if you were another person,
- roleplaying is accessible to everyone since it does not require acting talent,
- drama in the classroom proceeds largely by spontaneous improvisation, a process of creation.

Above all, teachers need to understand that classroom drama is an art form, as in the work of Peter Brook (1968) and Jerzy Grotowski (1968), and the outcomes cannot be predetermined. This is high-risk teaching and is the main reason many teachers avoid using drama. In order to overcome this, teachers need opportunities to experiment with the techniques in safe environments, and to become more comfortable with them. This can occur best in preservice and inservice settings.

In secondary education, we believe that drama specialist teachers will still exist, but their expertise needs to be shared with teachers in other subject areas so that the techniques of drama can be used in the classroom to encourage learning through direct experience. It should be noted that drama is always a group experience, where students have to negotiate, challenge, question, and convince one another through oral language. By doing so, they are developing generic skills that will be useful in any future occupation. Further, as learning is mediated increasingly by computers, we need to recognize that this relatively solitary mode could be balanced by interaction with peers in the context of dramatic explorations. Consequently, the preparation of secondary drama teachers must include models of in-school professional development that result in a sharing of expertise among various subject areas.

Learning through drama will not disappear from schools; it is an intrinsic part of the human experience. From the dramatic play of preschoolers to the rehearsal of a major presentation in business, the dramatic imagination is at work. Teachers knowledgeable in, and comfortable with, the techniques of teaching through drama will be valued in any school. It will continue to be the task of OISE/UT to provide the tools teachers need to engage students in this form of learning.

Part III

Communities of Inquiry

The Faculty Development Group Initiative

Mary Beattie is an associate professor of education at the University of Toronto. She holds a doctorate degree in education from the University of Toronto and master's degrees in English (York University, Ontario) and in education (University of Toronto). She has taught for seventeen years at the elementary and intermediate levels in the public school systems in Canada, England, and Ireland, and has also been a consultant of curriculum and staff development. Her ongoing research and writings focus on teachers' knowledge, professional development, and narrative inquiry.

This chapter gives an account of the establishment of a small group of faculty members committed to promoting excellence in teaching at FEUT. Our aim was to enrich the teaching aspect of faculty members' lives, and to institute an ongoing series of seminars, workshops, and newsletters that would focus on teaching and on the development of teaching. We (Mary Beattie, Carola Conle, Anne Millar, and Annette Yeager) have worked together for three years now, so this chapter is a retrospective account of our efforts to create a framework and setting for the support and valuing of teaching, and of providing resources and ideas for faculty who were interested in their ongoing development as teachers in a university setting. In our first three years together we did three things—instituted a seminar series, published several issues of a newsletter Teaching News, and accessed a research grant that resulted in ten small research projects focused on teacher education and on teaching in urban settings.

The chapter will deal with the way in which we worked towards our individual and collective goals, the activities we coordinated, and the vision which continues to pull us forward and which inspires our current activities and future plans. Three themes emerged from our work together, and they serve to explicate some of the issues, dilemmas and tensions we experienced in setting up this faculty development initiative. An exploration of the issues and tensions within these themes provides us with understandings of the process we engaged in and also with some direction for our future work together. The three themes are outlined on the next page:

1. Changing the Landscape: Teaching as a Collaborative, Improvisational Activity
2. Developing Teaching through Collaborative Research into Teaching
3. A New Kind of Academic Community, Where Teaching and Research are Interrelated

Following an explication of these themes, the section entitled Looking Back and Facing Forward provides the details of what we did, the lessons we learned, and the goals that pull us forward.

Changing the Landscape: Teaching as a Collaborative, Improvisational Activity

The seminar series involved four or five sessions each year, and topics ranged from the use of practical strategies such as portfolios in our teaching, to ways in which to create classroom experiences to promote equity and multicultural understanding among students. The seminar series provided the Faculty Development Group with a way of modelling a collaborative approach to faculty development, in that the series was designed and facilitated by faculty members for their colleagues. We invited faculty members to suggest topics to be addressed, to suggest sessions that we would plan and present, and to share their expertise, ideas and resources. The sessions that evolved from this approach were good examples of teachers talking to teachers about ways to develop professionally. The seminars also provided us with specific opportunities to discuss the realities of being a teacher educator in a multicultural, racially diverse urban setting, and of helping our students to learn to teach in this context.

For the most part, those who attended the seminars were already recognized as good teachers, were open to talking publicly about their teaching, and were willing to engage in discussion and in collaborative practices. As a faculty development group, our hope was that news about the nature and value of what took place in the sessions would spread, and that with time, new members of the faculty would attend and participate in their own way and according to their own agendas. We wanted people to hear that the sessions were a worthwhile investment of time and energy, and to be attracted to them because of this. We believed that our purpose was to offer a service to our colleagues, to promote good teaching for the benefit of our students and to raise the profile of teaching within the university. As a group, we observed movement towards increased sharing of ideas about teaching, talk about teaching, and a conceptualization of teaching as a collaborative activity. However, we also knew that we were working against a well-established view of teaching as a solitary, isolated activity where teachers work behind closed doors, and where interaction with other teachers has not been a cultural or institutional norm.

For those who attended the seminar series, the sessions provided valuable opportunities to talk about teaching in informal settings, to hear from other teachers, to interact with others who were experiencing similar concerns, and to get advice, ideas, and support. Seminar participants spoke of new modes of engaging students in learning about teaching, and often described ways to link the theory and the practice of learning to teach. Different metaphors of teaching, different philosophical perspectives, and different ways of relating theoretical frameworks to practical activities were addressed. The seminar presenters represented a range of different departments, groups, and academic disciplines. This was a major benefit, because a topic, idea, or suggestion not fully understood could always be returned to in an informal meeting or private conversation. A teaching strategy that proved to be more complex than originally expected, need not be abandoned because of obstacles encountered in practice, as support and suggestions could be accessed within the building and among colleagues.

For those who presented seminars (and many did so reluctantly at first, not wanting to promote themselves as experts), several found that the actual process of presenting, was itself a learning experience. Some faculty members spoke of the value of being recognized by their peers as affirming, and as an acknowledgment that they were making a contribution to the professional development of their colleagues. Many faculty members showed their willingness to prepare, present, and discuss the range of issues that impinge on our ability to teach in a university setting, and to link the work of the university classroom to the practices necessary to teach in the urban schools around us. As a Faculty Development Group, we were conscious of maintaining an attitude of inclusiveness, of valuing diversity, and of respect for all philosophical perspectives on teaching and learning.

Developing Teaching through Collaborative Research into Teaching

The theme of "research into teaching as a way of developing teaching" was a central part of our work in the Faculty Development Group. Collaborative research projects, which enabled faculty to work together on issues related to teaching, provided frameworks for inquiries into practical aspects of teaching, and provided opportunities for practice to inform and be translated into theory. The funding of small research projects where faculty members could work towards the resolution of tensions between teaching and research, between theory and practice and between collaborative and solitary conceptions of teaching was facilitated through a grant from UNITE (Urban Network for Teacher Educators). UNITE is a network of faculties of education and schools in urban settings in the United States and Canada dedicated to educating teachers to teach successfully in urban schools. The network has a major faculty development focus; and it was through this branch that we were able to access funds for research projects that would support faculty development and which would also provide the basis for future seminars on making links between research and teaching.

The grant from UNITE was administered by a subcommittee of the Faculty Development Group, and funds were given to faculty who proposed collaborative inquiries into issues of teaching and learning in urban settings and the education of potential teachers for these settings. For several faculty, these small-scale inquiries provided frameworks for interaction and research with colleagues, with professionals in the field, and with teacher candidates. The projects allowed faculty to be engaged in research activities they valued and believed in, to choose the colleagues with whom they would work, and to represent their findings in methods of their own choosing. The grants provided faculty members with situations for professional development, which had several dimensions and advantages, including opportunities to learn from and with others, to relate theory and practice on an ongoing basis, to develop new teaching practices as an outcome, and in some cases to publish the results. For junior faculty members the grants provided situations where research and teaching could be interrelated, and where scholarly research and subsequent publications could emanate from the work. This was a special incentive for many faculty members in tenure-track positions, whose teaching loads cut into research and writing time, but who saw a way of combining research, teaching, and publication through conducting research on aspects of their own teaching.

A New Kind of Academic Community Where Teaching and Research Are Interrelated

The centrality of teaching in a teacher educator's life is an almost unarguable premise, yet teacher educators differ greatly in the conceptions of teaching they hold, in the extent to which they believe that teaching is an important part of their work, and in the relationship between theory and practice that they live out in their lives. The reward system of a professional faculty requires both scholarly production and pedagogical excellence, and this presents each faculty member with an ongoing dilemma regarding the amount of time and energy to devote to the teaching part of their lives, especially when heavy teaching loads are the norm. Time spent on planning for teaching, meetings with students, grading assignments, and researching new topics are all added to the weekly hours scheduled for classroom meetings. For many faculty members, especially for those in tenure-track positions and under pressure to be productive in scholarly work, these hours devoted to the necessary aspects of teaching count for a disproportionate amount of time being spent on teaching. For those who engage in innovative teaching programs (e.g., field-based options), which require additional hours spent in administrative and coordinating activities related to curriculum design, interdisciplinary studies, and outcomes assessment—the hours spent in "teaching-related" work make the development of their teaching through attendance at seminars a low priority in their lives.

One of our goals as a Faculty Development Group was to work towards a new image of a teacher educator that contrasts with the traditional image of the university professor who is a highly motivated, independent individual, but whose espoused theories and lived classroom practices are not necessarily congruent with each other. We worked towards changing that image and of putting forward an image of a teacher educator who values both independence and interdependence, who works both individually and collaboratively in a culture of sharing and interaction, and whose classroom practices and espoused theories are in harmony. There is a tension felt between the practices involved in this image, and in the realities of the reward system of the university, which is set up to recognize and acknowledge individual products and individual success, and is often competitive and individualistic in both its incentives and rewards. Collaborative writing, team teaching, joint projects, and co-created products are as yet, not fully recognized within the university reward system. However, it is within these labour-intensive processes and products we must engage if we are to model in our own lives that which we espouse for our students and for practitioners in the field. If we are to recommend the creation of situations and frameworks within which practitioners reflect and work towards the improvement of practice, we must be able to create these conditions in our own lives, and to model and explain the process of doing so. As teacher educators, we must be prepared to challenge and change a reward system that does not fully credit good teaching, and we must be prepared to work towards the establishment of innovative, creative ways of assessing, documenting, and presenting our work. Unless the reward system changes, nothing changes; therefore the processes and practices of assessment and the creation of new ways to account for success in teaching and in teachers' work, provide us with major opportunities for reform in higher education and in public education.

The creation of a new kind of learning community has been at the heart of our efforts in the Faculty Development Group. In our teaching at FEUT, many faculty members advocate practices for students, teachers, and schools that grew out of a concept of school as a learning community. We emphasize the necessity for teachers and students to be involved in continuous inquiry and meaning making, and the need to establish a culture of sharing and of interaction. We also encourage our students to be reflective about their practices, to be continuously engaged in the monitoring, assessment, and development of their practice and to work together towards shared goals. It follows, therefore, that we should model this behaviour and these practices in our own teaching and research, and that a good faculty development program would support and enable individual members with this aspect of their professional lives. Through an inquiry orientation, where practice informs theory and theory informs practice, teaching and research can be interrelated in a teacher educator's life. To the extent that they are connected, they enhance the creation of a new kind of academic community, the development of a new image of the teacher educator, and opportunities to produce new kinds of knowledge about teaching and learning.

Looking Back and Facing Forward

The Faculty Development Group (FDG) has its roots in a series of informal conversations about the importance and complexity of teaching in higher education settings. These conversations took place in the halls between classes and in impromptu meetings in the spaces between discussions about other "official" topics. Our dialogues were based on the almost unarguable premise that those who teach future teachers should be good teachers themselves, and that good teachers deserve conditions and support for their ongoing efforts to become better. This all happened at a time when the organization itself was undergoing a process of major change, major restructuring and reculturing, and major budget cutbacks. In short, there was no time, space, or money for the introduction of a new initiative in faculty development—we knew that we would have to use our creativity to do what we believed needed doing, and virtue would have to be its own reward!

The formation of our group was set within a context where a number of different things were happening at the same time. At a strategic planning retreat in July 1991 for all faculty, we discussed our vision for the future, ways to develop our expertise in teaching and to create new knowledge about teaching and learning, and to work towards the reform of the education system. An inspirational article entitled The Best Faculty of Education in the Country: A Fable (Fullan, 1991) was provided to initiate discussion and to put forward some ideas about how we could begin to do this. The details of the fable resonated for me then, captured my imagination, and provided both a framework and direction for thought and action. Following the retreat, we had ongoing discussions about how to promote and support teaching among our members in the Department of Educational Policy and Foundation Studies. As a new faculty member, I was actively seeking a way to make a contribution to my colleagues' professional development, in the way that my development as a researcher was being supported by others. As an "old" teacher and "new" researcher, I had come to the Faculty with many years of classroom teaching experience, experience as a department head of English, and experience as a consultant in curriculum and staff development. These professional situations all provided ongoing support, resources, and encouragement for new and experienced teachers to develop their teaching, and I wondered about the absence of this for new teachers in settings of higher education. I believed that the institution of a forum for the improvement of the quality of teaching, the sharing of ideas and experiences on teaching, and working towards raising the status of teaching in the university setting was a way to make a contribution and to be of service to my colleagues. In a memo to the dean, I proposed the creation of a program that focused on teaching and on self-initiated faculty development. Soon afterwards I was contacted by Carola Conle, Anne Millar, and Annette Yeager, and we agreed to form the Faculty Development Group. Prior to this, faculty had attended to their own professional development individually through attendance at conferences and workshops, and through grant applications. The coordination of available grants and conference funds had been handled by the associate dean's office and the Personnel Committee. A program that focused on the faculty development teaching aspect of a faculty member's life was missing, although the teaching of prospective teachers is a central component of our work.

As a newly formed Faculty Development Group, we agreed that we would emphasize the teaching aspect of faculty development. We spent time finding out what kinds of programs were in place at other universities and made contacts with the people involved in these programs. We also received support from John Kirkness in the provost's office, whose mandate and interest was in the improvement of undergraduate teaching at the University of Toronto. We received the support and encouragement of our own administration at FEUT, who believed that a grass-roots initiative focusing on faculty development was far superior to anything imposed from above. We began to meet as a group as the 1992-93 academic year was well underway, and we shared ideas and perspectives, considered ways to translate our big ideas in small incremental steps towards a culture of teaching without time, resources, or funds. We made a plan for the following academic year, and began tentatively and hopefully to enhance what was already there in the culture, but which needed to be emphasized and made more prominent.

In retrospect, it now seems clear that the members of this group came together because of a shared belief in the value of teaching. We found that our individual philosophies were informed by constructivist theories of teaching and learning, practical inquiry, and reflection. In our work together, we found that we shared a perspective on faculty development that focused on learning through discussion, and interaction. We found that we all subscribed to an approach to faculty development that sought to enhance what we already had, to acknowledge the expertise and talents in our midst, and to work towards the creation of a more enriching, supportive, and nurturing environment for both new and experienced faculty members. This made our initial and ongoing work together both productive and satisfying, as we learned to voice our differences, to clarify our understandings, and to build a sense of trust, of respect, and of unity of purpose.

Through community-building events such as the seminar series, and through collaborative projects between ourselves and other university departments and between ourselves and the field, progress was made by individuals, by groups, and by our faculty as a whole. By entering into relationships with our colleagues, we learned from each other and could see new ways forward that offered more creative and innovative options than we had previously seen. Some faculty members saw ways in which organizational structures and the individual's purposes could be more closely aligned, and how closer and deeper connections could be made between the research and teaching dimensions of a faculty member's life. As we worked towards the creation of this kind of learning community, we found that the struggle itself could be both exhausting and invigorating—a challenge and an opportunity, a series of irritating dilemmas, or an enjoyable journey of personal and professional growth and development. As a faculty development group, we drew insights from the work we had done, and learned that the development of teaching and the methods used to promote teachers can be as diverse as the people who use them. We have learned that we help our colleagues by encouraging creativity, innovation, imagination, and the continuing desire to be better at what we do. We have also learned that we need to find new creative ways to support research into teaching, to continue to access research funds, and to share and disseminate the results of our work.

Planning seminars together and discussing the ways in which we could best support our colleagues as they developed their teaching were occasions for reflection and analysis of how we were doing this in our own lives. Our planning sessions provided new information, new ideas, and occasions to interact and learn from others. Although frustrating and difficult to deal with, the restrictions we experienced with regard to lack of budget, time, and resources were also challenging in that they forced us to examine our core values and beliefs and to focus on what was important for us to do, in spite of all obstacles. The situation forced us to be creative with all available resources, to consider the strengths and areas of expertise that we and our colleagues already possessed, and to be improvisational, adaptable, and alert to new possibilities. To do this with a group of trusted, respected colleagues was itself a learning event and a source of ongoing professional development.

The process of shaping and documenting the journey we have taken was one of meaning making and of new learning. Through the writing, I have come to see new connections between my work in the construction of professional knowledge within the context of faculty development. I have a new understanding of the significance of providing different settings, frameworks, initiatives, and outlets within which faculty members can develop their teaching, and to see that teaching and research can work synergistically in a faculty member's life. I have learned anew that continuous inquiry into teaching and into ways to develop as a teacher, is a holistic and creative process involving the construction and reconstruction of professional knowledge, whether the teacher is beginning a career in teaching, becoming a teacher educator, or committed to his or her own faculty development and to that of others. It is these learnings and this vision that pulls us forward and inspires our current activities and plans for the future.

The Joint Centre for Teacher Development: The Freshness of Transformation

C. T. Patrick Diamond is a professor and dissertation supervisor of arts-based educational research at the Joint Centre for Teacher Development (JCTD) of the Ontario Institute for Studies in Education of the University of Toronto (OISE/UT), Canada. He teaches courses on teacher development, cooperative learning, and arts-based educational research. In Teacher Education as Transformation: A Psychological Perspective, *he explored the reconstruction of teachers' meanings through the uses of narrative inquiry, roleplaying, and writing.*

The Centre

After thirty years of teaching, I am now working with teacher colleagues from Canada and many other countries at the Joint Centre for Teacher Development (JCTD) of the Ontario Institute for Studies in Education (OISE) and the Faculty of Education, University of Toronto (FEUT). I first came to the centre as a visiting professor in 1990. I found that it specializes in helping teachers and faculty make a fresh start. The centre is now a home for me and for teacher growth.

The JCTD is a special place, in and around which, teaching and research activities relating to teacher development are concentrated and from which they spread. The centre was created in 1989 through an agreement between OISE and the University of Toronto. Under the leadership of its director, Michael Connelly, the centre was granted independent program status in 1995, following a successful appraisal by the Ontario Council on Graduate Studies (OCGS). In 1996, OISE and FEUT are merging to become OISE/UT. Although the centre may become known as the CTD, it will continue to have reflection, inquiry, and improvement of practice as its distinctive themes. We come together in a communal way to preserve and extend the stories of individual members and of the centre itself.

The Vision

Michael Connelly and Jean Clandinin (Centre for Research for Teacher Education and Development, CRTED, University of

Alberta) are leaders in exploring narrative approaches to inquiry. At the centres they have each developed, growth is pursued as a career-long process of awakening in which teachers and their faculty helpers contribute to learning about how to teach. We have designed our program in graduate studies to provide individually driven and collaboratively guided professional development. Because we believe that we can help others to learn to develop only by first understanding how we ourselves learn, we use self- and other-study approaches to inquire into how our education has shaped us and our practice. There is an increasing degree of self-direction in this work. We seek to establish mentoring and collegial relationships that are as engaging and reciprocal as possible. We pursue thesis supervision as a process in which we journey together, seeking to discover and not to impose. The arts-based writing of accounts by and about teachers informs our practice.

The meaning of teacher experience is enriched through reflecting on the themes, metaphors, and images yielded by the narrative of self. Such literary inquiry provides a way of making our personal practical knowledge more accessible and revisable. We use a range of forms, including: progress logs, timelines, morning notes, personal diaries, visuals, response journals, unsent letters, autobiography, paradigm parables, collages, duography, dialogue, puzzles, fables, poems, and magical short stories. While established theory provides us with critical reference standpoints, we particularly seek to follow and rechart the individual course of our understandings. These grow from the personal and shared struggle to grapple with and improve our experiences of teaching.

Because we believe that we each construct ourselves as a "centre" for shaping meaning, we use ways of displaying and examining our lived experience that also encourage its reconstruction. By treating these accounts as works in progress, we extend our present points of view to generate new ones for the future. Through our inquiries, we learn to entertain different versions of our teacher selves and consider which of them are the more promising, as for example: what we think we are, what we want to be, what we are afraid to be, what we pretend to be, or what we think others (colleagues and students) think we are or want us to become. Every teacher consists of many teachers "incorporated" as a self in community.

To promote such exchanges and reconciliations, the centre provides us with a supportive space where we can be tentative and provisional. We gain in empathy through sharing our common and different processes. I have collaborated, for example, with teachers to reinvigorate our teaching through scripting and enacting alternative classroom scenarios. In a writing circle, I also shared in stories, poems, visuals, and responses produced by teachers and administrators from the Peel Board of Education (see Diamond & Dixon, forthcoming). By providing considerate comments, we deepened and widened each other's understandings. Such replotting is central to the transformative work of stories. The goal and means of teacher growth is for us to become narrative inquirers or arts-based authors and educational critics of our practice. However, it is not easy to discard the traditional guise of a teacher or academic and to appear among others as an evolving self. Whenever we teach or write, we need to resist the cloak of impersonal anonymity. Such a cover story muffles our authentic voices and slows their development.

Countering the Stress

Teacher stress is so common an experience that faculty can first help teachers (and themselves) to develop by finding ways to relieve the daily pressures. In such a countering form of teacher education, we learn to take charge by first articulating the sources of our stress and then by finding resources to reduce their impact, lessening the feelings of aloneness. Through sharing and responding to stories of practice, we regain self-control and community, learning to deal with the system and to improve the conditions under which we work. Coping with crises leads to greater self-development and awareness of others.

A complex array of demands continues to encroach on us as teachers. If our sense of control has been eroded, that of chronic overload has escalated. One way out of the conflict and uncertainty is through restorying experience. We then stand a better chance of surviving and may even thrive. Experiencing or living through describes the inner activity by which means teachers can learn to withstand the onslaught of stress. We then regain the equilibrium that was threatened or even lost. Through self-reclamation, we are enabled to deal more effectively with conflicting demands.

Renewing the Self in Community

Any viable community of teacher selves, whether individual or collective, needs to acknowledge its many components and partners in schools, including colleagues, students, and parents. All of our teaching is suffused with their multiple presences. Development originates as actual relations between us all at the centre and within aspects of our separate selves. To learn more about teaching, we each assign part of ourselves to others (as in response trios, comprehensive examination groups, and co-authoring or conference-presentation teams), who share many but not all of our stances. By writing and reading, telling and listening, we learn what forms of teaching and research are being enacted, are possible, still need to be imagined, or have gone stale. We escape from stress and loss of hope through developing self in community.

Greater independence and interdependence result from emphasizing collaboration and at-one-ness. Our isolation as embattled teachers and academics can be overcome without succumbing to either self-centredness or group conformity. Rather than separating experience from those with whom it is shared, we seek growth through close contact with the self and trusted others. We can each address the paradox of being a self located in a centre. We explore the possibilities that are afforded by our being drawn together like a cast of players. We perform a mutual drama, involving the exploration of past, present, and future obstacles and developments. Some of these other aspects of teacher self and others include: the person I am, the teacher I am, the teacher I fear to be, the teacher I want to become, colleagues, and students (Diamond, 1991). We seek to enjoy greater familiarity with self and colleagues. We tap memories, hopes, and anxieties to project our teacher selves across other teachers and across time.

This first task is attempted by using the centre as a collective mirror of the self and teaching. We each share our stories, taking turns to compose and recast experience. It is just as important also to project the self back into the past and then forward into the future. This process involves reflecting upon, or re-evaluating, past meanings from fresh perspectives. A teaching life is not simply given coherence by the passage of time. Growth is achievable only by deriving a configuration out of events so that we can experience them. By considering the past to redefine the self for the future, we rediscover our selves as, for example, enthusiastic, beginning teachers, recalling the helpful or hindering presence of former teachers, faculty, administrators, parents, and students. Dialogue between aspects of the self and others helps us to broaden and deepen our understandings. Tales provoke further retellings and other shapings. We become more alert to possibility, able to speak for and to declare our individual and group selves.

Finding the Way of Wonder

This is perhaps the most neglected form of teacher development, one that has to do with ensuring that each of us, in all of our aspects, can become more present and even transformed to ourselves and others. In the way of wonder or of reformed sensibility (Jackson, 1992), "things as they are / are changed upon the blue guitar" (Wallace Stevens, 1953, p. 52) of imagination. More active, altered awareness is established as new thoughts and feelings are called forth by and in community. Growth consists of entertaining, altering, and experimenting with different combinations of voices and viewpoints. To ensure joint progress, we provide opportunities to foreground personal understandings against the frameworks with which change and others have presented us. The range of our voices is amplified by using personal, arts-based inquiry modes. Our overall and personal stories of teacher development at the centre take many forms, releasing different emotions and insights.

Many of us may have learned previously to distrust the self, its disclosure, and the apparent immodesty of interest in personal development. In growing ourselves as teachers, we need to try to guard against both narrow self-centredness and imposed silence. Inauthenticity can result from our too readily and completely either ignoring or complying with the wishes of others. Rather than always adapting to external demands ("What do they want of me?" "What will they think of me?"), we also need to balance them against individual needs ("Who do I want of me?" "What will I think of me?"). Stories consist of both shared and competing accounts. As storytellers of our own practice, we can take and make what we want from the responses of others. Their suggestions for further change need to be framed as positive appreciations. The challenge for us is to reconcile and fulfill our personal vision with the professional mission. Through our inquiries at the centre, we find our separate and shared voices, learning to act alone and together. When opposition from traditional sources such as teacher or researcher, thesis candidate or supervisor, staff or administration, newly or very experienced practitioner, "us or them" is overcome, we no longer feel besieged or lost.

Through the giving and the taking of stories, we find that we can better voice and provide access to our personal and group imaginings. Expression and response promote further reconsideration and reconstruction. For each of us, the major theme or point of the self becomes what we find we are through inquiry. This is the crucially important "me" that is me alone. We learn to summon up the individual and shared, unfolding and patterned stories of teacher education. Together we are refreshing our experience of teaching, enticed by tunes as yet beyond us as we are.

A Centre to Live Through

While only some teachers may face the daily threat of violence, for many more there is the constant reality of exhaustion and loss of confidence. These teachers need to find their own community of selves and then develop ways of nourishing it as well. At the JCTD, we can become both reconciled with our life of teaching and reassured that we are part of a greater whole. The chief feature of this shifting of inner equilibrium and change of personal centre of energy is the transition from tenseness and worry to receptivity and calm. By taking time out, we can regain greater control of our teaching and so convert formerly difficult classrooms and schools into retreats for restoration and growth.

By contributing to the centre, we identify with and respond to our own special people and places. By establishing refuge and respite, we become more able to protect and promote our professional growth. Reconstituting the self within community, we are able to temper and even reverse the effects of conflict and stress. The centre helps us to hold things together until we can achieve a more satisfying harmony or more insightful vantage point. Progress for teacher self and others is achieved through telling and sharing personal and collaborative stories. Non-fictional educational storytelling is a powerful and persuasive form of inquiry that also provides a counter-narrative to dispel cruel myths about teachers. In one of these colliding stories, teachers and their helpers are depicted not only as understressed and negligent, but even as responsible for the supposed decline in standards of achievement. By sharing their stories of lifelong commitment, teachers increase public empathy for their position, reducing the threat of externally imposed regulation. We enhance our professionalism by gaining a greater role in deciding how best teacher education is to be replotted.

The centre represents an advance in teaching development and research that may herald greater acceptance and more widespread growth of other centres for teachers. The more "rational [or] click-clack" (Wallace Stevens, 1953, p. 107) forms of teacher education need to be complemented by the development of other centres using arts-based inquiries to make the work of teacher growth more accessible, fresh, and affecting. Such procedures transform teachers into educational artists. Rather than relying exclusively on expository forms and transmissive modes, we can capture and brighten facets of teacher education through personalizing, fictionalizing, and rendering the experience of teaching in new ways—and with greater impact and intensity.

At the JCTD, we seek to help individual teachers and schools to create their own rights as centres of integrity, despite the incoherences and assaults of classroom life that they may face. By coming more fully to understand ourselves and others, we are better able either to continue or to begin again. We can each develop in self-fashioning ways, becoming more self-alert and other-empowering. More than any formal account can suggest, the centre helps refresh each of us, even as we join in its transformation. In our celebration of growth,

> The freshness of transformation is
> The freshness of a world. It is our own,
> It is ourselves, the freshness of ourselves.
>
> (Wallace Stevens, 1953)

Five Personal Models for Professional Growth

David Booth has been a professor at the Faculty of Education for twenty-five years. A former elementary teacher and program consultant, he specializes in literacy and the arts in education. He is the author of many books for teachers and parents, as well as award-winning picture books and anthologies for children, and is a well-known speaker at international conferences for parents, teachers, and administrators.

> In Teachers for Our Nation's Schools, I referred to John Dewey's 1904 admonition to schools and colleges of education: seek lessons from the "matured experience" of other professional callings. They did not. Instead, they sought largely to model and be approved by the arts and sciences departments. Today, in the reward system of universities, there is less attention to the unique demands on professors engaged in the education of educators than is the case with respect to those preparing lawyers and architects.
>
> (John Goodlad, Educational Renewal, 1994)

John Goodlad draws our attention to the "unique demands" placed on those educators engaged in teacher education with preservice and graduate teachers. The balancing act I must play, especially in working in a one-year B.Ed. program with the immediate demands of student teachers entering a classroom for the first time, and presenting them with the necessary background and perceptions required for a lifetime in teaching, remains a constant dilemma. In my personal struggle to deal with teacher education, I am confronted with the demands of my own professional renewal and research, as well as with the need to encourage and support the student teacher and teachers in field schools where I work. What I research, read, write, and teach in the university setting must apply to what my students explore in teaching practice. How to continue developing as a professional may require integrating these aspects of learning into a more inclusive frame, as suggested by these recommendations in the

Holmes Report:

Schools of education, "to a great extent," should:

1. integrate faculty from schools, school districts, and other educational settings into the research and development activities of the school of education,
2. create opportunities for faculty research in a variety of field settings affiliated with the school of education,
3. create opportunities for faculty research in collaboration with field-based practitioners.

(Holmes, 1990)

In this chapter, I want to examine five personal models for my own professional development that link me with practising teachers, students in their classrooms, student teachers, and university research, allowing me to participate in all aspects of education while at the same time connecting me to the significant network of educators in the international community. Each of us involved in education will need to create a set of models that will apply specifically to our particular life situation. The following five models comprise a framework for my personal professional growth.

Model One: Working with Teacher Researchers

In 1988, the Ontario Ministry of Education and the Peel Board of Education established a three-year project to explore talk within the context of classroom learning. It seemed to those of us who organized the project that talk is a vital component of learning in every area of the curriculum, and that its benefits had not been scrutinized by teachers in a practical way, for the simple reason that they hadn't been given the opportunity. The TALK project was designed to support teachers as they began to examine their classroom practice by observing their students in action, and then analyzing and reflecting upon their observations in order to change their teaching.

Over the course of the first year of the project, the project consultants met with teachers in various contexts—at conferences with individual teachers, in school meetings, during catalyst committee meetings, at ministry courses, and in principal seminars. No strict guidelines were set down; each teacher was free to explore whatever facet of talk interested him or her. This proved to be the most difficult of all our tasks, for the balance of encouraging independent growth while enabling participation by as many teachers as possible was difficult to maintain.

Teachers from eight schools took part in the project in a variety of ways, from the private reading of resources supplied by the consultants to the public sharing of classroom research. The schools were given access to audio and video equipment, and some brief training sessions were offered to volunteers. Over three years, eighty teachers were committed to classroom-based research projects, and a resulting book[1] was a compilation of many of the papers that were received from the participants. They reflect the individual interests, styles, and experiences of the teachers: some are formal in tone, others informal; some use scientific research models, others are highly personal. We encouraged this diversity by refusing to establish predetermined standards about subjects, treatments, and so on. Although we tried to offer support when it was needed, we also tried to give the teachers free rein—much the same as many of them were trying to give their own students in the hope that they would pursue interests that would make a real difference to them and to their students.

What their work demonstrates is the extraordinary enthusiasm, intelligence, and originality that teachers can bring to classroom research. They all reveal the enormous range of possibilities teachers can explore on their own or as part of collaborative teams, with or without the help of consultants and elaborate equipment. These teachers represent forces and ideas in a period of great change and challenge in education, teachers helping one another to become more professional in their dealings with children; teachers becoming responsible for the effectiveness of their own programs; and teachers talking with one another, with children, and with educators concerned with talk in the classroom.

What has struck me most about this work is the constantly recurring statement that what matters most at this crucial time is the need for us to listen, not only to experts and to our own instincts, but, first and foremost, to the children with whom we spend our working lives.

Reclaiming the Classroom (Gaswami & Stillman, 1987) suggests that teachers should control their own learning. For many of us—teachers, teachers of teachers, and researchers—this concept comes as a breath of fresh air. Carol Thornley-Hall (in Booth, 1994), who headed the TALK teacher-research project, agreed wholeheartedly:

> How can teachers transmit a sense of worth to their children if they do not have it themselves? Most professional development activities have been organized and often mandated for teachers by others, a phenomenon that does not seem to occur in any other profession. This leaves the teachers with the feeling that they have been "professionally developed" rather than that they have expanded their own professional expertise and knowledge. Workshops and presentations, traditional forms of professional development, are stimulating and informative, but have short-term or little effect on the classroom.
>
> There are other disadvantages to such top-down, laid-on programs for implementing curriculum change or new ideas. Teachers often respond wearily with the comment "What next?" or "Now, what's coming down the tube?" They dutifully try to assimilate the new knowledge, but frequently find the changes required in adjusting their practice to fit new ideas can be discouraging and lower self-esteem.
>
> The uncomfortable business of changing patterns and procedures which have been successful over the years can make some feel, temporarily at least, utterly defeated.

Consultants such as Gordon Wells, Bob Barton, and I helped the teachers to come up with questions that were significant to them as teachers, and to develop research models for gathering and interpreting their data. The results were so stimulating that many teachers continued their classroom inquiry interest groups for the next few years, meeting together to look at certain aspects of programs. Personal inquiry, and eventually group inquiry, can only add to the professional growth process. It changes the conversations in the staff room and in the hallways. New books and new information pass through the school. If someone finds something, whether it is a new children's literature book or an article pertinent to some of the things that people are talking about, then others will soon be sharing the information.

The teachers in the TALK project created research booklets, ran workshops, and made videotapes showing what they tried to do in their own classrooms, what they had thought about, observed, and concluded. Many have shared their personal inquiries with the larger community of teachers and encouraged others to use their own classes as resources for research—teachers involved in sharing their journeys as they grow professionally.

As well, the TALK project sponsored two international conferences on classroom talk that included presentations from local teacher-researchers as well as those from various guest educators. In their evaluations of the first conference, those attending suggested that the next year they wanted to spend much more time with the teacher presenters. The voices of our peers pull us so much faster into new contexts for learning. When our colleagues ask us to join them, somehow the challenge of change and the risk implicit in classroom-based research seem to fade. What we hear is the excitement developing as teachers learn together with other teachers and through the help of our own students. Steven Lieberman (in Booth, 1994), a resource teacher, found it contributed to his own growth as a teacher:

> Teachers' own investigations, demonstrations, and articles are the heart of the TALK project. As a resource teacher working in several schools, I enjoy being part of an open learning community. I have been invited to professional dialogue sessions as a fellow researcher, not an outside expert. I have been with the staff on a retreat at which Gordon Wells was a guest, and I also participated in a teleconference between the staff and Donald Graves. The teachers had planned these events carefully, preparing ahead of time individual and group questions based on their

> readings and classroom experiments and therefore were able to make the most of the time available. Each session ended with a period for reflection and discussion.

The classroom is the best site for research into teaching, and the teacher is at the core of the research team. As they examine their own classrooms and tell stories about their children, teachers begin to gain an understanding of how children develop and how social needs determine language. As a participant in their research projects, my own professional awareness grows by leaps and bounds.

Model Two: Writing with Teachers

In Queenston Drive Public School, 600 children and thirty staff members form an educational community. A few years ago, I became involved with Queenston when I set out to write a book about an actual school functioning in a real community. Queenston was a natural choice for me. Time was my toughest obstacle: these were busy teachers committed to their children. The principal's organizational scheme, however, allowed me to meet them as groups and individuals, to observe in their classrooms, to read their journals where they articulated their thoughts as teachers, and to share their children's writings and classroom-based research. Some teachers bravely audiotaped or videotaped their classes and transcribed tapes of children talking for later analysis. Others collected data and observations from thematic units and special events. Teachers began to tell their stories, and together we created a book,[2] Classroom Voices (Booth, 1994).

The children at Queenston were using language for real purposes, with no "dummy runs." Not only were they communicating but they were able to talk about the language they used to do so. Their teachers had individual styles of teaching but shared similar beliefs and goals. Thus my understanding of a language-based school developed from the excitement and chaos of a school full of real professionals and real children struggling to grow and change.

Through journal writing, collaborative talk, classroom observation, and research, the voices in this book were those of the principal, teachers, resource personnel, parents, and students of Queenston, of the visiting educators suggested by staff members, and of the dozens of writers on language teaching who had inspired the teachers.

We make time for what we feel is important. Everything we do in the classroom, in school, and at university is founded on a set of assumptions about learning and teaching, about knowledge. These beliefs and values, however, are all too often tacit and unacknowledged. We need to uncover and examine them if we—and our teaching—are to change and grow and develop. One way of doing this is to look at our current instructional practices. We can analyze "critical incidents"—those special moments in our teaching experience when we and our students know that real teaching and real learning are taking place. We can observe and learn from our students' responses and then reflect on our teaching, our setbacks, and our successes with colleagues who, like us, want to become better teachers. We can accompany our own classroom research by reading books and articles by other professionals whose work illuminates, strengthens, and redirects our own approaches to teaching. We need to see ourselves as learners. One teacher, Lois Roy (in Booth, 1994), commented on an interesting facet of this particular school:

> The one thing I find at Queenston in contrast to some other schools, is that there is always an interesting dialogue going on—sometimes positive, sometimes negative—but always discussion. You don't walk into the staff room and hear a lot of conversation about the baseball game last night; it's beyond that. I think the teachers here probably have more investment in doing classroom research on their own, too. You have to be thinking about where you are going in your own process of learning as well. If you want your students to be risk takers, you have to learn to be a risk taker as well. I've been astounded at how many teachers out there are not risk takers.
>
> We can't have apathy in education—that's happened for far too long. This school is never apathetic. There are lots of strong individuals with lots of strong ideas.

We often ask our students to keep journals as records of their lives, observations, and learning. Teachers and student teachers who do the same may find it a useful and rewarding activity.

Over the years, I have worked with hundreds of teachers and student teachers who were striving to understand how children learn language, how children learn through language, and how children learn about language. Today, we have a fundamental change in our view of professional growth. We have come to realize that teachers, and that includes student teachers and university educators, must see themselves as language learners and language users—as real readers and writers—if they are to understand how children become literate. In other words, we must work from inside the reading and writing processes, from inside the conversation. This book was the result of teachers writing alongside me, telling our stories together. I continue to learn from inside the teaching circle, a participant alongside the teachers, coming to understand our profession.

This approach changes not only how teachers view their students, but it also changes the way they behave in the classroom. Students see their teachers, at whatever level, as participants in the literacy activities of the classroom, discovering and sharing stories, revelling in the rhythm and images of a poem, writing down an important thought, reading what others write with interest, enjoying a real conversation, exploring how words sound in the air, and how they appear on paper. They recognize that this is what literate people do; they want to become literate people themselves. They learn by example to value books and writing and talk; they view projects and themes and units as sources of excitement and commitment; as individuals, they feel part of an authentic, language-rich learning community.

In the classroom-based projects where I participate, I see the same model working so well. Teachers and student teachers choose their own area of interest and begin to explore it by reflecting on students' work, taping their talk, discussing with them what happened, and writing about their experiences in their classrooms. By talking with experts in the field and with colleagues, by reading and by writing, teachers learn what it is to be a changing teacher, and continue to try to reach each year's students in new and better ways. As we write together, we are engaged in authentic learning, sharing our reflections and our plans, altering what we thought we knew, and constructing new patterns of knowledge.

Model Three: Reading with Teachers

When I began teaching, there were very few methodology courses for teachers, few reference books on classroom theory and practice, and often a single textbook in each subject for every child in the district. To keep up to date, I relied heavily on colleagues, consultants, and the occasional inservice program. Even so, I felt very much alone, with little to measure the success, or lack of it, in my teaching. Today, teachers have a wealth of materials and resources to assist them, yet some still have difficulty knowing where to turn for information on appropriate and effective strategies for helping students learn and for advice on what will be most useful in their classrooms. Conscious reflection on their teaching practices and planning their future growth often lead teachers to identify thin spots or even gaps in their understanding. We know that significant change seldom occurs incidentally or accidentally.

To keep abreast of significant developments that could help us in teaching, we must be on the lookout for the latest publications—books, articles, reports, and newsletters. Today's teacher-authors give us plenty of opportunities for professional development. Everyone benefits as we cruise the world through reading, visiting schools in New Zealand, Australia, Britain, the United States, and Canada. We come to know the writers as our colleagues; we sit in their classrooms; we appreciate their practices; we recognize their successes.

Reading suggestions from colleagues, conferences, seminars, and courses, along with our personal choices, provide an enormous informal reference library. Teachers pass on articles they have read that they know would attract wider interest. They lend or even buy one another books that they feel would strengthen and support their colleagues in particular areas of concern or exploration.

If our reading is wide, we can quickly select those authorities whose work applies to a particular challenge we face. Of course, this requires knowing where to turn. We need to know who the reliable writers are in the areas of education that interest us and be on the lookout for their publishing ventures. By recognizing the specialists who inspire us, we can build our own personal philosophy of teaching by interacting with their ideas.

However, many teachers attempt blindly to replicate the recipes offered in professional writings. Others react defensively to what they see as an unrealistic vision of the teaching experience. The classroom activities and the context in which they are presented on paper often imply a coherence few teachers meet in their own work. They are sometimes overwhelmed by the disparity and dissonance between these "perfect" classrooms and their own. I have met and worked with teachers who, for various reasons, have frozen their teaching in time; I have met others who continue to seek significant change and progress all their lives. Reflective teachers are always expanding their professional knowledge base and developing their philosophy of teaching so that the strategies and activities they employ benefit the children with whom they have been entrusted.

A series of intricate networks are necessary: teachers need to work with other teachers in groups; they can collaborate on projects for professional development courses they are taking together; they can discuss new children's books during planned book-talk lunch sessions; individual teachers can prepare school-wide inservice sessions based on their reading and the expertise they personally bring to the school and the classroom; and they can form book clubs that meet regularly to share interpretations, and responses to a professional book they all have read.

With the support of a network of colleagues and the encouragement of a caring and enlightened administration, teachers can begin to examine their own behaviour as teachers through interacting with colleagues about books and articles that affect change in education.

Model Four: Teaching Children

This model may appear controversial for someone involved in teacher education at a faculty of education, but it is such an integral part of my life that I must include it.

For twenty-five years, I have worked with children loaned to me by cooperative teachers as demonstration classes, while groups of teachers and student teachers both observed and participated in the experience.[3] Teaching in such a context provided me with opportunities to work with teachers from inside the learning, as we visited schools or brought children to our teacher-education centre. I find it difficult to believe that so many years have passed, but as I reread my notes, the children's faces pop into view with each transcript, captured in teaching moments. When triggered, I can recall faces and incidents from almost every group of children with whom I have worked, moments that have seeped into my unconscious and that reappear, seemingly from nowhere, during subsequent teaching encounters. As well, I have had the good fortune to spend hours with teachers and student teachers after the children have left, discussing the ideas explored, the children's words and phrases, the questions that remained unanswered, the strategies that awaited implementation with the next group.

Teachers need to teach, and children need to be taught by teachers who reflect on what has gone on, so that their future work can be informed and illuminated by past experience. It concerns me deeply that so many educators working in preservice and inservice courses for teachers no longer work with children. When I was a young teacher, my role models frequently taught children, relating their mistakes and successes, analyzing the classroom dynamic, working alongside classroom teachers like me in order to grow in their own understanding of how children learn, at least in a particular situation at one moment in time. I would hope the stories we tell each other about working with children will cause us to change as teachers. We need mentors to point the way and guide our reflections but more than that, we need others who continue to find joy and satisfaction in the struggle to teach, who extend and enrich us with their own explorations, working together. As Maxine Greene says (in Noddings, 1996), "It may be that education can only take place when we can be the friends of one another's minds."

Over the years, in these teaching situations where all of us are engaged in working with children, I have noticed a range of styles among teachers, from energetic young apprentices who become the whole lesson, leaving children to stare in wonder, to thoughtful practitioners, who draw from these youngsters concentrated and focused affective thought. This is worth pointing out because teachers often tell me that they can't replicate my results in the classroom. After all, I appear for a few hours or a few days, armed with plans and stories I have prepared well in advance, and without all the other responsibilities classroom teachers have. "What will the children be like when your novelty wears off?" "You have the time to prepare for one two-hour lesson; we have to keep teaching." And, most often, because I ask the adults observing to work with the children whenever possible: "We don't have a bunch of teaching volunteers in our classrooms."

These are valid points, but it is worth noting that a visiting teacher's session can suggest new ideas and approaches, as does any guest's involvement with the children, from an excursion to a gallery, a theatre performance or a trip to the classroom across the hall, or to a celebration on parents' night. Children learn all the time in different ways, and an interactive demonstration lesson can give the classroom teacher an opportunity to observe the children in a different setting. From this opportunity, many teachers have commented that they have learned something new about one or more of their children.

At times, the classroom teacher is nervous in a public setting with a guest teacher, focused on wanting the children to do well and to feel valued. I remember my first years of teaching, when my language arts supervisor, Bill Moore, would ask if he could work with my class. I would retreat to the back of the room, still controlling each child with invisible threads to be manipulated by me in secret. When eventually I let loose those ties, and relaxed as Bill set free the children into new patterns of behaviour, new status roles, new dynamics of interaction, only then did those children emerge into fully rounded human beings for me; it was a bit like watching a Polaroid picture developing over time. On each occasion when Bill Moore visited, I learned more about teaching and more about my children.

When I work with children and teachers, I quickly lose myself in the classroom, but the children are front and centre in the learning. Educator Dorothy Heathcote (O'Neill, 1984) taught me to ensure that those watching not respond as an audience being entertained, but as participants engaged in the struggle to understand the teaching/learning dynamic.

Because of the format of a typical day of demonstration teaching, where we work as a whole group, in small groups, and with partners, teacher participants can begin to develop their subsequent contributions from the feedback the children give when I draw them together from time to time. The strength and abilities teachers possess never cease to amaze me, and I watch both them and the children, taking direction for the work from their hesitant yet productive interactions. A young teacher once complained to me that during discussions, I was not calling on her for suggestions, and when I explained that my focus was on the children's work, she replied that she, too, had ideas to contribute. Certainly the dual roles of participant and observer can be frustrating, but moments of learning can grow from that tension. During reflection, first with the children, and then with the adults, the opportunities for growth multiply. When the community listens to its members revealing and commenting upon their experiences, everyone can benefit from the variety of observations being offered, selecting those reflections that will illuminate their own journeys. As well, children often write to me about our visits, and a new set of observations appears for further consideration. Teachers, too, bring back their thoughts in journals and papers, distanced from the moment and placed in context within their own teaching lives.

Over the years, as teachers pondered the demonstrations, together in class and alone in their journals, I recognized that their collective reflections reveal all of the concerns we have in education today. If we would listen to those educators working with children, and if we could become part of the negotiated meaning-making that grows from these interactions, then the teaching/learning process could be revealed and clarified from within the truth of the classroom, the voices represented in the variety of responses that emerged from teachers as they brought their own experiences to both participatory classroom demonstrations and seminars. Many teachers had worked with or read many educational authorities in contemporary education; some were new to teaching but brought finely-honed curriculum-connected strengths.

I now videotape and transcribe the work of the children, and learn from their reflections and thoughts about their experiences in letters that I have received from them, after they returned to their classrooms and their own school programs. These letters often reveal a teaching moment I had missed or had misjudged, or demonstrate further insight by the children from the cool distance of "after the events." I treasure them, and each time I read through a bundle that a teacher has been kind enough to send along, I am struck again by the clarifying that occurs for all of us when we take time to consider the implications of the events in which we have participated.

Model Five: Reading What Children Read

It hit a little close to home when I read that Margaret Narwin, the 9th-grade teacher in Avi's Nothing But the Truth, was considering taking a summer course in whole language because she found herself unable to relate to the young people in her English classroom. How dare an author of books for young people move onto my professional turf! And yet, during my career, I've encountered and found bits and pieces of myself in hundreds of teachers in children's books. This time, the image stared back at me from the page and I couldn't look away.

When we see a film or read books about us, about our worlds of education, we respond often with indignation or frustration. Is this who they think we are? I look carefully for myself as a teacher in the media daily, struggling to find out if the mirror lies.

How close to us as teachers are the characters drawn from the imaginations and life experiences of the writers of children's literature? Do children build their images of us the way a writer creates a composite story teacher? When they grow up, what bits of us will be left in the toy box, what bits taken on the journey?

Not all teaching in books is what we would choose. Have I made a child disappear as Mr. Rawlings did in Kin Platt's The Boy Who Could Make Himself Disappear, when he asked Roger aloud in class whether he had ever thought of doing something about his speech defect? Have I been as unaware of my students as the experimenters who flashed phonics on a screen in Robert O'Brien's Mrs. Frisbee and The Rats of NIMH (the rats learned much faster than their instructors suspected and soon began decoding the notes written for the lab technicians). Did I assign book reports as a young teacher? Does my son do book reports now? In Dear Mr. Henshaw, Beverly Cleary slams the book report again and again as Leigh Botts reports on the same book for four years in a row. Was I sure I knew the newest and best system for teaching, without reference to my students? In Harper Lee's To Kill a Mockingbird, Miss Caroline Fisher taught Scout's class ignoring their knowledge and advice because, as Scout's brother Jem pointed out, she was teaching by the Dewey Decimal System.

Whose side am I on? Didn't I join in the cheer that went up when the biggest student in the class thrashed the bullying new master in Ralph Connor's Glengarry Schooldays? Don't I still taste Anna's terror in Jean Little's Listen for the Singing when the role-call stopped after her name as the jingoistic and sadistic Mr. Lloyd singles out those students with German backgrounds just after World War II? Didn't I hide a secret grin when the hero of Paula Danzinger's The Cat Ate My Gym Suit gave her thirtieth excuse for not bringing her phys-ed uniform to class with her? Who got my sympathies in Louise Fitzhugh's Harriet the Spy when Harriet rudely told Miss Elson that she wasn't going to be an onion in the school play?

Who are the teachers, anyway? In Virginia Hamilton's The Planet of Junior Brown, it's the janitor, Mr. Pool, who helps Buddy Clark. (I remember the caretaker who taught me drama in grade 8.) Katherine Paterson leads me across The Bridge to Terabithia to meet Miss Edmunds, who takes Jess to the Smithsonian, on her own time, and alters his life forever.

Perhaps I'll retreat more than a century to the prairies and look at the schoolroom through the eyes of Laura Ingalls Wilder. After all, I too boarded with a couple in my first two years of teaching as Laura does in These Happy Golden Years. But I did not suffer as she did when the school day ended: she had to go back to a home where the husband was abusive. And yet I know it happens—in teachers' homes, in students' homes. Where shall we find the ideal setting for our teaching dreams?

Beginning readers, of course, rest safely with Leatie Weiss in the knowledge that My Teacher Sleeps in School. But Harry Allard and James Marshall make them realize that Miss Nelson Is Missing! And teachers are human: has Eve Bunting told them that Our Teacher's Having a Baby? And once they've learned from James Howe about The Day the Teacher Went Bananas, how can we wipe it from their minds?

The pages of these books play tricks on me; they keep revealing glimpses of my face, my class, my colleagues, shadows of my life. Did I teach Roger, Leigh, Harriet, and Junior Brown? Was I so blinded by my own preconceptions that I saw children as physical defects, as Nazis, as onions? And the students, how do they remember those years? Do they remember all of our times together, or just the mean ones, the ones that hurt—the ones that are just plain funny?

These writers were children once, students in my classroom. What are they saying about schools and teachers and students? Would these stories be so gripping, for teacher as well as child, if there were not truth within them? And how would I know who I was if there were no more children—and writers—to tell me? When I recognize that truth, I am already moving on. Yet my reality is still formed by these books that have been part of my life with school children, with teachers, and with my own son. I smart from the sharp jabs some writers have given me; I am soothed by the honeysweet images of teachers depicted by others.

I think I'll take my chances with Ernestine Blue in M. E. Kerr's Is That You, Miss Blue? Students at Charles, a conservative religious school, had their days brightened by her unusual yet effective teaching methods. However, when her own, unorthodox relationship with Jesus began to dominate her life, she was asked to leave, and the girls realized their enormous loss. As an adult, one of them recalls her years with Miss Blue, and like all of us who mourn the passing of a loved one, conjures her image in the crowds on the streets of New York, and longs to be recognized in return: "Miss Blue," I say, "It's me. Is it really you?"

We find ourselves in story, as does everyone who looks. The picture is always slightly out of focus, and we have to adjust our rose-coloured glasses. For those of us in teacher education, looking in the mirrors of our classrooms and struggling to make out the often distorted reflections provided by the children—and the artists writing for the children—is our starting point for tomorrow. We must therefore read with the children and help our student teachers read with the children, noticing the story and the writer and the children and ourselves—all at once. Or else, who will conjure us up when we have made ourselves disappear?

Final Thoughts

How can we continue to become good teacher educators? How do I continue growth for life? Let us remember, as Gordon Wells (1994) says, that reflection is not enough by itself. To benefit our children in schools, our reflection needs to lead to specific plans for change that are put into action and then subjected to observation and further reflection. We want school improvement in action. It's this ongoing cycle of research with which we can hope to change our schools from within.

Michael Fullan says (1991) that schools will never succeed until teachers, individually and collectively, become inquirers, learners, and improvers, as a normal part of their everyday work. When teachers join a community of practice, and work with others who have already acquired some expertise, when the children in those classrooms are involved and see themselves as learners who can look at themselves learning, when the results are shared with colleagues in forums that engender supportive, cooperative interaction, then teachers will see themselves as learners as well, and the classrooms will be the centres of change. I want to be part of that change, part of the culture of school, learning about teaching from inside out.

I look around at my own good fortune. I have access to the faculty library with the best materials and the most helpful librarians one could possibly find in education today. Thirty journals and periodicals come across my desk monthly and I can read, select, and copy those articles that will help me in my work. I have opportunities to meet with educators from all over the world at conferences, in my own office, and on e-mail. I work with colleagues at OISE and the Faculty of Education who are authorities in their own fields; they broaden me, they include me as a team member, they push me. I observe the classroom work of professional, dedicated teachers and I watch student teachers struggling to turn theory into practice. Last and most important, I work with children in schools. All these resources are necessary for my personal professional change and growth.

As the millennium approaches, we who will be grandparents, senior citizens, white-haired teachers, having lived our lives in school, trust that the new teachers will ask to hear our stories and to see our photo albums of what life was like in the last century inside the classroom. And then, all of us will have to follow the breadcrumbs of childhood back through the forest to where all children truly live, so that we can remember who we were, once upon a time, entering school, letting go of our parent's hand, and joining society.

Endnotes

1. The teachers' research has been collected in a book I edited with Carol Thornley-Hall: Classroom Talk. Markham: Pembroke Publishers, 1991.
2. The story of one school's performance growth is recounted in my book Classroom Voices, Toronto: Harcourt Brace, 1994.
3. The recollections of my teaching times with children and teacher-participants is taken from my book Story Drama. Markham: Pembroke Publishers, 1994.

The Role of Research in a Faculty of Education

Nancy Watson is involved in coordinating and supporting research at the Faculty of Education, University of Toronto, and is also senior research associate on a study, funded by the Rockefeller Foundation, of school district professional development initiatives. She recently served as senior researcher on the Ontario Royal Commission on Learning, a major review of elementary and secondary education in the province, and as senior research associate on a year-long evaluation of the work of the Holmes Group, a consortium of American research universities focused on teacher education reform.

Context

In this chapter, I explore the role of research and inquiry in the Faculty of Education, University of Toronto (FEUT), highlighting the changes that took place in the years following the University of Toronto Provostial Review of 1987 and the appointment of Michael Fullan as dean in 1988. The chapter provides a framework for considering the changes, an overview of organizational initiatives aimed at fostering educational research and inquiry, and a discussion of some of the issues and tensions around the role of research in the institution. Although the specific strategies used to support research and scholarship at FEUT are listed and discussed separately, they operate, in fact, as an interconnecting web of activities, linked to all the change initiatives at FEUT. I have been involved as a participant and an observer since 1988, first as the coordinator of the Learning Consortium (see chapters 13 and 14), and since 1990, on a part-time basis, providing research support and coordination through the associate dean's office. This chapter was written in September 1995, less than a year from the planned integration of FEUT and OISE.

The Faculty of Education, University of Toronto is not the first school of education to wrestle with the role of research in an institution that is usually seen in terms of teacher education. Such struggles seem remarkably similar to those that go on in other professional schools—all caught between the demands of the university and those of the profession.[1] Like their counterparts in other universities, faculty members at FEUT have struggled with questions such as: How important is research, and why? Do we need new research models in education? How do teaching and research relate to each other? What organizational supports are necessary? How can such support be provided during a time of often-declining resources?

The place of research at FEUT has changed considerably over the years. For much of its earlier history as the Ontario College of Education (OCE), the institution had both graduate programs and a department of educational research. With the founding of the Ontario Institute for Studies in Education (OISE) in the late 1960s, however, the situation changed dramatically. All OCE's graduate activity and research were transferred to OISE, forming the initial core of the new institution. Inevitably, educational research came to be associated with OISE rather than with FEUT. This shift left the Faculty in an awkward position with regard to both scholarship and its role within the university. Rather than a full-fledged professional school, with all the complexities that role entails, the Faculty was seen purely as a place for preparing teachers.

For the twenty years prior to 1988, then, research was not seen as a major component of FEUT's mandate. Although some faculty members were involved in research, such work was regarded as peripheral to the primary function of preservice teacher preparation. Service to the profession was important, but was interpreted largely in terms of providing government-mandated courses for additional ministry certification, writing textbooks, or participating in professional-development sessions for school boards. Research and scholarship were not considered critical. One Faculty member, looking back to that era, observed, "No one cared; research was not where it was at. There was some lip service, but nothing in practice."[2]

Another colleague agreed, "Some people were engaged in research, but it was individual interest only. It wasn't an organizational priority. It was on the side rather than central to the job here."

The position of FEUT as a non-research faculty was somewhat anomalous in the University of Toronto, an institution that declares:

> We are a *research university*. The nexus between teaching and research is absolutely central to our mission. What distinguishes us is not only our strengths in research and scholarship but also the reflections of those strengths in our undergraduate, graduate and professional teaching programs.
>
> As a research university, the University of Toronto provides a strong base for professional education, both in established professional areas and in emerging areas that cross established professional and disciplinary lines. Nowhere is the translation of research strength into problem-solving capacity more apparent than in these professional areas.[3]

At least during the 1970s and early 1980s, it would have been difficult to see how such a mission was demonstrated in the Faculty of Education, except perhaps through the professional service activities described earlier. The 1987 Provostial Review, however, demanded change. From 1988 onward, following the appointment of the new dean, the situation began to shift, with teaching and research both considered as essential and complementary aspects of FEUT's role. For the first time, education was to be connected to the mission of the University of Toronto as a major international research university.

The Problem

The concept of organizational culture provides a framework for considering the broad change efforts at FEUT since 1988 and, more specifically, efforts to change the role of research in the organization. Culture has been defined as:

> A pattern of basic assumptions—invented, discovered, or developed by a given group as it learns to cope with its problems of external adaptation and internal interaction—that has worked well enough to be considered valid and, therefore, to be taught to new members as the correct way to perceive, think, and feel in relation to these problems.[4]

Culture involves not only "the way we do things around here," but also "who we are around here." Organizational cultures represent webs of beliefs and values built up over time, underlying how people view themselves and their relationship to the environment. Such cultures are highly resistant to change, and yet that is what is attempted in major change initiatives such as that undertaken at FEUT.

A situation somewhat comparable to that at FEUT can be found in many colleges of education in Australia. Policy changes in Australian higher education have changed many institutions with teacher-education units into universities. A recent article describes efforts in one of these colleges of education to "create a research culture."[5] Although many of the specific initiatives and activities are similar to those undertaken at FEUT, the context appears quite different, as the Australian efforts focus on creating a research culture without much reference to other elements of the organization. The efforts at FEUT, covering a much broader front, might better be described as attempts at organizational transformation rather than creation of a research culture.

Shifting the role of research and inquiry at the Faculty of Education represents just one strand of multifaceted efforts to develop a new professional identity for the institution, with corresponding changes in the beliefs and values of members of the organization. With regard to research specifically, the task has been to create a new inquiry-based professional culture in which research plays an important role. Faculty would draw on research, be involved in research, and disseminate the results of research.

Strategies

Faculty development and renewal, accomplished both through hiring and through ongoing professional growth, have been key to enabling FEUT to be a professional college within the setting of a major research university. The intent was not to make teaching less of a priority, but rather, through engaging in scholarship, to enrich the context in which teacher preparation occurred. As other chapters in this book have demonstrated, a key link between the "old culture" and the "new culture" has been the focus on teaching as an appropriate subject for inquiry.

In the first few years after 1988, the emphasis was primarily on raising the profile of research and making it easier for people to engage in inquiry. Such an approach encouraged all faculty members, regardless of their previous experience with research, to become productively involved in new initiatives. The emphasis on inquiry, "reflective practice," and action research was linked with program reform, giving more faculty members a way to participate and feel a growing sense of achievement about their own practice.

As the words of one faculty observer indicate, many faculty were attracted by this approach, "[The] change agenda was taken up by the old guard with a passion.... You create a new work context and you can make your work your research."

Faculty were encouraged to spend more time in schools, to work with people from schools, and to participate in partnership activities. At the same time, a number of external connections were being established, most of which offered a variety of professional opportunities to faculty members. These included the Learning Consortium, international development projects through the Aga Khan Foundation, and the Urban Network for Improving Teacher Education (UNITE). All these, although not specifically focused on research and scholarship, provided new perspectives and strengthened FEUT's links to other professional communities. As noted below, faculty hiring was also bringing in new people to support these directions.

Paralleling these broader shifts in organizational focus, a variety of initiatives were adopted to strengthen the role of research. These research support strategies, however, cannot be considered in isolation from the other organizational change initiatives.

Hiring: Research expertise is one of the hiring criteria for new tenure stream positions, with research and publication now important criteria in tenure and promotion decisions. Since 1988, twenty-nine tenured or tenure-stream appointments have been made (although six have since left for other universities), with a further three being hired for the 1995-96 year. During the same period, more than thirty faculty retired. Those appointed since 1988 now make up nearly half of the fifty-five tenured or tenure-stream faculty.

*Administrative support:*A faculty reorganization resulted in the appointment of an associate dean for field services and research. The mandate of the associate dean includes enabling research support to faculty members and coordinating research activity. The creation of a part-time position with specific responsibilities for planning and carrying out a range of research support activities facilitated this work.

Information: Research-related information is collected and disseminated in a variety of ways. A bimonthly newsletter, FEUT Research News, provides information about upcoming research and funding opportunities, as well as capsule comments on current FEUT research projects, faculty publications, and recent grants and contracts awarded. Data bases have been developed to track information about faculty interests, proposals submitted, and progress of research projects. The administration and administrative support staff frequently contact individual faculty members about scholarly or professional opportunities they might be interested in, but of which they are unaware.

Professional development: Over a period of several years, seminars and professional development sessions targeted various aspects of the research process, with topics such as: preparing proposals, becoming aware of funding opportunities, dealing with ethical issues, developing a research program, and preparing literature reviews. When large numbers of faculty members were making presentations for the first time at a national scholarly conference, "dry run" sessions helped them prepare, and also served to inform colleagues about each other's work. More recently, professional development sessions have focused on preparing external grant proposals, and seminars have been organized where researchers present their current work.

Personal and technical support: One-to-one assistance in preparing proposals and developing budgets, available on an as-needed basis, has been used primarily by those relatively new to the grant-seeking process. Several faculty have noted that access to research support at FEUT has been, in the words of one, "personal and comfortable."

Computer support facilities have been developed over the last several years. At an early phase, to meet the research needs of faculty who did not yet have them, several computers were purchased for faculty loan, specifically for research use (proposal preparation, inputting field notes, analyzing data, and writing final reports). As more faculty members were provided with computers in their offices, such support became less necessary. Electronic mail service, increasingly essential for academic researchers, is now available for virtually all staff.

Although statistical and methodological consulting services are not available through FEUT, faculty can access them through the University of Toronto computing services.

Small-scale funding: Relatively small amounts of money can often make a significant difference in getting research underway. All faculty have access to a competitive pool of university funds for small-scale and pilot research projects. The pool had been administered centrally, but in 1993 the university decentralized the administration and allocation of the funds. The amount available was originally determined largely by FTE, but now depends more on the number of research proposals generated and funded. Because FEUT has a large FTE, but as yet a relatively small number of researchers seeking external funding, the amount available for such small-scale projects has decreased. Recently, faculty members responsible for allocating the pool decided to give priority to supporting projects likely to lead to viable proposals for external funding.

There have been other sources for small-scale funding, but these have been somewhat sporadic. Some funds have been available through UNITE, through the Learning Consortium, or through other partnership initiatives.

Organizational recognition: Beyond the formal tenure and promotion system, the organization has provided other forms of recognition, including notices in university and faculty publications recognizing faculty achievements. As noted by one long-term faculty member:

> In the post-1988 world, it was clear that research performance was recognized and to some extent rewarded, through letters from the dean, merit pay, and other acknowledgment. Also the new faculty appointments gave a clear message that research was now important.

Support for new faculty: Several types of support are available for recently hired faculty. The university makes available an automatic start-up grant of up to $6200 to help new assistant professors establish their research programs. New faculty also have a slightly reduced teaching load, teaching eight to ten hours per week rather than ten to twelve. In the last few years, a mentor system has been set up, matching junior faculty members with more senior colleagues for ongoing informal support and assistance as they move toward the tenure review process.

External liaison: As noted earlier, FEUT has been active in establishing and expanding links within the university, with school boards, with other faculties of education, with the Ministry of Education and other provincial agencies, with charitable foundations, and with international projects. Such links can provide up-to-date information about funding priorities and opportunities and may also provide opportunities for linking practice and theory. FEUT's membership in UNITE has fostered greater awareness of teacher education initiatives in other universities. Some of these connections have also led to additional funding for both professional and research initiatives at FEUT.

Synergy: Research and inquiry are linked to ongoing strategic planning, with an inquiry emphasis woven through much of the work of the Faculty. An emphasis on research can be seen as a way of building impact, making it more likely that people think of research and inquiry as an "ongoing part of the way we do things." Faculty are encouraged to integrate research with their teaching, strengthening both themes in their work, but for those with specialized research programs, such integration with preservice teaching has been difficult.

Impact

The impact of research support efforts can be traced in two major ways: first, the reported experience of faculty members, and, second, data on research projects and publications, as well as other less formal indicators.

An incident that took place in 1990, relatively early in the change process, illustrates the difficulty of identifying "impact." Several professional development sessions on various aspects of the research process were scheduled. The meetings were well attended by faculty, most of whom, at this early stage, predated the "new era." Their responses on a participant evaluation of the research sessions indicated they found the information both interesting and helpful. However, when asked how they planned to actually use this information, it was interesting to note that virtually none planned to develop research proposals. Apparently they were eager to learn and to be included in new opportunities, but their plans did not include engaging in formal research.

It was in this context that the emphasis on inquiry into practice took hold and flourished. Inquiry and reflection allowed people to build on what they knew, to add another dimension to their experience, but to remain within a sphere in which they felt relatively comfortable. "Inquiry" has been interpreted in various ways, but usually includes systematic attention to one's own teaching. Inquiry has served as an accessible channel that has revitalized the work of many faculty members and given them ways of communicating with the broader academic community. In 1988, there were virtually no FEUT representatives at the annual meetings of Canadian academics, while by 1992, thirty-two people attended and gave presentations.

One long-term Faculty member, who was both personally and professionally revitalized through involvement in this kind of inquiry process, described it as gaining and using "eyes I never had before." In the words of another colleague:

> Inquiry means looking at our practice to learn more about its impact. You feed back into practice and teaching, build on it, and take it out in the field. It's collaborative and that's a change from the past. We're connected with the field and with students.

FEUT is a large organization, with Faculty members varying greatly in background and perspective. Thus it would be expected that they would experience the research/inquiry context differently. For new faculty, the situation was often difficult. The demands of the university tenure and promotion process place productivity demands on new tenure-stream faculty, making their situation quite different from that of the longer term faculty who had been awarded tenure already under an earlier system. Although all newly hired Faculty members had completed, or nearly completed, doctorates, not all of them had much research experience. Yet if they were to meet tenure criteria, they would have to become productive scholars.

One assistant professor, coming from a strong teaching background, was excited to be coming to the university to teach and to be involved in working with schools, but came with an orientation to practice rather than research. She initially felt:

> Overwhelmed in the university situation, out of my league. I'd completed one study in my life—big deal! If I hadn't had support and encouragement in the first few years here, I would have gone back to practice. People here made it safe to experiment and I felt some initial success... . And I now see research differently than I did at the beginning. I've added a qualitative dimension, but I also have more ideas about the quantitative.

Several Faculty members have become involved in action research, defined by one as being:

> Grounded in questions that emerge from the working context of individuals, to test personal theories, gather information, ...explain, rethink, and then lead to change in theory or practice. Research then is not separate, it's connected with teaching and work with the field. Exploring questions is part of that work.

With the exception of one part of the organization (the Institute of Child Study, described later) it would not be accurate to describe FEUT as having developed a research culture. On the other hand, it might be described fairly as an inquiry-oriented organization, where most Faculty members are aware of developments in teacher education in Ontario and elsewhere, where they are experimenting with new approaches in their teaching, and where they are communicating their experiences to each other and to the broader teacher education community through attendance and presentation at conferences.

Within this context, an increasing number of faculty (including those hired since 1988) are involved in what might be seen as the next level of scholarship, writing for both professional and academic publications. Some of these are working with methodologies such as action research, narrative, and life histories for instance, that may not easily fit within the traditional research university standards.

Finally, a relatively small number of Faculty members are deeply engaged in research programs of the kind recognized and rewarded by both research universities and granting agencies.

Although there have been tensions around the different approaches to research and inquiry, the changes seem to have taken place without FEUT being sharply divided into balkanized subgroups. This somewhat surprising result is probably due, at least in part, to the emphasis on inquiry into teaching as an appropriate and organizationally valued activity. Such recognition gave scope for all faculty to use their own teaching as a basis for developing an inquiry orientation. Since no one was explicitly excluded from participating in this inquiry focus, there was less opportunity for resentment about research taking a higher priority.

What follows are some examples of research activity that give a sense of the scope and variety of projects that are underway at FEUT.

FEUT faculty carried out the Ontario portion of a large Canadian study of exemplary high schools. The purpose was to document practices that work well to improve the learning environment of secondary schools, and to make this information available to education policy makers at the provincial and local level. In this study, funds were available to release faculty from some of their teaching responsibilities while they did ethnographic work in schools over a one-year period.

In 1995, FEUT researchers were awarded six three-year grants from the leading Canadian federal funding agency in the social sciences. Annual funding on these projects ranged from just over $20 000 to close to $50 000. An idea of the range of issues addressed can be gleaned from a glance at the project titles:

- Young Children's Theory of Mind and Its Relation to Their Success in School
- Teacher Self: Stories of Preservice and Induction
- Teaching Rational Number Sense: An Approach Based on Cognitive Developmental Theory
- Parental Appraisal, Social Reinforcement and the Development of Children's Emotionality
- Cultural Negotiation of Minority Students and Teachers
- Studying Narrative and Propositional Modes of Moral and Social Reasoning within the Context of the Three-Generational Family

As well as research grants, FEUT personnel also receive contracts to carry out activities defined by the funder, usually provincial or federal agencies, but also private foundations. For example, teams are examining integration of children's health and social services, evaluating the work of the Holmes Group (a consortium of research universities focused on teacher education), and evaluating occupational training programs in Canada and abroad. During 1995, FEUT had thirty externally funded projects, including seventeen research grants and thirteen contracts. In addition, there were another twenty small-scale projects funded by money originating from external funding but awarded within the Faculty.

So far, reference has been made to FEUT as if it were one organization in terms of research. However, this is not strictly true. The Institute for Child Study (ICS), although part of FEUT, has established quite a different academic research culture, building on a history of child study going back to 1924. Located several blocks from the main FEUT building, the ICS faculty share space with the Institute Laboratory School, which also serves as a site for some of their research. Through the Dr. R.G.N. Laidlaw Centre, established in 1992 to support interdisciplinary and inter-institutional research on children, ICS has established a culture in which a critical mass of researchers work together on a focused research agenda that includes both basic and applied research. Within the overall theme of "children's understanding of the social system," the centre has attracted substantial funding for both basic and applied research, primarily in three broad areas: the child and the law, the child and the school, and the child and the family.

Adding to existing personnel, strong appointments have been made at The Institute for Child Studies, both at junior and senior levels, with faculty complementing each other in terms of expertise and interests. These researchers have been highly productive in terms of both quantity and quality, continuing to attract new resources for the systematic study of children's development in areas that are of pressing social relevance. Examples of topics include: young children's ability to instruct legal counsel, students' knowledge of the Young Offenders Act, improving children's performance in early mathematics, peer tutoring with children at risk for school failure in the middle grades, familial roots of psychopathology, siblings in families with a chronically ill child, and the mental health of children of refugees. One faculty member recently received the Raymond B. Cattell award for programmatic research from the American Educational Research Association for work on children's theory of mind. The highly prestigious award, presented annually for the most outstanding program of research carried out in the ten years following the doctoral degree, is an indication of the calibre of the research being done.

Issues and Tensions

Much progress has been made in strengthening the role of research and inquiry at FEUT, but some problems and tensions remain. Some of these issues are common to most education faculties, while others are specific to this organization. Constraints such as time and workload are major concerns. As well, several people referred to a lingering sense that commitment to research is perceived as being incompatible with commitment to teaching. Finally, although an emphasis on inquiry has opened professional opportunities for many faculty members, there is some tension around the relationship between "inquiry" and "research."

Workload: A major issue, workload was mentioned by virtually all those interviewed as this chapter was being written. The basic problem seems to be a perception that the teaching load has not been adjusted to take account of the fact that research and scholarship are now an expected part of the faculty role to an extent that was not formerly the case. FEUT faculty teach approximately ten hours per week in three or four courses, more than either their University of Toronto colleagues or their counterparts at OISE. Release time occasionally has been provided for research, with reduced loads available for new faculty or for those whose time has been funded by external research grants. A number of faculty have been highly productive in terms of their scholarly output in spite of the teaching load, but there is widespread agreement that in the long run the workload issue must be addressed. The recent report of an external review done in preparation for the upcoming institutional merger concluded:

> The weakness that now exists at FEUT ... is that faculty seem to be doing too much with too little. The research mission fostered in recent years has been furthered by high energy, committed scholars who will assuredly either burn out or leave the institution if the current loads in teaching/supervision and service and high expectations for scholarship are maintained. Since the standards for scholarship should not be compromised, it seems that adjustments in teaching assignments, some reduction in the number of students served, or some restructuring of the institution itself is called for. Signs of faculty fatigue and awareness that the current rate of development could not be sustained were clearly observable.[6]

Cultural ambiguities: FEUT has a long tradition of service to students. In an institution devoted to preparing teachers, it is hardly surprising that teaching is highly valued. There is an on-going tension between what could be seen as a "teachers' college perspective" and the development of more of a research culture. Although in theory, teaching and research support and enrich each other, in practice they are often seen as conflicting, particularly in the case of those people whose research programs do not directly relate to teachers or teaching. One research-oriented faculty member noted:

> There's a tension—are you a teacher *or* are you a researcher? Somehow you feel you have to choose. There's a halo effect around the people here who love teaching *so* much. You're supposed to do research, but you're not allowed to love it. If you love research, then [some colleagues believe] you're not committed to teaching.

At least some of those most strongly committed to teaching and service to students expressed some uneasiness about formal research. This uneasiness, which seems to be based on ethical misgivings, is particularly strong in relation to experimental research designs, on the basis of these being "research *on* people rather than *with* them." For a few faculty members, these types of studies seem not to fit well with an ethos of service to students and schools.

Such concerns seem rooted in long-standing traditions, and organizational cultures are hard to shift. FEUT had a strong culture prior to 1988, centered around preparing student teachers. One faculty member noted that:

> Some things don't change—they're in the walls. The older people protect the culture they created.... They are holding on to something that is good. September to May is for students, and the research culture pushes against this.

These older faculty members are sympathetic to the new faculty members and the pressures they are experiencing, but they do not want to weaken the commitment to teaching and to students that they believe should continue to characterize FEUT. At the same time, the value of commitment to students continues to be fostered through the intensive and time-consuming program reform efforts that have characterized the institution over the last few years. Junior tenure-stream faculty members have often taken leading roles as program coordinators, further lessening the time and energy they have available for research. As a result, an uneasy balance between teaching and research continues.

Standards: During the first few years of organizational change at FEUT, the aim was to stimulate interest and involvement in research and inquiry. Now that the level of activity has increased, the stage has been set for a second phase. It is time to become more critical. The dean has suggested that in the future, people must ask "what are the standards... and how do you subject your work to scrutiny?... Let's be tougher on ourselves about what constitutes good work."

For some researchers, the emphasis on *inquiry* rather than research is seen as contributing to concerns about establishing and maintaining standards:

> The broadened definition of research often means less definition, and although some of the work can be rigorous, often it is not.
>
> Research requires a knowledge of specialized techniques. Inquiry seems not to require skills and specialized knowledge.
>
> Inquiry can be navel-gazing more than intelligent observation of education. They assure us there are standards of quality but I don't see it.

Infrastructure: Although considerable progress has been made in building institutional supports for research, much remains to be done. Regular availability of graduate assistants, involvement in graduate studies, technical support including methodological consulting and sophisticated computer services—all these were mentioned by faculty members as necessary supports for those establishing and maintaining a solid research program. Unfortunately, provision of such supports has been difficult if not impossible. The absence of graduate programs has been particularly constraining. Although many FEUT faculty are members of the University of Toronto School of Graduate Studies, any involvement in graduate teaching at OISE is usually done on an overload basis, rather than as part of the regular teaching load. Although faculty members can and have hired OISE graduate students to assist with research projects, this is done on an informal one-to-one basis, rather than as part of an organizational initiative. For hiring research officers or research assistants, the University of Toronto services are not usually appropriate because staff with educational research expertise are more likely to be at OISE than at the University of Toronto (the two organizations have been completely distinct in terms of personnel services).

The more specialized manifestations of a research infrastructure, such as methodological and statistical consulting or specialized computer or media services, have not been available, and would not be feasible without a critical mass of potential users, larger than is likely to be the base at FEUT. Even finding room to house assistants and any equipment for research projects has not been easy, because space at FEUT is limited (and organized more for teaching than for research).

Most of the opportunities and supports provided at FEUT are more useful to relative novices than to established researchers. For the most part, it has been providing help with the basics, rather than the highly developed infrastructure that experienced researchers need if they are to maintain their research programs.

Expectations and reality: Some recently hired faculty members found that FEUT provided a less positive research environment than they had anticipated. Although they were well aware of the teaching expectations, they found they had less time for research than they had expected. Many are involved in field-based program options that require time in schools, planning time, and travel time. For some, the organization was seen as less supportive of serious research than they had hoped:

> The culture in FEUT is not geared for research. It's second or further down the list. There's no real understanding of what research involves .... there's no way to run a research program here.

Other new faculty are attempting to find their way through the maze of research possibilities, and may not always be aware of guidelines, constraints, and opportunities.

Conclusion

Faculties of education, like other professional faculties, are in a difficult position, located at the intersection of the teaching profession and the university. The ongoing tensions between the role of a professional school and the traditional role of a university create particular difficulties in the area of research. Faculty are often pulled between the demands of academic research and more client-oriented research, as well as between research and teaching. At FEUT, the notion of "inquiry," especially inquiry into one's own practice, has added yet another dimension. Although FEUT is encouraging faculty to engage in all types of inquiry, confusion and tensions are inevitable.

The last eight years at FEUT have seen both large and small changes. From the perspective of strengthening the research aspect of the Faculty's mandate, these changes have been significant, but many issues remain to be addressed. FEUT faculty are much more connected to the academic and professional community in education and are now part of many ongoing dialogues concerning inquiry-oriented practice. With the exception of researchers in the Dr. R.G.N. Laidlaw Centre, however, they have been less involved in the creation of new knowledge.

The challenge is to develop models that ensure the continued support of both professional and academic inquiry, and to change the balance between program and research without damaging either. What is needed to support a culture of professional inquiry may be different from what is needed to support more traditional programs of research: if the organization cannot do both, it may be in danger of losing its best researchers through burnout or to other organizations.

The report of the external review referred to earlier noted the fragility of the research enterprise at FEUT:

> The commitment to establishing a presence in educational research, though recent, is certainly appropriate and laudable. To this point it would have to be characterized as provisional and unless its development is nurtured and accelerated, the desired outcomes will likely be in jeopardy.[7]

The merger of FEUT and OISE should help to address these issues. With the addition of OISE's graduate programs, particularly those at the doctoral level, and its well-developed research infrastructure, the new institution will have a solid research base, and in many areas will be a world leader. For FEUT faculty, the challenge will be to take advantage of these new opportunities without losing the benefits that have come from the emphasis on practice and on inquiry into teaching.

Endnotes

1. Harman, Kay M. Using Culture to Understand Conflict within a University: Professional versus Academic Values in University Professional Schools in Australia. Paper presented at the American Educational Research Association Annual Meeting, San Francisco, April, 1989.
2. All faculty quotations are from interviews done during the summer of 1995 as part of the preparation for this chapter.
3. University of Toronto, 1994 Provostial White Paper, "Planning for 2000."
4. Schein, E.H. *Organizational Culture and Leadership*. San Francisco: Jossey-Bass, 1985, p.9.
5. Poole, M. "Establishing a Research Culture." *Higher Education Research and Development News*, 13 (2), 1991, pp.3-5.
6. Birch, D.R., Lanier, J.E. & Mortimore, P. *Report of the Provostial Commission on a Design for an Integrated Institution in Education*. University of Toronto, June, 1994, p.9.
7. Birch, D.R., Lanier, J.E. & Mortimore, P. *Report of the Provostial Commission on a Design for an Integrated Institution in Education*. University of Toronto, June, 1994, pp.4-5.

Part IV

Partnerships in Teacher Education

A Collaborative Partnership with the Field

Ethne Erskine-Cullen, in addition to working in five countries as a classroom teacher, school administrator, and school district coordinator, spent three years with the Ministry of Education in British Columbia. She lectured in the Faculty of Education, University of Victoria for nine years in the area of evaluation of student performance. At present, she is the coordinator of the Learning Consortium, a partnership program among four school boards in the greater metropolitan Toronto area, the Faculty of Education, University of Toronto, and the Ontario Institute for Studies in Education.

The Faculty of Education has established a number of partnership programs over the past few years. This chapter describes one of these programs, the Learning Consortium, a partnership among FEUT and four large school districts in the greater metropolitan Toronto area. Factors contributing to the success of this collaborative venture are discussed, as well as the challenges of such a partnership. Some of the change initiatives that have benefited both the school partners and the Faculty are identified.

Background

Over the past few years, the Faculty of Education has spread its connections to wider communities through the establishment of a range of partnership programs. These have included connections with local schools and districts, and through global connections with institutions and universities in other countries. This participation in multiple partnerships has served to broaden our connections, our research base, and our learning opportunities, and has strengthened our collaboration with the field.

We have learned how to use these networks in a mutual give-and-take model that provides a win-win situation for all partners. We have learned to see teachers as collaborative colleagues in a learning community where collaboration and collegiality are guiding principles in our redesigned teacher-education program, and schools and districts view us as partners in the education of teachers.

One such partnership is the Learning Consortium. Reaching into classrooms to make a difference to students, the Learning Consortium is a partnership among six organizations—four large boards in the metro Toronto area and two universities. The partners are the Durham, Halton, North York, and Scarborough boards of education, OISE, and FEUT.

The Learning Consortium is a proactive way of harnessing collective strengths and expertise to initiate, implement, and institutionalize change. The opportunity to share financial and human resources in a synergistic approach to teacher development and school improvement is a positive collaborative venture. We believe that together the partners can accomplish, confirm, and extend what they cannot do alone. The Consortium brings together teachers, administrators, and professors in a collegial partnership that focuses on the sustained development of educators. This, in turn, is directed at improving students' experiences and learning. This sharing of resources and expertise provides not only a saving in time and finances, but creates a synergy when different people bring ideas together, cross the cultures between boards and universities, and pursue innovations as a partnership.

Context

The context in which the partnership developed was a positive one, favourable to innovation and growth. A variety of factors led to the formation of the Learning Consortium. In 1987, as part of a wide-ranging review of teacher education in Ontario, a position paper on teacher education in Ontario was widely circulated throughout the province (Fullan & Connolly, 1990). It outlined the need for increased collaboration among those involved in teacher education, and the importance of the teacher-education continuum. As well, school districts, already active in developing quality professional development programs, were interested in collaborating with one another and with universities to support these initiatives—to go beyond what they were already doing. At the same time, the Faculty was beginning a process of renewal following a long period in which there had been few resources and little growth. There was also interest in developing closer links between OISE and FEUT. Such a favourable context represented a window of opportunity for all six member organizations to build on their individual accomplishments and to refocus for the future.

Rationale

The Learning Consortium was established in 1988 as a partnership of the six organizations in the greater metropolitan Toronto area. The aim of the Consortium was identified as the improvement of the quality of education in schools and universities by focusing on teacher development at all levels. The partnership agreed that school improvement and teacher development were inextricably related, and that staff development was a key strategy for organization and school change. Two basic assumptions became central to the thinking of the relationship between school-faculty change and teacher development. These assumptions were:

- that teacher education and development was a career-long continuum from preservice, through inservice and leadership,
- that teacher development and school improvement go hand-in-hand.

As well, it was recognized that realizing these two assumptions, taken together, would require greater system development and coherence. School districts and the universities would have to change in ways that provided greater system support and coordination within their organizations, as well as across institutions.

Our model, therefore, instead of binding the universities to specific schools, took a broader systemic approach and linked with school districts. We also deliberately rejected a single model for school improvement and teacher development in favour of a more multifaceted approach.

Structure

In establishing a collaborative venture such as ours, we were well aware of the pitfalls that such a partnership posed, and the barriers to success that existed. Much time was taken to examine the past experiences of other partnerships to see what could be learned that could guide our enterprise. We were impressed by Gray's (1989) identified critical features of collaboration:

- collaboration implies interdependence, an ongoing give and take,
- solutions emerge by dealing constructively with differences,
- collaboration involves joint responsibility for future direction of the domain,

- collaboration is an emergent process. Through negotiations and interactions, rules for governing future interactions are actually restructured.

These features were adopted by the Learning Consortium partners and guided much of our early direction in establishing design principles, as well as a framework for operation. We knew that collaboration was necessary where all parties had a shared interest in solving problems that none of us could resolve alone. Collaboration made sense where all stakeholders recognized the potential advantages of working together—we needed one another to execute a vision we all shared, and we needed the others to advance each partner's interests. Such a partnership represented for us, an ideal, a goal toward which our collaborative venture could aspire.

We also read with interest Goodlad's (1988) essentials for structuring partnerships for success. He maintains that partnerships need:

- a governing board,
- a modest secretariat paid from the partnership budget,
- an operating budget providing money and personnel,
- top-level endorsement and support from each partner,
- task forces to develop strategies for critical issues,
- an orderly process of endorsing all projects,
- documentation, analysis, and communication of success and failures,
- arrangement for sharing information, ideas, and resources within and across the partnership.

These became our guiding principles. The initial commitment to the partnership was three years, during which each partner agreed to contribute money, time, and personnel to support what soon became an expanding and increasingly complex set of initiatives. A modest secretariat was established to provide a mechanism for implementing initiatives. The primary decision-making body is the Planning Group, composed of representatives from each of the six member organizations, with monthly meetings chaired by the coordinator. This group plans collaborative activities, and takes initiatives forward in ways that honour the unique culture of their respective organizations. A Steering Committee, composed of the superintendents from the school districts and the deans of the universities meets annually to review the year and to identify priorities for the future.

Focus

On the basis of the assumption concerning teaching as lifelong learning, and the necessity of viewing teacher development as inextricably linked to school improvement, the Consortium set out as its mandate:

- to plan, initiate and implement teacher development and school-improvement programs,
- evaluate and produce new knowledge about teacher education and school improvement,
- disseminate what has been learned.

Such a focus set out our overall agenda, but we were also committed to launching specific initiatives. Through processes both serendipitous and deliberate, we began with an emphasis on cooperative small-group learning, a theme that appealed to teachers at all grade levels and in all subject areas. This provided a concrete instructional agenda to get the partnership underway, and influenced other program developments over the next years as we built on this focus with conflict management and anti-racist professional-development opportunities. Over the past seven years, inservice professional-development programs, such as summer institutes on cooperative learning, peer coaching, conflict management, anti-racism, and student evaluation have followed.

At first glance, such a set of teacher development initiatives might seem somewhat unrelated to one another. However, the Consortium has attempted to link these programs by paying attention to consistent themes that weave through the various initiatives including teaching as lifelong learning, fostering collaboration in the workplace, and focusing on instruction as the link between teacher development and school improvement.

In addition to the formally established activities and programs, a variety of less formal practices have evolved, also aimed at integrating a set of varied Learning Consortium activities. These include networking among and between the partners, bridging partners' borders, and joint problem solving around emerging issues. The implementation actions taken by the Planning Group on a regular basis, with the unique cultures of their respective organizations and the ongoing linking of school-improvement efforts by participants in the various programs in their places of work, have resulted in noticeable school district, school, and faculty change initiatives. By the end of year eight of operation, the Learning Consortium activities have evolved into a connected web within and across the six organizations.

Commitment

The commitment of resources of time, money, and personnel from each of the partners acted as a concrete indication of the value each member placed on the partnership activities. However, each of the organizations entered the partnership with different expectations and priorities, and each brought different organizational structures and realities. These factors of self-interest and common goals became paramount in structuring the partnership.They were met through identifying a common vision of the future together and the establishment of a process of shared decision making. The partnership became an opportunity to build on our individual accomplishments, to develop a broader view of the educational picture, to share and interact with wider audiences, and, particularly, to refocus for the future.

A long-term commitment of three years (now in year nine) provided the opportunity for programs to be established and early success to be enjoyed. A "think big, start small" (Fullan 1991) approach was followed with early initiatives starting at the same time as a long-term vision was being developed. Fullan (1991) recommends a "ready-fire-aim" approach, and this worked for the Consortium. In this way, we got "ready" by setting our basic aim and structure in place. Initial activities were then started (three months after the formation of the partnership) and these helped to identify the overall direction of the partnership.

The early successful initiatives lent momentum and focus to later projects, providing the base for early change and reform at the school, district, and faculty levels. The motivation and commitment that sprang from this cannot be overestimated in gauging the success of the partnership. The early success of the first initiatives and the resulting immediate impact on classrooms, schools, and the faculty led to expanded projects and diversification of initiatives.

Process

Although some attention was given to structures and procedures at the beginning of the partnership, the priority was more on starting some initial activities. This approach was based partly on the notion that a broad agenda, combined with specific initial activities, would encompass the kind of developmental or evolutionary planning needed—at the same time, that it would address the need for short-term accountability experienced mainly by the school-district representatives.

Strong partnerships will not happen by accident, goodwill, or establishing ad hoc projects. They require new structures, new activities and relationships, and a rethinking of the internal workings of each institution, as well as their interinstitutional workings. With this in mind, much time has been given to encouraging positive personal and professional relationships among representatives from the school and university partners, with a balance of power and influence being perceived as equitable. A concerted effort has been made to understand and respect one another's cultures, and to use shared experience to problem solve by incorporating the strengths of each culture.

Collaboration, communication, and mutual trust have become the keys to accomplish what we had set out to do. However, I would be remiss if I led you to believe that this has been an easy journey. Those of you who have worked on collaborative projects will appreciate that it takes time, effort, and ongoing problem solving to surmount the constant challenges of personal interest and immediate concerns to perceive the benefit for the larger organization.

Do not be misled into thinking that our collaboration has been an easy task. Like most partnerships, the Learning Consortium has had its share of difficult moments, times when we have struggled with consensus, have had long discussions around conflict of interest, and have made difficult decisions around the nature of our initiatives. Members have had to learn that what is best for their individual organization may not be what the other partners need. We have learned to give and take, to buy into initiatives to a greater or lesser extent, or sometimes not to participate at all—but always to be supportive. We have had to learn to balance the dual perspective of our individual organization's focus and the larger picture of the mission of the Learning Consortium. Ultimately, however, the partnership is only strong if it serves the needs of its members, and this we keep at the fore of all decision making.

The organizational cultures of school boards and universities are different. With the Learning Consortium, we have variation not only between the university and school-district partners, but also between the two university partners and among the four school districts. Such cultural differences have led to many misunderstandings, and have necessitated ongoing negotiation and adaptation as the Consortium has developed. Both school-district and university participants agreed that school districts were more preoccupied with "front-line" issues of budget and accountability, and were more likely than the university partners to be subject to shifting pressures from their organizations. This has become more noticeable as recent budget cuts have affected organizations.

The Planning Group meets each month, with the agenda emphasizing implementation of joint program initiatives. However, time is set aside to focus on discussion of interesting programs and ideas in each organization, on considering knowledge arising from research and evaluation, and on planning how best to build on previous accomplishments. Between meetings, communication among the group has been largely through telephone and fax, although group members may meet for specific planning purposes and see one another at various workshops and conferences.

With six partners, communication is always a challenge. Given our belief that all partners have an equal status in the partnership, we endeavour to ensure that all parties are always in the information loop. With the considerations of distances in Toronto, we are now exploring ways in which technology can assist us in our communication and so facilitate easier and more frequent conversations.

Membership in the Planning Group has changed somewhat over the time of the Learning Consortium. In year seven, only the Faculty representative and those from two districts were in the original group. I came in as coordinator in 1991, replacing Nancy Watson. One district, Scarborough, joined in 1991, and another district has replaced their representative on the Planning Group. Although the transitions associated with changing membership have been relatively smooth, the new representatives have needed time to catch up with the history and purposes of the group. On the plus side, we have found that the input from new members has helped us to break from the mold of "group think," and has brought a new enthusiasm and energy to the partnership.

Joint Initiatives

The first initiative of the Learning Consortium was to sponsor a two-week residential summer institute. The first week covered cooperative learning and coaching; week two focused on the need to attend to understanding and managing change. This first institute brought together ninety educators from the Consortium's four school districts and the two higher education institutes in the summer of 1988. The Planning Group chose cooperative learning because of the evidence that it stimulates student learning. Coaching and mentoring were emphasized as vehicles for sharing expertise and for encouraging collaboration in schools. These concepts and processes were introduced because of their effect on stimulating teacher learning. Teams from schools were encouraged to attend as the most successful implementation occurs when they work together and provide a nucleus for change in the school setting.

The summer institute model has been so successful that the Consortium has continued to sponsor them for each of the past seven years. Over 800 educators from Consortium organizations have participated in four- and five-day intensive workshops on cooperative learning, conflict management, anti-racist education, assessment and evaluation, and school councils.

Besides the very successful summer institutes, the Consortium sponsors ongoing professional development opportunities throughout the year. These include one-day workshops and conferences on a wide range of topics including, outcomes-based education, assessment and evaluation, portfolio assessment, the transition years, and using the internet. As well, a number of international experts have been brought to Toronto to work with large groups of Consortium personnel, particularly with a train-the-trainer model.

In 1993 and 1995, the Consortium sponsored two international conferences on evaluation that brought together the most knowledgeable experts in the field from around the world. The roughly 850 persons who attended each of these events rated them as highly successful and worthwhile professional development opportunities. The emphasis of these institutes, workshops, and conferences has been on helping educators broaden the range of teaching strategies used in classrooms and schools.

Ongoing follow-up throughout the implementation process has been a key feature of the Consortium initiatives. Planning Group representatives work together to ensure support at the local, system, and Consortium levels. Follow-up activities in schools are wideranging: support from peers, from administration, from consultants visiting schools to provide assistance, and, increasingly, from other teachers who have been part of the team training. As well, the Consortium offers structured follow-up that provides both new learning and problem-solving opportunities. Such central support includes follow-up workshops and a regular newsletter.

In building on the train-the-trainer model, one program was designed to create a cascade effect within each district. In 1989, the Consortium trained a "cadre of trainers" (fifty persons from the partners' districts). The objective of the training was to train a core of "experts" in key elements of effective teaching. The program focused on classroom management, instructional skills and strategies, as well as on consultative and conferencing skills necessary for coaching and teaching others. These trainers were charged with the task of training future trainers and offering support at both the system and school levels. This aimed at building the professional capacity of school systems by providing a number of "experts" at the local level. These trainers took an active role in providing workshops and informal support for colleagues.

Another very successful initiative of the Learning Consortium has been the mini-project program. This program funded projects between Consortium members, and was designed to support professional growth and collaboration between the partners. A number of these projects connected faculty and field educators on collaborative research initiatives. Erskine-Cullen and Kilcher (1992) report that these projects were viewed by all participants as being highly successful in bridging the cultures between universities and schools.

Spinoffs

Within each of the partner organizations, a number of additional initiatives have emerged, closely related to Consortium activities and influenced by Consortium work, yet outside the partnership framework. Related activities include induction programs for newly hired teachers, mentorship programs to support new teachers, inservice workshops or courses jointly taught by faculty members from the university and school-district personnel, and leadership programs for principals and vice-principals. The summer-institute program has been so successful that all the partner districts now sponsor summer institutes within their own districts, on a variety of topics of interest. Each partner makes spaces available to member districts, as well as to the Faculty, with the result that a wealth of summer options are made available to all educators within the Consortium membership.

Another spinoff is the cooperation and exchange across the four school districts. Districts rarely have access to one another's internal planning and policy considerations, or to one another's internal expertise and external resources. In the Learning Consortium, school districts now issue invitations to participate in or find out about one another's work. When an outside consultant is brought in, for example, other districts are often invited to send participants. These mutual exchanges are above and beyond the joint activities carried out collectively by the Learning Consortium.

Preservice Connection

One of the mandates of the Learning Consortium is to broaden the definition of teacher education to include all stages of the teaching continuum, from preservice student teachers through highly experienced teachers and administrators. To support the preservice components, two of the program options at the Faculty have operated in collaboration with the Learning Consortium. The Learning Consortium option, a junior/intermediate option, and a secondary option were developed within the Learning

Consortium partnership. These two programs had a strong teaching-experience component that was integral to the programs; a blending of the in-faculty and practicum elements of the program. This strong school support has been provided by a number of schools in each of the Learning Consortium partner districts.

In 1995, these options were developed into the new two-year pilot program and continues to be supported by the Learning Consortium. A group of urban schools has been identified in three of the Learning Consortium districts that create an Elementary and Secondary Academy of Schools, in which this new program operates. (Because of geographic considerations, the fourth district is not participating in the program.) The elementary component of this new urban-focused program is described in chapter 14, Partnership and Program Renewal: Moving Forward.

To support the preservice activities of the Faculty, the Learning Consortium sponsored two very successful workshops on supporting beginning teachers. These three-day training sessions were designed to provide information, support, and skills for associate teachers who sponsor and act as mentors to new teachers in their classrooms and schools.

In the area of induction for beginning teachers, two working conferences brought universities and schools together. In many of the member districts, mentorship programs have been developed; in the Faculty, an induction project was developed that combined information, support from two faculty members, a series of one-day workshops, and a computer conferencing network that enabled beginning teachers to discuss issues with one another and with faculty members.

Research

All activities undertaken by the Learning Consortium are invested with the spirit of inquiry. The Consortium makes use of previous research and produces new research findings of their own in the "living laboratories" of member schools. As one member remarked, "I think that the research conducted in Consortium districts has been particularly useful to us in that it reflects our own unique experiences, the challenges that we have encountered in implementation, or in introducing new innovations. It has certainly bridged the gap between theory and practice, and has given us licence to challenge practices within our own boards and to forge ahead with confidence to do what we feel needs to be done to effect change in schools."

A spinoff of this research focus has been the changing attitude toward research on the part of the school districts. One member spoke of how research on Consortium programs has provided a "mirror on our work," giving information that is only available from such a perspective, and stressed the value of having such feedback, not about professional development in general, but about "our own programs." Other members spoke about becoming avid and discerning consumers of research, and described how the research literature was influencing their work within the districts.

For the Faculty, the Consortium has provided multiple opportunities for conducting research, both through opening up access to schools through the formal partnership mechanism, and inviting faculty to evaluate various initiatives undertaken. When working on collaborative research projects, the Consortium members have welcomed and appreciated the expertise of the Faculty's strong research skills.

The Universities

In the case of the university partners, the impact of the Learning Consortium has been less direct than it has been on the school districts. However, membership in the Consortium has contributed to program changes in both universities, with opportunities for field research also increasing.

FEUT has been involved in a process of change and renewal over the past eight years, during which time programs have been reviewed and expanded, new tenure-stream faculty have been hired, and personnel have been involved in more joint work with school boards, with an increased emphasis on research. The Learning Consortium has both supported and provided a vehicle for this organizational change. A large proportion of the faculty have participated in Consortium programs, with considerable impact as they expand their range of teaching methodologies for the student teachers at the Faculty.

The Consortium has provided multiple opportunities for professional development for the faculty, and many have taken advantage of these opportunities. It has been unique to see student teachers, inservice teachers, and faculty members as learners together, grappling with current educational issues and supporting one another in the learning process and growing together professionally. The partnership has provided a channel through which faculty members can stay closely attached to school and classroom issues, and can learn from educators in the field. On the flip side, the Consortium has tapped the expertise available in the Faculty, and many high-quality professional development sessions have been conducted by Faculty members, and sponsored by the Learning Consortium.

The preservice Learning Consortium options represent a powerful model for linking teachers' preparation with school development. The faculty coordinators of these options have been closely connected to the Consortium schools, not only supporting the preservice teachers, but also working with school staffs on professional development, program planning, and school change. This has led to an enhanced credibility for the Faculty with the field, and closer ties with these schools.

An OISE doctoral program was started in the fall of 1991. It was designed to integrate field development and research inquiry more closely than has been possible, fostering the development of more sustained research initiatives within the Learning Consortium. In collaboration with the Consortium school districts, graduate student dissertation research is closely tied to Learning Consortium and district priorities, as well as their professional interests. A number of teachers in Consortium districts have taken advantage of this new and innovative graduate program.

Conclusion

By the end of the eighth year of operation, membership in the Learning Consortium can be seen to have enhanced and strengthened the strategic direction for all partners. The joint initiatives have provided springboards from which districts have developed programs to meet their individual needs. All partners report that the impact of past Consortium endeavours has been significant. They have shifted their professional development and school improvement priorities in the direction of more coordinated and focused systems of change. Learning Consortium ideas, priorities, support, and research have become woven into system agendas, at times making it difficult to say what is a Learning Consortium project and what is not. It has not been one initiative that has brought about the change but rather the cumulative effect of activities and partners spinoffs, linking and supporting other developments in each system and across systems.

For the Faculty, this partnership has provided knowledge to guide a range of other partnerships. It has not only provided a good template for collaboration, but also the experience and learning to take to other groups. Our close connection with the boards has built a trust that could not have been achieved in a less structured and formal relationship.

As the Learning Consortium looks to the future, we know that there will be new exciting initiatives and challenges to face. As funding to school districts is cut back, the need to explore new funding sources will be more critical. As partners search to find the resources to support the Consortium, they will need to examine the role of the partnership in their organization and how it supports their own mandate. As FEUT and OISE merge, we will need to find another role for this "new" partner.

Support for the work of the Consortium has not wavered during the past years, and there is every indication that the partners will agree to another three years of membership. As long as the Consortium continues to move forward with productive enterprises and initiatives, it will continue to thrive and be a powerful change influence for both the district and university partners.

We believe that the real strength of the partnership has been in using a combination of roles and systems to bring about large-scale systemic change, and to support initiatives through the combined effort of strong collegial support. Through the development of a shared vision and an agenda that goes beyond self-interest, the group has managed to encompass and perhaps transcend the more specific mandates of partner organizations and create bridges between the individual cultures of each partner. Through sustained interaction of key players in the partnership, the Learning Consortium has become a powerful vehicle for fostering significant change in teacher education, in schools, and in the Faculty.

Partnership and Program Renewal: Moving Forward

Dr. Carol Rolheiser is an associate professor at the Faculty of Education, University of Toronto. She is originally from Edmonton, Alberta, where she was an elementary school teacher, district consultant, and school administrator. Her doctoral work took her to the University of Oregon, where she completed a meta-analysis on the effects of various models of teaching, including cooperative learning. Currently, she teaches preservice teachers in partnership with school personnel in the Learning Consortium, and is coordinating one of the two-year teacher education pilots for the province of Ontario. As well, she works as an international staff-development consultant, focusing on classroom and school improvement, and managing educational change.

Partnership Beginnings

I have always been a person who thrives on change, craves experimentation, and savours collaborative ventures. A phone call received in 1988, while working as an elementary school vice-principal in Edmonton, Alberta, created an opportunity to experience just that. The new dean at FEUT invited me to come to Toronto to play a part in the changes that were being initiated at the Faculty. The proposal included the opportunity to teach on faculty in the preservice education program and to work in a staff development position for a newly formed partnership called the Learning Consortium. Having just completed a doctorate in the area of staff development, this offer combined two areas I was interested in—preservice and inservice education. My experiences in both these roles significantly shaped the changes, experimentation, and collaborative ventures I was to become involved in during subsequent years. The duality of responsibilities during my first year provided an important contrast, and the resulting insights encouraged my present interest and involvement in faculty program renewal through partnership.

The first set of insights emerged from my experiences that first year in a school-university partnership called the Learning Consortium. We know that efforts to improve the quality and impact of teacher education programs have included a range of strategies, with one of the most popular being the emphasis on school-university partnerships. Likewise, school-university partnerships have been central to many school reform proposals, such as professional development schools (Holmes Group, 1990), and professional practice schools (Levine, 1992). Such collaboration may comprise many activities, including preservice teacher preparation, inservice or professional development, research on teaching, and school renewal. Such were the emphases within the Learning Consortium.

As a large-scale school district-university partnership, the Learning Consortium began in 1988 as a three-year partnership between four school districts in the greater metropolitan Toronto area—the Durham, Halton, and North York public boards of education and the Dufferin-Peel Roman Catholic Separate School Board—and two higher education institutions, FEUT and OISE. At the end of the initial three-year agreement, the decision was made to continue the partnership for another three years, with the Scarborough Board of Education replacing the Dufferin-Peel board.

The formation of the Learning Consortium was a clear response to the challenge that "Schools and universities both have a stake in improving schools and in improving teaching, but neither can do it alone" (Watson, 1991). Watson, the first coordinator of the Learning Consortium, noted: "The partnership developed in a context favourable to innovation—both university and school partners were interested in opportunities for organizational growth. The Learning Consortium represented a "window of opportunity" for the member organizations to build on their individual accomplishments and to refocus for the future" (Watson, 1991). Part of the refocusing and a strong rationale for the partnership was the need and desire to improve both inservice and preservice programs.

The initial agreement was to commit to the partnership for three years, with each organization agreeing to contribute money, time, and personnel to work toward common goals. The partners agreed to share resources and to work collaboratively in initiating innovative programs in teacher education, consciously linking teacher development with school improvement, researching their own practices, and disseminating findings.

One of the guiding assumptions of the Learning Consortium was to view teacher education as a continuum of lifelong learning, with school districts and universities working in concert to support learning from preservice through induction, and continuing into inservice and leadership. The Learning Consortium continues to view staff development as a complex integration of conditions as well as content, where all educational stakeholders are valued, and where schools are viewed as places where children and adults learn together.

My work with the Learning Consortium began in the summer of 1988, when I collaborated with a colleague to design and facilitate a summer institute on cooperative learning and peer coaching. My colleague and I had both completed doctoral work in these areas and were excited to have the opportunity to take this line of inquiry further. The institute was the first initiative of the Learning Consortium, and our focus on a powerful model of teaching as a means of improving instruction was an important choice. The complexity and potential of cooperative learning, however, took it beyond being just a classroom strategy; it also became a vehicle for supporting teacher collaboration and a way to shape organizational partnerships. This area of focus acted as a springboard, pushing to greater heights the building of communities of learners. As Consortium partners concentrated on cooperative learning principles in classrooms, they began applying those same principles to their schools and organizations as communities. For example, as teacher-administrator teams went back to their schools after the institute and began the process of implementing cooperative learning in their classrooms, they realized the need for building on the same principles to support their own growth as a team. Building positive interdependence, individual accountability, and face-to-face interaction were essential to their team, sustaining the initiative and accomplishing their goal of classroom implementation. Likewise, they had a heightened awareness of their own social skills in supporting one another, and realized the need for regular processing of their group's accomplishments and goals. Regular follow-up sessions established in each district and by the Learning Consortium built in time for these teams to reflect on the functioning of their own school-improvement teams, as well as on their use of cooperative learning with groups of children.

Our additional focus on peer coaching was with a view toward increasing the transfer of learning in order to achieve a high level of implementation (Bennett, 1987). Likewise, we viewed coaching as a means of fostering collaboration in the workplace and influencing organizational norms. In addition to cooperative learning and peer coaching, a three-day strand on managing educational change was incorporated into the design and presented by three additional team members during the second week of the institute. Collectively, we believed that understanding and managing educational change would be at the heart of whether the Learning Consortium would be successful in initiating, implementing, and institutionalizing a range of future educational innovations (Fullan, 1991).

The initiatives of the Learning Consortium have included a wide range of ventures: program development, conference planning, networking, preservice and inservice work, research, and publications (see Chapter 13). The Learning Consortium began with a mandate and mission statement, rather than a carefully constructed master plan. It has used a process of evolutionary planning that is emergent in nature in its quest to improve classrooms and schools within the partnership.

Importantly, the journey of collaboration has naturally resulted in having to deal with conflict, and I believe it has been through this process of dealing with conflict that Consortium members have learned collectively and individually. Like any cooperative venture, the partnership struggles with the degree to which the partners need one another, and the extent of their individual give and take. However, the partnership has found ways to honour the uniqueness of each partner while simultaneously initiating projects from which all can benefit.

A Need for Program Change

At the same time that I was working within the Learning Consortium partnership, I had another component to my work portfolio at FEUT. I was assigned to teach a number of classes in the preservice program. Having worked previously with new teachers as a district consultant, I was excited about the opportunity to work with the teacher candidates in the post-degree one-year teacher-education program. The job entailed teaching a number of classes to different groups of teacher candidates. Each class met once a week for two hours. I quickly discovered three factors that created dissonance for me. First, I taught my course in isolation from the other courses in the students' program. Although I had a general idea what the overall program included, I did not have a clear understanding of it or the emphases of the individual pieces. I worried about how all of the program components became a coherent experience for the students. I struggled with making appropriate connections to other aspects of their learning. Second, the students I advised during teaching practica were not the students I taught. They did not know me, nor I them. At the same time, I had no idea whether the students I taught classes to were being provided with feedback relative to the content, strategies, and skills that were the focus of our study together. Third, I had no contact with team planning or working with other staff who were teaching similar courses. I felt very much alone in a new role. Although the satisfaction of working with the students was immense, the dissatisfaction of working in the structure and design of this university program was also immense. The good news is that the dissatisfaction encouraged me to approach our department chair (rather naively, in retrospect) and suggest that I had some ideas for another way of approaching the program. With tremendous support, he encouraged me to develop the idea further and offered his support in the initiative to develop a new teacher preparation option. It was at that point I realized I knew a lot and a little simultaneously!

Given the connections to the Learning Consortium and the support of those four boards in teacher development and school improvement, it seemed natural to create the new option in partnership with these organizations. In September 1989, the Learning Consortium option began with thirty elementary teacher candidates, specializing in the junior/intermediate division. During this same time a range of other alternative models for the delivery of the one-year B.Ed. program were also emerging at FEUT. This teacher-education program experimentation occurred within a number of different school-university partnerships, some with multiple boards and others with individual boards.

Partnership and Program Renewal

The Learning Consortium is but one example of a FEUT partnership in our local context. What has been significant is FEUT's focus on establishing multiple local and global partnerships. The simultaneous participation of FEUT in a range of diverse partnerships and varied initiatives and activities has resulted in the unearthing of issues and possibilities regarding what mutual benefit means and how to go about achieving it. What we know now is that we are all about making the best of networks, and with this emphasis the cooperative model has grown. Our experimentation over these last six or so years has resulted in evolving directions and ideas for program redesign. In the elementary department, for example, all programming now involves cohorts of students and faculty working in partner programs with one or multiple school districts. Insights and promising practices have emerged from our efforts and we are now building on these in our newly restructured two-year teacher education program. During this phase of experimentation, we have come to realize that if we are to have long-term successful impact then we must evolve to fully reciprocal relationships in our school-university partnerships.

History of the Two-Year Program Redesign

While our partnership team was piloting the Learning Consortium option, other FEUT teams were also developing alternative partnership and traditional models for the delivery of the one-year B.Ed. program. The models varied in their location (with some alternating between the Faculty and selected schools, some based in designated schools), time in classrooms (with most increasing the proportion of time in schools), staffing (with an increasing involvement of school-based teacher educators in program delivery), and orientation (with some focusing on the challenges of teaching in urban settings, some on the importance of information technology, some on the development of collaborative competencies, and most on a balanced and integrated set of priorities across contemporary issues and reforms). In addition to generating many innovative and promising practices, the insights gained through this diversification informed efforts to restructure the teacher-preparation program.

In June 1994, FEUT approved a post-degree two-year B.Ed. program in teaching and learning, with the intention that graduates would receive advance standing toward an M.Ed. This model provided the framework for a pilot program started in September 1995. This pilot is one of five in the province being funded by the Ministry of Education, consisting of 100 teacher candidates, approximately sixty elementary, and forty secondary. I am coordinator of the elementary component of the pilot, while another faculty member coordinates the secondary component. At the elementary level, we are working in partnership with the North York Board of Education (a Learning Consortium partner) and the Metropolitan Separate School Board. As the largest of these five provincial pilots, FEUT's documentation is essential to the informed debate that will emerge about the pilot program.

The two-year program is based on six images of the effective teacher (see below) and nine program design principles (see next page) that are consistent with and elaborations of the initiatives and teacher education directions in Ontario education (Royal Commission on Learning, 1994). It is organized developmentally within an integrated, coherent, yet flexible structure. It involves student cohorts and staff teams (school-based and university-based teacher educators) working in partnership in professional development schools (clustered into academies). It adopts an intellectually rigorous approach to theory generation and application, and includes focused and extended time in classrooms and schools. As well, it stresses such areas as assessment, equity, and information technology and their interactions with learning, teaching, and teacher and school development. (The preceding description has been adapted from The Proposal for the Two-Year Pilot Study.)

Key Images of the Effective Teacher

The following six key images of the effective teacher both inform the design of the two-year pilot teacher education program at FEUT and define the outcomes we strive for our graduates to exhibit:

1. Working with all students in an equitable, effective, and caring manner by respecting diversity in relation to ethnicity, race, gender, and special needs of each learner.
2. Developing and applying knowledge of curriculum, instruction, principles of learning, the use of technology, and

evaluation needed to implement and monitor effective and evolving programs for all learners.

3. Appreciating and practising the principles, ethics, and legal responsibilities of teaching as a profession.
4. Being active learners who continuously seek, assess, apply, and communicate knowledge as reflective practitioners throughout their careers.
5. Initiating, valuing, and practising collaboration and partnerships with students, colleagues, parents, community, government, and social and business agencies.
6. Developing a personal philosophy of teaching that is informed by and contributes to the organizational, community, societal, and global contexts of education.

Program Design Principles

These program design principles are aimed at meeting the needs of and providing benefits for preservice candidates, faculty members, and partners in the educational community.

Partnerships

1. The establishment of partnership agreements, primarily with school boards, but also with other organizations in the educational community, to promote collaborative program design and delivery.
2. The establishment of collaborative relationships with "host schools" where candidates and faculty members work in sustained apprenticeship relationships involving administrators, associate teachers, and mentor teachers.
3. The clustering, wherever possible, of candidates, faculty staff, and host-school teachers into cohorts based on factors such as families of schools, combination of teaching subjects, or the particular focus of a program option. This clustering will be flexible enough to allow candidates to experience a variety of school settings over the course of the program.
4. The linkage of the preservice program and inservice professional development in recognition of the continuum of professional development, and to support initiatives aimed at teacher development and school improvement.
5. Strategies to support the educational reform efforts of all partner stakeholders.

Nature of Program

6. The integration of theory and practice in all elements of the program by encouraging collaboration within the in-faculty components, by ensuring that all courses incorporate field experiences, and by involving both faculty and educational community staff, including associate and mentor teachers, in the delivery of the program.
7. A developmentally based and coordinated series of knowledge, attitude, and skill development experiences that extend and strengthen the program so that candidates are prepared to meet both current and future needs of learners and of the educational system.
8. The provision of opportunities for candidates to begin developing their personal philosophies of education based on an understanding of the ethical, legal, and professional aspects of teaching, of curriculum and pedagogy, of the nature and diversity of learners, of the varied roles of teachers, of collaborative practices, and of the social contexts of teaching and learning.
9. A program that is actively concerned with inquiry and research, that draws upon the best of scholarship, that provides time for reflection, and that contributes over time to the growing theoretical and practical knowledge base of teaching, learning, and teacher education.

The elementary two-year pilot begun in September 1995 was also significantly influenced by FEUT's involvement in an international partnership of nine universities and field partners, entitled UNITE (Urban Network for Improving Teacher Education). The UNITE project is a network of faculties of education and schools in urban settings in Canada and the United States dedicated to improving the education of teachers who will teach in urban schools. The network is also committed to the reform of those schools and assume that faculties of education play a vital role in that process. Each of the UNITE partners has a leadership team responsible for coordinating four strands of the initiative at their site: 1) faculty development; 2) clinical (or field) development; 3) program renewal; and 4) leadership and change. As one of FEUT's five-member UNITE leadership team, I sit on the program renewal strand, although we have approached the project as a coordinated effort that unifies the strands at our site, and builds on our other initiatives and directions.

In addition to the funds and resources provided, UNITE became instrumental in helping us look at how we could specifically focus our two-year pilot to better prepare our future teachers to deal with challenges that range from poverty to cultural and racial diversity and multiple languages. As Erskine-Cullen and Sinclair (1995) state, "Faculties of education are realizing that prospective teachers need more than a general education. They need 'specialized knowledge of the life and learning styles of the urban child, first-hand experiences in urban schools, and an understanding of the community from which the child comes'." (Reed & Simon, 1991 p.32). To this end, some of the integrating themes in the pilot include anti-racism and ethnocultural equity, as well as urban education.

The pilot program is a significant change from what has gone before. As someone who first experienced a fragmented traditional program, then the Learning Consortium option, and now the two-year pilot, I am both exhilarated and challenged by the changes we are making (see also Rolheiser, 1996). The following section highlights some of the strengths and challenges identified in the first year of our work as we came together to plan and begin our partnership. The list is by no means comprehensive, but is certainly illustrative of the early phases of implementation that the FEUT-school district staff have gone through.

Two-Year Teacher Education Pilot: Initial Joys and Challenges

Part of school-university partnerships are the inevitable tensions that play themselves out on a regular basis. While tensions might be viewed as negative, I also see them as a positive force, providing the necessary impetus for change and growth. In fact, we might view these as necessary for meaningful school-university collaboration. Some of the tensions that have characterized our beginnings are as follows (Johnston, 1995):

University Culture versus School Culture

It will be of no surprise to the reader that this is the first tension I identify. Ross (1995) identifies one of the five main obstacles to the institutionalization of professional development schools as the cultural clash between universities and schools. They differ in beliefs, practices, and values that present themselves in real ways on a day-to-day basis. Ross goes on to say, "Conflict between school climate and university ambiance has frustrated many partnerships. School functions centre around the pragmatic realities and action orientations that govern school life. Solving problems in this environment is often from a "ready, fire, aim" stance, whereas the university is more inclined to the "ready, ready, ready" mode of problem solving. In the school world, it is challenging to find time to reflect, inquire, or just dialogue. Practice rules in this culture and ways of knowing often stem from custom and practice.

The primary client in this environment is the student, whereas the university culture focuses on the needs of the teacher candidate. This is an important point and relates back to the beginning of this chapter where I mentioned the dual focus in partnerships such as the Learning Consortium; that is, preservice and inservice program improvement. There are necessary tensions that arise in partnerships, and these arise from different clientele and aims—school improvement and preservice teacher development. As well, in universities there is value placed on knowing through disciplined inquiry, and theory is not viewed as a bad word. Taking time to make connections to broader issues, to ponder "why," or to reflect for depth is valued. There are different norms in these two environments regarding work priorities, and frictions often arise related to status discrepancies—for example, parity in the status of knowledge (Ross, 1995).

One of the structural innovations we are experimenting with to promote a collaborative work culture is a two-year committee entitled the Academy Advisory Committee (AAC). This committee was formed as soon as our eleven school sites were determined, and is used as a structure to guide our work and facilitate communication and planning within the pilot. This committee is comprised of the program coordinator (myself, a university-based teacher educator), field coordinator (a district-based teacher educator), three university-based teacher educators, the principal of each of the eleven academy schools, a teacher liaison from each academy school, and three elected teacher candidates.

As the AAC came together over the 1995 summer to begin specific planning for the fall, we felt this tension of cultures emerge. Part of the tension was likely present because of the stereotypes that each of us held about the other. We needed to start, therefore, on common ground. We took time to focus on getting to know one another, conducting interviews about our work and our interest in changing teacher education, and making school improvement. This attention to community-building was essential, in that we wanted to begin our interaction in ways that would foster appreciation and acceptance, respect and trust, care and commitment (Bennett, Rolheiser & Stevahn, 1991). We needed to build in time, even though it was scarce, to talk about things that really mattered, and to build some common language and understandings regarding teacher education and school improvement. At the same time, we needed to capitalize on learning from our differences.

Part of the challenge during this time was learning how we could collectively impact change in teacher education, while unlearning the ways we had approached the design of teacher education in the past. We wanted to hang on to the best of what we had learned over the last number of years, but also feel the freedom to change that which was perhaps no longer viable or meaningful. To do this, we started with few assumptions regarding what should be. We brainstormed what we felt should be part of a two-year experience, how these learnings could be developmentally structured, and how to alter or remove structures that bound us in the past. We also began exploring the ways in which we would work collectively. How could we create changes in our roles, as well as the perceptions behind those roles? Part of our decision in using new terminology for our roles was to remove the stereotypes of what those roles might mean to others.

In our AAC discussions, we are working toward the voice and choice of all members of the committee being valued. Such a goal is not always easy, and I am constantly aware of how delicate our journey is given the historical baggage, assumptions, and personal agendas we all bring to the table. At the end of our first planning meeting, however, I was struck with a statement made by one of the teacher liaisons. She stated that she had come expecting that university personnel would "tell her all about the design of the program," and she would be told what her role would be. She had a smile on her face when she said, "It felt good to be listened to—I felt like we all had equal voices in our discussion." I was humbly aware of the implications of her statement. Likely, her previous experiences in "partnerships" with university personnel were not all that equal, and I realized that this was but one of the realities many teachers would be bringing into our partnership.

You versus Us

This is a tension that I suspect will take a substantial period of time to work through. When problems in a partnership emerge it is much easier to say, "You need to solve this problem from your end (i.e., the university or school)," rather than "We need to address this issue out of collective interest." During a meeting with an academy school principal, for example, I addressed some concerns that had arisen in a meeting with the student cohort working in her school. The conversation that afternoon left me with a high degree of frustration. I realized that at the core of my frustration was the feeling that communication was occurring in terms of "you versus us." One statement in particular, "Well, then you need to address that issue," left me feeling that there was this void between the two partners in the program. In reply, I said, "No, *we* need to address the issue together." As we move from a relationship that traditionally had two different worlds contributing "their part" to a program, to a place where we view it as a connected, coherent, and mutually developed program, we also move to a place where greater responsibility is assumed by all.

Especially in times of conflict, I suspect this tension will re-emerge. However, given the different cultures, it may be important to reemphasize the tension between "you versus us" even while trying to work toward a model where responsibility is assumed by all. For example, while working toward the partnership model it may be reasonable to expect that teacher educators solve different problems that arise based on their cultural affiliation, even while being reminded that the responsibility lies with everyone.

Constructivism versus Skills-Training

In teacher education there are a range of philosophies about teaching and learning, just as there are in our profession as a whole. As two cultures come together to design experiences for preparing teachers, these differing philosophies and views often clash. This clash became very apparent in the recent work of a subcommittee within the elementary pilot. A group of university professors, a teacher, a principal, and a field coordinator formed a committee to struggle with the area of literacy, and to design components, sequence, and dimensions that would best come together in a two-year program designed to graduate teacher candidates who were prepared for the challenges of teaching literacy in an urban context.

At one end of the continuum, we had represented on the team a constructivist view of teaching—those who believe that through a range of experiences, interaction, and talk learners will construct their own meaning. A part of this orientation is to trust that the learner will move through discomfort to a stage of deeper understanding. At the other end of the continuum is the belief that others can be the experts who guide learners in structured, direct, learning experiences in order to develop specific skills and knowledge. This view of teaching operates from the belief that there is a fixed curriculum that needs to be transmitted to the students. The committee struggled to find a middle ground from which to operate, and indeed, to even talk to one another. At times, I suspect, it felt like they were never going to bridge the two ends of the continuum. Their commitment of time and capacity to listen and understand one another resulted in representation of merged spectrum views to be experienced by our candidates throughout their teacher education program. For example, a constructivist-driven, school-based literacy project was used to develop teacher candidates' inquiry skills in the first four months of the pilot. This was followed by a number of full-day skills-oriented workshops focused on comprehension and word decoding skills.

The complexity of this subcommittee's work, as they struggled with inquiry and reflection regarding how best to teach and learn, and as they tried to demonstrate their valuing of partnership while living out the challenge of varying philosophical views, is not a complexity to be minimized. I believe, however, that this type of work will ensure that the program evolves in ways that meets the needs of both school and university personnel.

Individual Orientation versus Organizational Orientation

As we move to a program where we are not focused on the individual teacher candidate who works solely with one host teacher in his or her classroom to a model that is focused on a cohort of teacher candidates working in an organizational context, we feel the tension of breaking traditions and norms. Helping teachers see that they can provide a collective range of experiences for new teachers, beyond what any one individual can provide, means treading new water. We have run up against issues such as professional territory and pride. One teacher educator, for example, was upset when her teacher candidate went to another teacher as a resource. She expressed her concern that the colleague would feel that she was not doing her job as a mentor. The teacher candidate's intent was to access yet another resource in the school. The tension is also felt when school-based teacher educators view schoolwide responsibilities and activities (e.g., extracurricular clubs, professional study groups, school-wide inquiry projects) as less valued or deserving of time than the responsibilities in their specific classroom. Likewise, this tension is also felt as university instructors give up their individual view of "subject, discipline, or course" to look at the overall organizational goals in delivering a coherent and relevant program.

Another aspect of this tension is the very real pull of reward that individuals in a university structure feel, while at the same time wanting to contribute to the good of the organization through strengthening partnerships. According to Ross (1995), "The failure of universities to reward fieldwork inhibits partnerships with schools." Individuals on our pilot team find it very challenging to structure writing and research time, and attend to committee work of the university, while also developing quality field partnerships. On the one hand, they are pushing to bring about change in teacher education through a different kind of teaching and scholarship. On the other hand, they are pulled and sometimes constrained by what is often perceived as an institutional context that has not fully revamped their reward structures (e.g., tenure and promotion) to embrace a broader view of scholarship. As Elijah suggests, "University reward systems have lagged behind in supporting the reform initiatives" (1995, p.25) for which university personnel are assuming greater responsibility. Untenured faculty especially feel the tension that this situation creates. Their work on a pilot becomes more high risk, and the demands they feel may result in priorities being placed alongside the rewards. This can create internal tension, as well as tension with field partners who do not understand or appreciate this world.

The points I have raised regarding individual and organizational orientation not only illuminate the tensions within cultures, but across cultures as well. These tensions are also apparent in the following issue.

Structure versus Ambiguity

One of the first tensions we realized in the beginning stages of the pilot development was structure versus ambiguity. We wanted to begin the program without the structure laid out; otherwise we would not be acting on the belief that the structure should emerge through the interaction of the partners. In our initial meeting between FEUT personnel and North York personnel, we identified some mutual criteria by which academy schools might be identified. A range of schools were invited to the meeting, with the idea that after the meeting any interested schools would put in a proposal to become part of the academy. The meeting was a challenge. For many of the questions, such as, "How many days will the teacher candidates be in the school?" "When will the practica be?" and "What will the role of the teacher liaison be?" We had to be honest and say that the partners would determine that in subsequent planning. We had to restate the idea that buying into the academy meant that your school was interested in shaping what would be, not accepting a predetermined structure and process. We wanted emergent goals versus imposed goals. For the schools that eventually were selected for the academy, it was this open-endedness and opportunity to have a voice that was the attraction. For those who did not put in a proposal, they expressed their dissatisfaction with the meeting, feeling it to have too much ambiguity. They felt there was a lack of structure in the program and too many unanswered questions.

The tension between structure versus ambiguity continues to be present as we create school and academy structures that will support our work, yet leave opportunity within those structures to allow implementation to be contextually determined in each school. We struggle to provide enough direction to generate action and not provide so much that it inhibits our work. We suspect this particular challenge of partnership to continue, and feel that it provides a healthy tension.

Insiders versus Outsiders

While developing a pilot, life in the rest of the Faculty of Education continues. One of the tensions we are dealing with is the reality that we likely need to facilitate a shift to a full two-year program in 1997 for the whole faculty. Given this possibility, we need to develop an internal and external dissemination strategy. This will prepare our entire staff, as well as school staffs from future school board partners, in preparing for the intense and very different work involved in totally reconceptualizing and delivering a two-year program. While we are building on many of the principles and practices that we have been experimenting with over the last number of years in the one-year program, the reality is that this may be a new way of doing what we do. The issue becomes one of how do we involve the rest of the staff (outsiders to the pilot) in thinking through the issues, when they are very much involved in their own day-to-day programs?

We have been aware of this challenge and have attempted to build a number of bridges to create opportunities for dialogue. For example, we have hosted a day focused on rethinking the assessment and evaluation of the practicum. This involved sharing the process and product of what we did with all option coordinators and staff. The personnel in the one-year program also shared how they were rethinking assessment so that it became a dialogue regarding issues with which we were grappling. In wanting to keep the pilot connected to those not immediately involved in it, we are finding ways to communicate on a regular basis through forums such as round-table seminars (OISE / UT) and invitations to attend some of the academy functions such as a fall literacy conference put on by our teacher candidates. Additional strategies need to be considered, such as observing the pilot in practice, participating in seminars on key features, and for some, being members of subcommittees or advisory groups.

Competition versus Cooperation

A predominant orientation in schools and higher-education institutions is that of competition. Our systems have operated for so long with the norm of competition prevailing that a shift to adopting alternative norms becomes a hard road to travel. In the two-year pilot, we are grounding our operation as a community in the tenets of cooperative learning. With the vision of achieving common goals through our interdependent work, we know that we are also challenging beliefs versus supporting tradition. For most of our teacher candidates, they have achieved in schooling and admission to the faculty because of competition. To have them begin to value open sharing of ideas, expertise, and resources with their colleagues means having them begin to trust, and feel the rewards of, cooperation. Likewise, as evident in a collaborative practicum-evaluation meeting we had with our school teacher educators, openly sharing decisions and rationales for those decisions is not an easy task. Old competitive norms begin to emerge as we provide a new rationale for why such public sharing might enhance the collective work of our program. We would be naive to think that life is devoid of competition, yet we want to have our graduates leave our program armed with an alternative system of cooperative beliefs and values.

Growth versus Achievement

One tension that we knew we needed to address in a two-year program was the valuing of growth versus achievement. In our one-year program, there is a dilemma that all of us have experienced; that is, we try to instill in our teacher candidates the belief that teaching is lifelong learning, yet as early as October in their first practicum they are evaluated for their performance or achievement. This first evaluation is also a critical source used by boards of education for hiring purposes. The stress of the need for this first evaluation to be as "perfect" as possible is felt by all. Teacher candidates go into a survival mode, where they expect in their first practicum to be prepared with "all the practical stuff to do the job perfectly." Theory, therefore, does not seem to play a role, and risk-taking is minimal. School teacher educators are put in the unenviable position of writing a report that supposedly meets the growth and feedback needs of the teacher candidate, but that simultaneously provides hiring teams the information they need to make a decision.

In the two-year pilot, we wanted to deal with this tension in a proactive way and to have the teacher candidates shift from the stance of "being to becoming." We wanted them to embrace the notion that they would have time and support in becoming a professional. We did so by having the first semester structured around time in the entire school (two to three days a week), where the cohort conducted an inquiry that helped them see the bigger picture of schools and schooling, as well as teaching and learning. Furthermore, in their first year of the program, all practicum evaluations are focused on growth, and the evidence of it, as opposed to an achievement focus. We expect this will help them and their teacher educators adopt a risk-taking versus comfort stance. Year two will see a shift to performance or achievement.

Status Quo versus Change for Improvement

It is hard to change the "way things are," yet we also don't want to change just for change sake. We want our changes to be guided by improvement. That demands we document what we are doing at this early stage and make adjustments, applications, and additions over the remainder of the two years. Our documentation will provide formative evaluation to the program-in-use and a foundation for judging the merit, worth, and success of the model over the long term. We need to be constantly aware of questioning the status quo, and of not making assumptions in either direction; that is, that the status quo is good or bad. By questioning and documenting, we will be able to make informed decisions regarding what to keep doing, what to stop doing, and what to start doing. All of this needs to be grounded in a desire to improve what we presently do in teacher education.

Change in Teacher Candidates versus Change in School Teacher-Educators versus Change in University Teacher-Educators

We have to believe that a program such as the two-year pilot is about all of us changing, not just one stakeholder group. If we enter the partnership with the belief that all of us will be altered by the collaboration, then we will have created the right mindset for the type of work and change that is needed. It is not about what we need to do to make the "other person" change. It is about each of us changing.

At the beginning of this chapter, I emphasized the importance of university-district partnerships for school improvement and teacher development. Based on our emerging partnership, I feel we are moving closer to our collective goals. With all stakeholders now believing that what we are doing will result in better learning opportunities for all, we have found common ground. Through our partnership, I believe that teacher candidates will be better prepared for the demands of schools today, school teacher educators will develop new skills as mentors and teacher leaders, university teacher educators will become more effective teachers and stronger scholars, while also better understanding the workings of schools, and schools will become better learning environments for teachers and students.

Our unwillingness to have challenges defeat us and our collective "belief in better" continues to drive us forward to what we anticipate will be an improved version of teacher education.

Learning to Teach Inside the Classroom

Jill Lloyd-Jones teaches drama at Western Technical and Commercial School in Toronto. She has a bachelor of education degree from the University of Toronto, and a masters degree in arts education from OISE. Jill has taught additional qualification courses in dramatic arts at the University of Toronto, and has given workshops on many aspects of drama. Together with Frances Fagan, she has been involved for the past four years in an action research project, twinning elementary and secondary students together in story drama.

Frances Fagan is an elementary school teacher at Runnymede Public School in Toronto. Prior to her teaching career, Frances worked as a professional actor in the theatre. She received her undergraduate honours degree in fine arts from York University, her bachelor of education from the University of Toronto, and her masters degree in education from OISE.

This is our story of synchronicity, of how a chance meeting developed into an enriching four-year professional partnership.

We first met at OISE while working on our masters degrees in the area of arts education. Through class discussions, we recognized that we shared similar views and values regarding education, and later, discovered that we taught across the street from each other, one in a secondary school and the other in an elementary one. Undaunted by the fact that there was a ten-year age span between the students in our classes, our close working proximity and a shared vision of the arts encouraged our resolve to explore the power of drama as a learning medium, and collaboration became our vehicle.

We see collaboration as a means of maximizing the potential of who we are; collaboration for us is not just a meeting of two persons, but a shared possibility, a relationship that has become more than just the sum of two parts (Coles, 1989). Over the past four years, this initial alliance has matured into a professional partnership that has expanded beyond the classroom to our work with preservice teacher candidates at the Faculty of Education, giving workshops in the educational community and engaging in ongoing action research. We are, therefore, building on what we believe in, creating partnerships in the classroom, the universities, and the academic community (Ralph, 1992). It is this philosophy of teaching that has propelled us to embrace the role of associate teacher in perhaps the most personal of partnerships, because it is the sharing of who we are with potential teachers.

For the last four years, we have twinned our classes as part of an ongoing action research project. Our drama in education work is process-oriented, and therefore does not readily lend itself to replication or "performance." However, we believe it is important to give preservice teachers the opportunity to observe our process by inviting them to participate in "drama in progress." This is a working session that begins with observation and culminates in an interactive sharing, in which the process (both with teachers and students) is decoded so that preservice students will gain an understanding and appreciation of the ongoing learning that has previously taken place. Sharing our work, then, is one way in which we can tangibly demonstrate the power of collegial partnerships.

We believe that we teach the way we teach because of who we are. Every experience that we have had, and every person we have met who has had a significant impact on our lives, has contributed to the formation of our personal philosophy towards teaching. It is this personal understanding and the importance of being receptive to ongoing experiences and interactions with others that has furthered our understanding of the value of partnerships, collaboration, and associate teaching.

Our work has shown us that the following elements are essential in building these partnerships:

- a desire to learn,
- a willingness to listen,
- a willingness to give up personal control,
- honesty in communication,
- flexibility,
- a sharing of common goals and philosophy,
- a sense of humour,
- a willingness to change.

Frances's Story

Teaching means many things to me. It is founded in my love for children and in my belief in that simple ritual, the passing down of stories, stories that we learn from, stories of my Scottish heritage that took the form of beautiful ballads expressing the sentiment of the times in which they were sung. Teaching means exploration and discovery, and teaching was what my coal miner father did as he explained the mysteries of the solar system to me on my bedroom wall with the reflection of a light bulb and a tennis ball to represent the earth. This was a safe environment where questions were answered with patience and understanding, without ridicule. How do you become a real teacher like that, someone who touches lives the way my mother did as she unraveled my eighth attempt at crochet and threaded the needle yet again for my friend who was inspired, through necessity, to sew her own clothes. By example we learn, and through experience we try to emulate what has been modelled for us. Being given that opportunity to try and perhaps to fail with dignity was one of the greatest gifts I unknowingly was given, first as a child by my parents, and later during my preservice year.

My acceptance into the Faculty of Education at the University of Toronto came late in the summer of 1989. A new field-based option had been opened and I was one of thirty-four students who would have the opportunity to experience a preservice year housed primarily in a large elementary school. It was the vision of our option coordinators, Dr. Allan MacKinnon and Dr. Susan Sydor, that we acquire the skills, attitudes, and knowledge required for initial teacher training by participating as fully as possible in the life of the school. They encouraged us from the very beginning to keep a record of our experiences, our learnings, and how we were affected by these developments. It was this reflective practice that became most important to me, and one that was also used as a communication tool with my supervisors.

On our first practice teaching session, when we found ourselves removed from these familiar surroundings, unable to chat or commiserate with our fellow classmates, we used our journals to record those initial teaching experiences and to reflect on them. It is also a practice that I try to foster in my student teachers. Taking the time to revisit a lesson or conversation and recording it often becomes the pivotal learning point, as it is usually the next day when my student teacher will say to me that the "aha" happened, or the "now I get it."

The Faculty students that I receive from the University of Toronto work on a program similar to the one in which I was a participant. They are with the class one day a week for four weeks, and then they stay for a three-week practicum. By the time they do their placement, they are familiar with the students and the routines.

Following is an excerpt from my preservice journal:

> I'm so fortunate my associate is so nice and she has such a gentle way with her class. If I can just speak in that same sweet tone and give them those nods and looks the way she does then every thing should be under control. Yet I'm surrounded by six-year-olds. Remember now, they are only six, you're the adult here, you're the one with the power. You can handle these little kids. If I could just get them to stay seated and stop running around. "OK. Listen now, listening please. Excuse me! Excuse me! Everybody LISTEN." Being left alone with those children was the longest 15 minutes of my life. But my associate knew that it was the only way that I could gain control of the class, having to sort it out for myself. Will this ever come easy to me or will I always be a beginning teacher?

When will I stop being a beginning teacher? That was the question that I often asked when I was involved in a research project about beginning teachers, and it is a question that my student teachers ask of me. I can't remember the exact moment: did it stop after that first terrifying—exhilarating—day when the eager, sometimes shy faces of my first class looked up at me in anticipation of great things to come? Or was it when I had to state with great conviction to parents that their child would find a safe learning environment in my class, even though I wasn't sure what that class would actually look or feel like?

I don't remember the day that it happened, the day that I felt I belonged. I suppose as my confidence grew, as I became more comfortable with my students and their parents, that this sense of belonging evolved. But I wish I could have been outside myself to view that moment. Sometimes it is very subtle: the child asks the student teacher the question instead of asking me. Usually it has to do with the student teacher being tuned in to the children, anticipating their needs before they are articulated, or resolving a conflict before most know that there is one. I call that *developing teaching antennae.* Allowing our student teachers to risk, fail, and risk again is how they learn to develop their antennae. You can't get a sense of who you are unless you are actively participating, and we must give our new teachers that opportunity.

I always feel a certain amount of insecurity each year as September approaches. I don't believe that you pass the threshold one day never to return to the uncertainty of those first weeks of teaching. In many ways you revisit them each time you teach a new grade or move into a new divisional level. The unknown comes flooding back when you find yourself challenged by an uncooperative child who refuses to be motivated by your previously successful methods, or by a new curriculum that must be developed, or by the anxious face of your new student teacher. The questions then become, "How do you get over these hurdles that seem somewhat overwhelming in your initial teaching experiences?" "Where do you turn for advice, counselling, and practical hands-on help?"

Many of us learned from an experienced teacher associate that sharing ideas was worthwhile and sharing concerns was crucial to a healthy existence. Many of us were fortunate to have had a challenging learning experience during our preservice year that caused us to examine who we were and what it was that we could bring to this profession.

I was fortunate; I was encouraged to share my story:

> I remember my first student teacher and how composed and poised she appeared. It wasn't until we shook hands that I realized that she was as nervous as I was. "I don't know which one of us is shaking more." I said. She laughed, grateful to know that she was not alone. My insecurities continued.

Here am I encouraging my student teacher to write about the day's experiences in my class. Write about everything, the good moments and the mistakes that you say will never happen in your class.

> Am I living dangerously, telling them to report on everything? Warts and all? I wonder how I will be compared to other associates. Will he/ she like my style? Will we get along? What will be reported back to the professors at the Faculty? Will I be able to explain all the things I want them to know? Will I be good enough?

Becoming an associate teacher made me realize that we are all learners at different stages of our development. Some of us have been learning longer than others.

When you stop feeling apprehensive or insecure, when you begin to feel indifferent and apathetic, when you stop learning from your student teacher, then you stop being a real teacher doing real teaching.

Jill's Story

Whenever I think about teachers and teaching, I'm always reminded of the reasons we go into teaching in the first place. Why do we do it? What do we get? What do we give? And what is the cost? Of course I'm not talking about money; it's something much deeper than that, or at least it is for me. All I really have to offer is my story, my life experience, and yet it is everything I have because it is the very essence of who I am, and has been the catalyst that has propelled me on my journey to question, learn and share. It is the last one, the sharing, that is risky. It makes me feel vulnerable, my values out there for all to see and maybe to be judged! It is this willingness, this compulsion to share what I am, that is the cornerstone of my commitment to being an associate teacher.

It's autumn. Practice teaching time again. I'm always curious to see who it will be. I have the name only, and the gender, and I scrutinize carefully for clues. Miss, Ms. or Mrs. (does anyone still use Mrs.?) and rarely Mr., each title containing a hint of personality. Can I tell from the name, first and last, who this person is? Where have they come from, what are they like, what baggage will they bring with them? And then, that deep seed of doubt coming from way back, from some deep place inside of me, repeating itself in my mind: Will they like me? Will what I have to offer be enough? This is the baggage that I carry.

We are working together, student teacher and associate teacher, in a partnership, in the same way that the teacher in the field and the professor at the Faculty of Education work together in a partnership, to develop better teachers in the classroom. While the Faculty provides the academic and theoretical framework for teaching, associate teachers provide the environment in which student teachers "try out" what they have learned, and gather new techniques to practice in the classroom. For me, "try out" is perhaps the linchpin of what I believe is essential in practice teaching. I believe that the three weeks each student spends with me is the time to try out new ideas, and find out if and how they work. It is the time to make "mistakes," learn how to assess them and move on. It is the time to "risk" in a trusting and caring environment, and it is my responsibility as associate teacher to establish that. I always tell my student teachers that the three weeks spent with me is their time to take chances and ask questions, but because we are working together in a partnership, it is also their responsibility to tell me what they want from our time together so we can work towards those goals. I also let them know that I do not expect them to teach on their own, and that I will be there to provide ongoing assistance and feedback.

> The first meeting. Small, dark haired, friendly smile. I know she's nervous so I prattle on about the school and the students, hoping that the sheer volume of information will mask my own shyness at meeting a new person for the first time. I try to put her at ease, to let her know that I have been in the place that she is in, that I know how she feels, that this is a safe place for her, that it's all right to make mistakes. In fact, it is an essential part of learning that you *do* make mistakes. This I know to be true.
>
> I remember being eight years old. I live in a small town in the north of England with Mum and

> Nana. Nana doesn't like children very much. She thinks "children should be seen and not heard." I can't get away from her constant and unremitting criticism even when I'm quiet and lost in my own world. "You'll never get anywhere day dreaming." "You don't know how to be quiet." "You can't do anything right!"
>
> I could *never* do anything right no matter how hard I tried. The list of my "mistakes" was endless in her eyes. What I did know was that I could never be the person she wanted me to be, compliant, obedient, unquestioning, invisible. I was too much like her for that!
>
> It's forty years later, and there is still the occasional time when I'm tired or stressed, when my stomach turns, if I think I've made a "mistake," but mostly I've learned to acknowledge that a mistake is often an opportunity to make changes, and to move on and work toward creating a positive force. It's taken me a long time to discover this secret. If only Nana knew what a gift she really gave me!
>
> I see the similarities in my student teacher's eyes also. I can tell that she understands what life is all about, that she actually has *had* a life, rich, eventful, maybe not always what she wanted, but lots of lessons learned, and in the learning the compassion that comes with knowing what it's like to make mistakes. I feel it will be a good three weeks!

As we only work with our student teachers for a three-week period, there is very little opportunity to get to know them before we are into practice-teaching time. Yet it is important for me to find out who that person really is. I have to try to "fast forward" through the usual pleasantries and get to a place where we can feel comfortable enough to be able to think about, and discuss, what areas we will examine and what we will do in the next three weeks. This is by no means an easy task because we are both trying to overcome a very basic teacher instinct, fear of not being able to teach what is needed.

I can still remember my own practice teaching sessions not long ago with teachers who had varying attitudes, goals, and expectations of me, the student teacher, and that gnawing feeling deep in my stomach that I wouldn't be able to live up to their expectations. It is by reaching back in my mind to that time that I can relate to my own students' fears and try to reassure them as much as I can that these three weeks, although hard work, will be rewarding.

Once we get past the initial "getting to know each other" stage, it is time to get to know the classes. In my school, which is an inner city, multicultural, semestered school, I have three classes with very different characteristics. A large, adolescent, destreamed grade 10 class, a small, more mature grade 12 class, and a large mixed-age (adult and adolescent) English as a second language class. It is very important for my student teacher to understand that each student, in addition to the usual traumas of adolescent years, or returning to school as an adult, is also dealing with a number of other factors that have an impact on his/her attitude towards learning. They experience racism and the frustration of not being understood as a second-language learner, although perhaps well educated in their own country. There may be long-term unemployment in the family, juggling school work with a part-time job to augment family income, and lastly, perhaps the most tragic of all, the feeling that there is no future for them. The associate teacher, then, is responsible for helping the student teacher understand who the students are in their classes as individuals, before we can begin to talk about what and how to teach them.

> It's the spring, another student teacher, another story. It's the last class of the day, English as a second language (ESL), drama, and we have been listening to a student tell the story of his flight by sea from Vietnam to Malaysia. Five days in a boat with no food and only a little water. Everyone crammed together like sardines. You do not move from the spot you have claimed or it is lost. The sun beats down unmercifully on the open boat. Some people don't make it, the very old and the very young. Their bodies are

> thrown overboard, strangers, beloved relatives. No ceremony, only the ritual circling of the sharks to mark their passing. For us, the teachers, the magnitude of what is being heard brings us close to tears, afraid to glance at each other in case we lose control, concerned that for other students this disclosure will bring to the surface unspeakable memories, long buried away. These are the students who come to class daily, happy and smiling, eager to learn, carrying huge loads that we are completely unaware of. Later, in private, the tears come—it is the last time that I use the drama game "Shark" in any of my ESL classes.
>
> It's at times like these that our relationship as fellow educators, as student and associate teacher, falls to the common denominator. We are all human beings, our experiences, while individually diverse, are universally the same. We all laugh, cry, and feel. I think the acknowledgment of these very basic facts is essential to being a good teacher. The sharing and imparting of knowledge is not done in a vacuum to empty vessels, as some people believe, but to living breathing human beings. Each student, however young, brings important life experiences, and it is the honouring of those experiences by the teacher that allows each student to feel that what he or she has to offer in the classroom is worthwhile and valuable.

I have thought a lot about the difference between great teachers and those who are satisfactory. I think the distinction lies in life experience and how we deal with what we are given. While it is possible to be a satisfactory teacher who is able to convey the intricacies of the subject matter quite adequately, it is the subtle nuances of teaching—the personal connection with each student, the ability to make the subject relevant and meaningful—that can make a real difference to how our students respond to us, and ultimately, to their academic success. This is the kind of teaching that can only come from the heart, from the experience of understanding what has gone before.

Teaching is not a finite thing—something that you perfect and then continue to do for the rest of a teaching career. It is something that is continually changing and evolving, as are our students in the classroom. More than anything else, I want student teachers to understand this, and value the philosophy that we as teachers must have a thirst for learning and a curiosity to explore and effect change in our students in a positive way. I believe that by working together in the classroom in an atmosphere of mutual respect, we can make a substantial impact on the learning of our students, and that in the larger context, we are helping young people to become responsible and mature adults who will contribute to our country's future.

As an associate teacher I do not see myself as a supervisor because this role denotes one who controls. My relationship with my student teacher is one in which we exchange information, learning from our students and each other as partners, partners who are constantly thinking, learning, and refining our work together, partners with an appreciation of the value of life experience, of our stories.

I feel very honoured to have had the opportunity of sharing my stories and my teaching with others, and, in turn, to have had the privilege of being part of my students' stories, for it is within those stories that we see the intricacies of the web that connects us all (Robert Coles, 1989) captured this so eloquently when he said:

> Their story, yours, mine,—it's what we all carry with us on this trip we take, and we owe it to each other to respect our stories and learn from them.

What better advice could we give to our student teachers?

Teacher Training

Although individual educators have tried various innovative ways to change the methods used to train student teachers, until recently there had been little change in teacher training. As

Portman says, student teachers are essentially trained in the same way that we were trained, and our parents were trained before us (1993).

We are perhaps representative of a new group of associate teachers who believe that we are most effective when we work in a collaborative partnership, using new ways of knowing and understanding the world in an ever-changing classroom environment (Nolan & Francis, in Ralph, 1992). We now know that it has been far easier to change what we teach than it has been to change our thinking about how we teach preservice teachers (Portman, 1993). It is the latter that we must strive to alter. If we can effectively change how we teach teaching, then, as Dorothy Heathcote (1972) says, we can:

> Create a race of teachers who are unafraid to make relationships with classes; who are unafraid to admit they do not know; who never stop seeking to learn more about the dynamics of teaching; who bring all of themselves to school and demand that their classes do the same; who can actually change their models of work to suit the needs of their classes at any time so that learning is kept meaningful; who like to get on with the people they teach because they are unafraid of the dull, the aggressive, the unacademic, the naughty; who are able to admit they are tired today so that their classes can take some responsibility.

This, however, means we must change the premise of what it means to be an associate teacher. We must look at our practice, reflect on its effectiveness and constantly "re-view" who we are and what we value (Daley, 1978).

The New Associate Teacher

When looking at remodelling the program at the Faculty of Education, University of Toronto, Dennis Thiessen (1995) defined the key images of an effective teacher, as one who works:

> With all students in an equitable, effective and caring manner by respecting diversity in relation to ethnicity, race, gender, and special needs of each learner. [as] ...active learners who continuously seek, assess, apply and communicate knowledge as reflective practitioners throughout their careers.

While this gives us the philosophical framework from which to work with our student teachers, our own classroom inquiry has led to a working model that we believe is of primary importance because it is effective in communicating to others what we know about teaching. As associate teachers, we have a responsibility to provide a quality learning experience. An associate teacher using this model would, therefore:

- encourage initiative,
- create an environment for exploration,
- create a safe space to take chances / risks,
- establish a "no penalty" zone,
- give constructive feedback,
- value and encourage reflection,
- relinquish some of their control.

Initiative

Associate teachers should encourage student teachers to demonstrate initiative in planning, executing, and evaluating lessons. They should be a part of the decision-making process in as many aspects of their learning as possible. This allows them to take some ownership of the classroom, and makes evaluation feel less uncertain and is, in itself, an important learning experience. We need to find the balance that allows for student teachers to explore new ideas but continues to guide them forward on their continuum of learning. Often the most powerful learning takes place in an unplanned moment, a spontaneous, organic initiative that propels the learner onto a new plane of understanding. This process encourages risk taking, rather than relying on proscribed classroom formulae.

Creating an Environment for Exploration

Associate teachers need to be aware of the conflict between their own necessity to complete a unit of study, which is often driven by institutional curriculum demands, and the need for learning by the student teacher. While it is essential that curriculum be valued, it is equally important to ensure that there is time for exploration within the lesson, and by exploration we mean the opportunity for the student teacher to try innovative strategies. These adaptations of a lesson are often the brick that then becomes the building block for a new way of looking at what the student teacher is doing in the classroom. While we may have taught the same very successful lesson for a number of years, we want our students to experiment with ideas he or she may have so the opportunity exists for us to see the lesson in a new way. By allowing them to claim their own place, the possibility exists for both the student and associate teacher to be reciprocally enriched, provided that the environment is a safe one.

Creating a Safe Place to Take Chances

It is essential that the classroom environment in which we teach together as associate and student be one in which there is mutual respect, a place where learning takes place through working in real-life situations rather than from a theoretical base. This needs to happen not only during a teaching session, but also in the daily discussions that take place when we confer together about what has transpired. While an associate teacher should always be ready to provide a safety net if needed, the student teacher needs to know that in conference sessions a safe environment exists that encourages and supports creative decision making in the classroom. As a result of mutual sharing, the student teacher is given permission to be a novice, not responsible for knowing everything, and allowed to experience the consequences of their decisions without penalty (Ellis, 1993). Experienced teachers are also reminded of their own practice teaching experience, both negative and positive, and through this can relate more personally to the student teacher (Hadaway & Reinhartz, 1992-93).

Establishing a "No Penalty" Zone

When a student comes into our classroom, we acknowledge that they are at the beginning of their learning journey and to continue this learning there will be many missteps made along the way. We refer to the classroom as a "no penalty" zone, as it is important that they can make mistakes in an environment that will not penalize them for their exploration. What is important is to discuss, reflect, and internalize the learning so that there is deeper understanding. We also acknowledge to our student teachers that similar errors are often repeated, and that our own years of teaching experience certainly inform the choices that we make, but do not equal infallibility. A good associate teacher ensures that there are no penalties for trying out new ideas (within the context of an agreed upon lesson plan), or modifying an existing lesson to meet the needs of the students. Meeting challenges in the classroom and responding to them is something that should be encouraged and supported.

Constructive Feedback

Within the school day there is little opportunity to give constructive criticism, yet this is an area of primary importance, as time is needed to discuss the written feedback of what has transpired in the classroom. While we do have ongoing informal chats, they tend to be a passing on of information from associate to student, not a "sit-down" mutual discussion on how the day has gone. Daily conferences, then, are an absolute necessity, and whether they are done during preparation periods, lunch time or before or after school, they are essential to the learning continuum. There are two sides to this equation: we, as associate teachers, have to find ways of giving feedback in a constructive and non-threatening manner, so that the students will feel comfortable enough to acknowledge their lack of understanding and feel free to ask for help (Ralph, 1992); they, as preservice teachers, have a responsibility to find ways to hear the information and internalize it so that it will increase their understanding and enrich their learning. As feedback is something that teachers are always engaged in, this is also serving as effective models for learning how to proceed successfully with our students in the classroom. We encourage our student teachers to observe, note, and question our teaching methods, and to give constructive feedback to us in the same manner that we have modelled with them. This process helps them analyze their own work, and assists them in developing their rationale for further preparation. For us as associates, it helps inform our own work and by doing so either confirms or encourages us to revise our teaching practice.

Reflection

Griffin reports that:

> Ideal teachers are reflective, deliberate, and collaborative. They want to understand their practice to know why things work as they do and how to improve. Their teaching is based on knowledge about teaching, learning, children, classroom dynamics and contexts of schooling.
>
> (Griffin, 1984)

Often it is difficult to recall everything that happens when you are in the midst of a lesson, and it may be helpful for the student teacher to have the associate in the classroom observing and taking notes. From these, our mutual observations of the day can be discussed at the conference session and become the catalyst for reflection on the teaching-learning process. As we are striving to develop teachers who will come to value reflection as a natural tool to be used in their professional development, we encourage them to write about their experiences and to reflect critically on those events. Through continual reflection we know that they will be able to better understand and apply this learning in an effective manner in the classroom. It is important to remember, however, that reflection does not always happen "in the moment," but can, over time, develop into new understandings. It is this ongoing critical reflection, together with an understanding of experiences and relationships, that give beginning teachers a prime opportunity to develop their teaching practice, both now and in future years. In addition, reflection that occurs after collegial discussion promotes a positive attitude towards facing the isolation and uncertainty often felt at the beginning of a teacher's career (Ellis, 1993).

Control—Who Has it?

The issue of control is not one that readily comes to mind when examining the relationship between student teacher and associate; the associate has the power. But in order for the student teacher to be empowered in terms of his or her learning, the associate must be willing to relinquish some of this control. For many of us, letting go of the reins is an extremely difficult process as we have worked so hard to establish a positive, productive learning environment in our class. This "letting go" is similar in many ways to being a parent of an infant who is trying to take its first steps. You are there to guide and support, but eventually you must let go of their hands so that they will be empowered to experience the event on their own. You create a safety net of sorts, moving the obstacles back a few feet, covering sharp corners, and blocking off passageways that could lead to a fall. As the students gain more confidence through their experiences, and with our help, they will be able to find their way around.

When we are in the classroom, we need to make the choice to use our power selectively. As the one possessing the expertise, it is easy for us to give the answers, own the problem and resolve it immediately, instead of letting our student teachers struggle through to resolve it in their own way. If we don't give our student teachers time to work their way through all the steps needed, but jump in and do it for them, then in essence we are denying them the opportunity to learn. By giving up control, we acknowledge the possibility that the student teacher may encounter difficulties in the classroom, which we will then have to remedy ourselves (e.g., the reteaching of a lesson). As this is time-consuming, we are sometimes reluctant to empower the student teacher. However, as teachers who work together collaboratively, we know we must share the authority in order to have a successful partnership.

Evaluation

An area of concern for student teachers is the method in which they will be evaluated. One of the purposes of practice teacher evaluation is to identify students who have the potential to become superior teachers, as we have a vested interest as educators to ensure that only the best teachers, those who really love teaching and care about what they do, actually become teachers. Yet the necessity to evaluate each student can sometimes impinge upon their creative learning process (Cole, 1995). Student teachers are very aware of the importance of the practice teacher appraisal form, and are sometimes so apprehensive about the evaluation that they avoid taking risks in favour of a more conservative approach to their teaching practice. Our strategy is to try to shift the balance of motivation from extrinsic to intrinsic, from learning as a means to a reward for what we are most interested in—learning for its own sake (Kohn, 1994). We know that evaluating creates the possibility of tension and fear tht is counterproductive to the learning process, and so by removing the emphasis on the final evaluation and concentrating on the task of learning to teach, and of *wanting* to learn to teach, we hope we will encourage innovative, creative, and involved teachers (Wiedmer, 1995). In order to understand the criteria, we take the evaluation form (the appraisal of practice teaching, set out by the Faculty of Education) at the beginning of the teaching session, and go through it together point by point, outlining and discussing mutual expectations. It is this document that will be essential in garnering employment for the student teacher. It is, therefore, crucial that they understand the criteria by which they will be evaluated, as the process is one of mutual responsibility. While the evaluation document reflects the cumulative progress, what is going to help the student teacher day by day will be the ongoing daily conferences, written feedback, and informal chats that become the backbone of the learning process. Part of our task is to demonstrate successfully the value of collaboration as a natural part of professional activity and growth. As associate teachers, we work to assist student teachers in developing a personal philosophy of teaching that will reflect the experiences they have had in our classrooms.

Conclusion—Learning to Teach/Teaching to Learn

The continuum of the learning circle is part of our personal philosophy of lifelong learning. As students, we entered the Faculty of Education with a very narrow perspective, assuming that the only source of learning would come from our professors and textbooks. How wrong we were! You can study or read books, but in the final analysis it is the doing and the sharing with others that allow for deeper learning to take place. From the very first day at the Faculty when we began to share our stories of who we were, our backgrounds and histories, it was apparent that many of us had brought a rich diversity of life experience to teaching. This exchange of stories became the first step of our journey towards learning.

The Learning Circle:
from Student Teacher to Associate Teacher

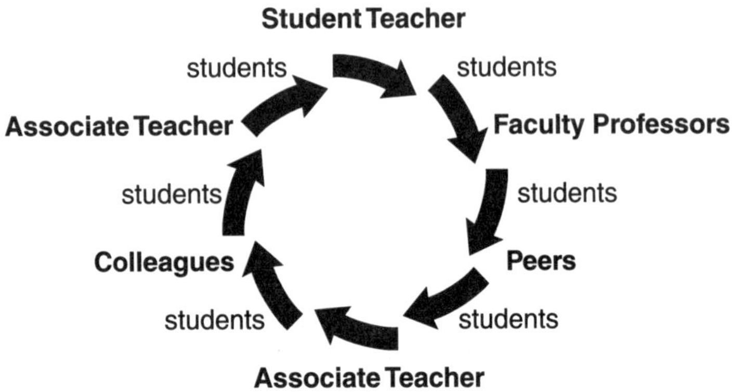

The diagram shows the path that we have travelled from being a student teacher at the Faculty of Education, to becoming an associate teacher. Each step along the way has been influenced by the students in our classrooms, professors and peers at the Faculty, the associate teachers with whom we worked during our practicum, and later, after graduation, the colleagues on staff. Knowing that the circle of learning is not a closed one, we continued to develop professionally by creating new partnerships with other educational stakeholders. These interactions included professional workshops, preservice and inservice education, action research in the classroom, and writing. Through these collaborative activities, we have realised that this cyclical process of partnership was the key component to the quality of our learning. It was a natural progression, then, to become an associate teacher, where the value of the relationship between associate and student relies upon the reciprocity of a partnership.

As we reflect upon our progress of developing associate teachers over the past few years, we know that we have progressed to a third kind of learning: our experience has transformed us into different kinds of teachers so that who we were in the beginning of our journey is not who we are now. The knowledge we have gained along the way continues to grow and expand as we continue our quest to assist student teachers inside our classrooms.

Ian Hundey

The FEUT-Aga Khan University Partnership

Ian Hundey has taught for almost thirty years, with teaching experience in four countries at the elementary, secondary, and university levels. At FEUT since 1988, he has taught in the elementary, secondary, and foundations departments, as well as in continuing education. Currently, he coordinates the two-year intermediate/senior pilot project and FEUT's program contributions to the FEUT-Aga Khan University project.

Introduction

Over the years, many FEUT professors have contributed to international educational initiatives. In recent years, the diversity of these initiatives is reflected in activities such as an English education project at the University of the West Indies, a professional development institute for department of education officials from Thailand, and consultations with South African teachers college staff. Since 1992, the scope of FEUT's international links has been greatly widened and enriched by the activities of the International Institute for Global Education with its initiatives in the Middle East, North Africa, Eastern Europe, and elsewhere. In addition to these institutional initiatives, many FEUT professors have developed individual connections at the international level through participation in conferences, visits to foreign universities, consultations in Toronto with visiting professors, and through electronic conferring with overseas colleagues.

One of FEUT's most ambitious undertakings in the international sphere has been its partnership project with the Aga Khan University (AKU) in Karachi, Pakistan, which began in 1992-93. This tripartite partnership involving FEUT, the Aga Khan University, and the Oxford University Department for Educational Studies (OUDES) is funded by the Canadian International Development Agency, the Commission of the European Community, the United Nations Development Project, and the Aga Khan Foundation (AKF). The focus on the partnership has been to promote teacher development and school improvement in Karachi specifically, and in Pakistan generally, through helping first to create, and then to support, the work of the Institute for Educational Development (IED) at the Aga Khan University. This chapter provides an overview of FEUT's involvement in this international initiative.

Background to FEUT's Involvement in the Institute for Educational Development Project

The Aga Khan Foundation was established in 1967 by His Highness Prince Karim Aga Khan, to support social, economic, and educational projects in the developing world. In the 1980s, the Aga Khan agencies were already engaged in school improvement projects and field-based teacher development initiatives in Pakistan, when it decided to set up a task force to determine how these various teacher education initiatives might be "better articulated and more purposely related to the development of education in Pakistan as a whole" (Aga Khan Foundation/Aga Khan University, 1990).

This task force, appointed in early 1989, was composed of representatives from the Aga Khan Foundation, the Aga Khan Educational Services (AKES), the Aga Khan University, and several international educational consultants. The context in which this task force worked was a complex one. At the Aga Khan University level, the framework for recommendations was clearly set by the 1983 report prepared by Harvard University's president for the university's board of trustees, which strongly encouraged the new institution (Aga Khan University had received its charter earlier in 1983) to concentrate first on building excellence in its health sciences programs, and recommended against forays into teacher training, especially preservice teacher education. This report went on to say that if educational programs were developed in the future they should be limited to in-service teacher education and the development of educational research, policy, and curricula (Ahmad Ali, 1995).

The Pakistani context in 1989 was one of a heightened crisis in education. The World Bank had just issued a gloomy report that concluded that Pakistan suffered from some of the "most acute educational problems anywhere in the developing world." The report continued: "Rural-urban and male-female imbalances are striking. Over 70% of the population is illiterate, with female literacy rates in the rural areas averaging only 4%" (The World Bank, 1988). At the same time, grass roots educational projects run by Aga Khan Educational Services and other groups that were tackling these problems with some success faced another sort of difficulty. A new generation of dedicated Pakistani educators was being developed, but "there was nowhere in Pakistan for them to advance their own skills and gain worthwhile qualifications and status which goes with them" (Aga Khan Foundation/Aga Khan University, 1990).

The international context was determined in part by the expertise and experience of the consultants on the task force. North American and British models of teacher education, with an emphasis on school-based teacher development, mentoring (the Oxford Internship program), and on clinical teachers working with visiting teachers (the Schenley model in Pittsburgh secondary schools) strongly influenced the final report.

The task force report in late 1989 recommended:

1. That the main focus in teacher education be on inservice training for practising teachers through short courses.
2. That the faculty or master trainers who would deliver these courses should themselves be practicing teachers who would receive further intensive preparation over an eighteen-month course delivered by senior faculty. Subsequently the bulk of the teaching in the short courses would be conducted by these master trainers, while the senior faculty would be involved in research.
3. That the affiliation with a university (Aga Khan University) was necessary to support the intellectual rigour of instruction and research and to confer appropriate status on faculty and participating teachers. Rather than a traditional faculty of education, however, the preferred designation was the Institute for Educational Development, which would operate in a professional development centre (PDC) attached to a Karachi school. Additional professional development centres could be "licensed" by the Institute for Educational Development elsewhere in Pakistan or in other countries.
4. That affiliation be sought with one or more overseas universities that had an established international reputation in the recommended mode of training and research (Ahmad Ali, 1995).

FEUT's Early Involvement

Aga Khan University accepted the task force report with few modifications and charged the Aga Khan Foundation to raise the necessary U.S. $12.5 million dollars as start-up funds to finance the Institute for Educational Development (IED) for six years. These funds were secured through the funding agencies referred to previously. Meanwhile, members of the task force visited prospective participating universities in early 1991, looking for institutions with international reputations in teacher education that would be in a position "to validate IED's training programs and research, and supplement the skills of the IED faculty in designing and delivering a variety of teacher education programs" (Ahmad Ali, 1995).

I was one of several FEUT staff who went into a meeting with this visiting team out of curiosity, but who came out with an appetite whetted for involvement in the Institute for Educational Development project. The task force considered the Oxford University Department of Educational Studies, the Faculty of Education at Michigan State University, and FEUT as partner institutions. The final selection resulted in a partnership among the Institute for Educational Development, FEUT, and the Oxford University Department of Educational Studies.

As a participating university, FEUT agreed to contribute 200 days per year of teaching and administrative time to the project over three years beginning in 1993-94. In the meantime, Associate Dean Dennis Thiessen began to establish the groundwork for FEUT's involvement by undertaking a preliminary visit to Pakistan in the fall of 1992, and by serving on a working group composed of task force members, other consultants, and potential staff for the Institute for Educational Development. This group held a critical meeting in Karachi in April of 1993, where initial plans were drawn up for an eighteen-month M.Ed. to prepare the first group of master teachers (previously called master trainers). This M.Ed. was designed both to improve the candidates' instructional practices in four core subject areas (English, math, science, and social studies) and also to develop their teacher educator skills. This dual focus would allow the graduates to work with a variety of subject teachers in their home schools and to contribute to short courses for visiting teachers at the Institute for Educational Development. Dennis Thiessen also was appointed as FEUT's representative on the Academic Advisory Council (AAC), which was set up to oversee the work of the Institute for Educational Development.

Besides his general role as AAC member, he was appointed to two AAC committees—the Research Committee, (which he chaired) and the Appointments Committee.

While Associate Dean Thiessen undertook general administration of the project and related Academic Advisory Council work, I, from the secondary department, began to work as informal coordinator of FEUT's program contribution to the Institute for Educational Development. The first step in this coordination involved consulting with Oxford's program coordinator, especially in regard to the draft proposal for the Institute for Educational Development's M.Ed. program which had been developed at the April 1993 meeting of the task force/working group. The next step involved my visiting Karachi in late August-early September 1993 to work with Terry Allsop, the Oxford coordinator, the newly appointed director of the Institute for Educational Development, Kazim Bacchus, and Associate Director Sadru Pardhan, to refine plans for the M.Ed. program that was to start in January 1994. These meetings resulted in the production of a detailed outline for the first six months of the program, a rough outline for the following academic year, and a schedule for contributions to be made by visiting faculty from the participating universities.

FEUT Instruction in the M. Ed. Program

Beginning in January 1994, FEUT professors began to travel to the Institute for Educational Development in Karachi for periods of two to four weeks to teach in the M.Ed. program and, in the case of the program coordinator, to finalize plans for the 1994-95 component of the program. When they arrived they found an interesting mix of M.Ed. course participants (CPs) drawn mostly from Karachi, with two from the northern areas of Pakistan, one from the provincial city of Peshawar, and four international students—one from Bangladesh, two from East Africa, and one from Tajikistan. Of the twenty-two course participants, thirteen were females, an unusually high number for an advanced degree course in education in Pakistan. Course participants were drawn from government schools, Aga Khan Educational Services schools, and private schools, and ranged in age from twenty-two to forty-seven years. (Bacchus, 1994). All had gone through a rigorous application and screening process that included interviews and observation of their teaching, before being selected.

I was the first FEUT instructor to teach in Karachi, working with the program coordinator from the Oxford University Department of Educational Studies for most of the month of January 1994 in the introductory module of the course. The goal of this module was to build understandings about reflective practice and collaborative learning, which would serve as a scaffold for later course activities.

The next FEUT professors to teach in Karachi were Barrie Bennett and Linda Cameron, who contributed to the English language module in the period March to May 1994. Barrie Bennett concentrated on cooperative learning, which was well received by the course participants, despite their tradition of teacher-centred instruction. Linda Cameron provided a range of student-centred strategies for teaching English. Their efforts were followed by Mark Evans and me, who taught in the social studies component in May and June. Besides developing a range of instructional strategies for social studies, we highlighted the teaching of thinking skills and developed a variety of assessment procedures.

Further contributions were made in March 1995 when Steve Anderson taught in a module on effecting educational change. Mark Evans returned in May 1995 to lead a component on effective management of school-based professional development.

During nine weeks in October to December of 1994, as part of their M.Ed. program requirement, course participants completed an overseas residency with roughly half the group travelling to Oxford and the other half to Toronto. A description of their program follows:

> In the nine-week overseas experience at the Faculty of Education University of Toronto, the Institute for Educational Development course participants (CPs) took part in both university-based and field-based activities. Orientation and introductory activities (to the university, to Ontario schools, and to teacher development) in the first and second week were undertaken both at the university and in off-campus sites in central Toronto schools. In the third and fourth weeks, the course participants experienced a

range of activities in the Durham Board of Education—attending formal sessions on staff development and school improvement, visiting schools, observing classes, meeting with teachers and administrators, and interacting with students. In week five, the candidates synthesized what they had learned in their field activities and began to focus more fully on their research papers. Activities in weeks six and seven explored staff development initiatives and programs, with workshops at FEUT and site-visits to education centres in two other school boards, Peel and Scarborough. As well, in this two-week period, course participants took part in methodology sessions dealing with ESL, language arts, and multiple intelligences. Sessions in week eight concentrated on mentoring and coaching and on equity issues. Activities in the final week of the residency were based at the university, and focused on synthesis of the whole experience and on report preparation.

Besides visits to schools and education centres over the course of the program, the candidates also visited the Art Gallery of Ontario, the McMichael Gallery, the Royal Ontario Museum, and the Ontario Science Centre to learn about education programs offered at each site.

As well, it should be noted that course participants made good use of the opportunities for research (at FEUT and OISE libraries) and consultation with faculty members throughout the program.

(Hundey, 1995)

What the description above does not highlight fully is the wide involvement of FEUT staff in the course participants' program in Toronto. Altogether, fifteen FEUT professors and a number of library support staff provided the visiting course participants with instruction, consultation, and other support that totalled more than eighty days of staff time. The impact of this overseas experience on the course participants was significant. Those faculty members who read and responded to course participants' journals would agree that the residency was a transformational experience for many of the visitors. Those Faculty members who visited Karachi following the residency would propose that it provided the course participants with the confidence and vision not only to complete their studies, but also to contribute to subsequent teacher education courses at the Institute for Educational Development. What was also clear in their journals and in their program evaluations was how much the Institute for Educational Development students appreciated the support provided by the FEUT staff during the residency. As one course participant wrote: "... we thank all the faculty members who worked with us... . They gave us a great time and learning facilities. They are all really true facilitators (true teachers)."

Continuing Program Involvement

The completion of the M.Ed. program in the summer of 1995 did not bring an end to FEUT's involvement in the Institute for Educational Development programs. I had already completed some planning work overseas in the spring of 1995 for the first of the proposed short courses for visiting teachers. In August and September 1995, Mark Evans and Antoinette Gagné visited the Institute for Educational Development and contributed further to the planning of these eight-week visiting teacher (VT) courses that started in October. In November, Antoinette Gagné returned to help with the English visiting teacher course, and Mark Evans and I taught in the social studies course and attended meetings in Karachi.

FEUT staff has also taken an active role in supporting the Institute for Educational Development's planning of a second M.Ed. program to start in the fall of 1996. Professors Evans, Gagné, and I have already responded to the program outline produced by the Institute for Educational Development, and have taken part in planning meetings with Institute for Educational Development staff in Karachi and Toronto in the period March to April 1996. At the time of writing, tentative plans have been made for FEUT professors Anderson, Evans, Gagné, and me to teach in various components of the M.Ed. in 1996-97 or 1997-98. It must be noted that far more of the teaching responsibility in the 1996-97 M.Ed.

will be carried by the Institute for Educational Development staff, including some of the graduates from the first M.Ed. class. This transfer of responsibility is entirely proper and very welcome, since the overall intent of the project has always been to encourage the development of a true partnership among equal participants.

Other Project Activities

Most of FEUT's activities in the Institute for Educational Development project have centred on program development and delivery. The research agenda has not been ignored, however. Steve Anderson is completing a preliminary study of the organizational culture of schools based on a sample of government and private community schools in Karachi. He and his co-researcher, Iffat Farah of the Institute for Educational Development, intend that the product of the study will be a series of case studies to be used in future programs. Additional research proposals are being developed by several staff members who were involved in the first M.Ed. and visiting-teacher programs.

FEUT professors are beginning to take part in professional conferences linked to the Institute for Educational Development initiative. Dean Michael Fullan gave a keynote address in April 1996 in Karachi at the Institute for Educational Development's conference "Innovative Approaches to Teacher Education." Mark Evans chaired a forum session at the same conference. In the same month at the American Educational Research Association in New York, Dennis Thiessen presented a paper jointly with Mehrunnisa Ahmad Ali from the Institute for Educational Development on international collaboration within the project. In June, at the Canadian Society for the Study of Education conference at Brock University, professors Evans, Gagné, and I will join colleagues from Oxford and the Institute for Educational Development in a round-table presentation on the partnership project to date.

Dennis Thiessen has been appointed to the second Aga Khan University task force on education to determine future directions for the Institute for Educational Development. As well, he is serving as FEUT's representative on the Partner University Forum that came to replace the Academy Advisory Committee as the partnership evolved towards a forum of equals.

Mark Evans and I are developing a proposal to present to the new task force to develop, along with Institute for Educational Development faculty, social studies curriculum and assessment materials reflective of the M.Ed. instructional focus. These materials would be used both in the visiting teacher courses and in schools participating in the Institute for Educational Development programs.

Wider Involvement

There have been several interesting spinoffs from the original Institute for Educational Development project to which FEUT staff have contributed. In 1994, Steve Anderson undertook for the Aga Khan Foundation a formal evaluation of the school improvement program of Aga Khan Mzizma Secondary School in Dar Es Salaam. In 1995, I travelled to the northern areas of Pakistan as part of a task force subcommittee to investigate possibilities for establishing a second professional development centre. At the time of writing, preliminary steps have been taken towards the establishment of this professional development centre in Gilgit, under Aga Khan Educational Services auspices, with the Institute for Educational Development and partner universities providing planning and teaching support. In early 1996, Steve Anderson visited Kenya, Tanzania, and Uganda as part of an initiative developed with Dennis Thiessen for Aga Khan Foundation Canada. Following his visit, Steve Anderson wrote a discussion paper and proposal for the professional development of teachers in East Africa. With its focus on "collaborative professional development of groups of teachers working in specific school settings" and on "access for credible sources of professional expertise and assistance for targetted focuses of professional development" (Anderson, 1996), this report offers clear possibilities for participation by FEUT staff in the future.

Challenges and Responses

FEUT staff contributing to the Institute for Educational Development project have faced a number of challenges. For many, it was a new and demanding experience to work in temperatures of up to 40 degrees Celsius at times of the year when power outages rendered air conditioners useless. For many, too, there were challenges in facing the relentless poverty, violence, and overcrowding in a city which the Institute for Educational Development admits is "a difficult city to live in, even by Pakistani standards" (Ahmad Ali, 1995). Other challenges arose in working with Institute for Educational Development students whose first language was Urdu or other vernacular languages, and whose work culture was based on hierarchical structures and a strict transmission form of teaching. Finally, there have been the challenges associated with making a long-distance partnership work, especially when two partners represent the traditions of the western developed world and the third partner represents the traditions of the southeast Asian developing world.

The physical challenges of Karachi have been mitigated by a combination of good humour, shared information among Toronto travellers to the city, and the care demonstrated by Institute for Educational Development staff for the well-being of FEUT visitors. Challenges associated with language have been partially overcome by modifications in style and content of FEUT program contributions, and the occasional use of translation services, but more fully by the incredible patience, commitment, and determination of the Institute for Educational Development students. Challenges associated with the partnership have been addressed openly and have resulted in structural change (e.g., the transition from an Academic Advisory Council to a Partners University Forum). On the other hand, partnership challenges inevitably will remain as part of the dynamic tension of this international venture.

Personal Reflections

Many of the FEUT contributors have fond memories of their experience and were profoundly affected by contact with visiting course participants or by their experiences in Karachi. Several of those who have participated in FEUT-IED partnership activities were asked to provide for this chapter personal perspectives on their involvement. Barrie Bennett, who worked with the course participants in both Karachi and Toronto, provided these comments:

> I had the opportunity to rethink in terms of both altering and confirming what it means to be a teacher. Issues such as class size, facilities, and resources were redefined in terms of importance. The critical importance of education to a society was re-established.

> I can still remember one week after I had returned, a teacher in Ontario made a statement related to class size, "But what are you supposed to do when you have thirty-four students?" I smiled and said, "You are asking the wrong person. Last month I watched and taught in classrooms of sixty and seventy students—no overhead, no textbooks, no video, etc." I don't complain any longer.

Antoinette Gagné who taught the course participants in Toronto and contributed to the planning and delivery of the English visiting teacher course in Karachi wrote:

> I was pleased to find out that the teachers giving and taking the course enjoyed having fun while working as much as I did. They took their work seriously while sharing in the belief that teaching and learning occur much more effectively when the teacher and the learners enjoy what they are doing... . I realized that many of the assumptions that I had about the teaching/learning environment in the average class in Canada did not hold true in Pakistan. These assumptions directly affected the way I functioned as a teacher educator. For example, in most Canadian classrooms it is safe to assume that teachers and students have access to a variety of materials ranging from textbooks to pencils and papers. In many Pakistani schools, this is not the case. I therefore had to reconceptualize what it is possible to do in a language classroom with very few resources and with groups two to three times larger than average groups of students in Canada. This reconceptualization was healthy because it led me to reflect on what is fundamental to language teaching and learning in the classroom setting.

Mark Evans, who has worked extensively with the Institute for Educational Development students and faculty over the last two years, provided these insights:

> This experience has challenged my notions of teaching and learning on a variety of fronts. The opportunity to work in an environment that is significantly different from our own, both culturally and contextually, has moved me to reconsider my own notions of diversity and contextual expectations that we sometimes take for granted.
>
> On the one hand, I've been surprised by common concerns voiced that exist between Canadian and Pakistani educators... issues around equity, literacy, technology, quality of teaching and school improvement work. On the other hand, the significant inequities that exist have also become quite evident to me. I admire the will and resilience of the teachers in the IED programs and their overriding sense of optimism that they bring to their work. All in all, it has reinforced my feelings about the value of developing a broader, more global perspective in terms of reconceptualizing our work as educators in the Canadian context and around the world.

Annette Yeager, who in the fall of 1994 welcomed the Institute for Educational Development visitors to her classroom, and acted as a mentor to one of the course participants, wrote:

> The visit of the teachers from Pakistan to my Family Studies Education class was very memorable. In that class, we were addressing the topic of "the educator's response to change." As part of the class, we examined several metaphors. The activity was highly interactive and the discussion was lively. Voices from Ontario and Pakistan blended equally and with ease. Experiences described and ideas shared were met with common recognition. We were reminded that the issues and challenges educators face are not separated by geographical boundaries! In education as in most aspects of life, there is more that connects humankind than divides it.

As program coordinator for the project, I offer these final comments. Although I have gained immensely from my experiences in the partnership and my friendships with the participants, I frequently find myself wondering about one central question: "How much practical value does our western approach to education provide for the teachers we work with at IED?" Despite the obvious receptiveness of the course participants and visiting teachers to my sessions, I return again and again to this question. In preparing this overview of the FEUT-IED project, three reassurances regarding this question have stood out for me.

First, a review of the literature on development education confirmed my beliefs that the best educational ideas from the west are worth sharing even when they are radical: "radical reform is what is needed... . Any program that really serves the needs of the poor must challenge the sacred tenets of the school" (Bennett, 1993).

Second, I found reassurance by rereading the feedback provided by course participants regarding the M.Ed. program. The two East African students provided the following comment on the value of the methodology that was presented to them. "We find ourselves like the selected few who have been given all the food from a starving village so that we may have strength to go to a distant village to bring supplies to our colleagues whom we have left behind" (Bacchus, 1994).

Finally, I found inspiration in the words of the IED's valedictorian at the M.Ed. graduation ceremony in November 1995: "...thanks to all these visionaries who keep in a small but significant handful of Pakistanis, a light burning. Yes we are but a drop, but it is many drops that form a cloud, that leads to a thunderstorm. ...Thank you for giving us the right amount of push to develop both self-confidence and self-knowledge" (Mehta, 1995).

In the years ahead, more FEUT professors may find satisfaction in keeping the "light burning" and in providing the "right amount of push" in the FEUT-Institute for Educational Development partnership.

Part V

A Century of Images

From the formality of pre-World War I,
to the contemporary activities of 1996,
almost a century of photographs tells the story of
the Faculty of Education.

The next phase of teacher education will celebrate a
new centre—
the Ontario Institute for Studies in Education
University of Toronto.

The Faculty in Photography 1906–1996

Gerald A. Whyte studied at the universities of Carleton, Syracuse, and Princeton before becoming a history teacher in Ottawa and Peterborough. He joined the staff of the Faculty of Education in 1968, served as assistant and associate registrar in the Faculty, and sat on the admissions and awards committees throughout his career.

1 *Members of the Class of 1915*

2 *Executive Committee of the Literary Society, 1907–08*

3 *The First Graduating Class, 1907–08*

1.

2.

3.

The 1922 Picnic to Niagara Falls

Women's Physical Education Class, 1932

A Dramatic Production of
She Stoops to Conquer
1915

Deans of the Faculty of Education

J.G. Althouse
1934–1944

A.C. Lewis
1944–1958

The First Dean
W. Pakenham
1907–1934

B.C. Diltz
1958–1963

D.F. Dadson
1963–1973

H.O. Barrett
1974

J.C. Ricker
1975–1981

The Last Dean
M.G. Fullan
1988–1996

M.A. Millar
1987–1988

J.W. MacDonald
1981–1987

Snapshots from the 1970s and 1980s

VARSITY
BLUES

Snapshots from the 1990s

References

Aga Khan Foundation/Aga Khan University. *Project Overview: Aga Khan Institute for Educational Development (IED)*, Karachi, 1990.

Ahmad Ali, Mehrunnisa, Ghzala Aslam & Murphy, Kelly. IDRC Report #1, 1995.

Allard, H., & Marshall, J. Miss Nelson is Missing! Boston: Houghton Mifflin, 1977.

Anderson, S.E. *Professional Development for Teachers in East Africa: A Discussion Paper and Proposal*, 1996.

Andrews, I.P., Holborn, P. & Wideen, M. Becoming a Teacher. Toronto: Kagan and Woo, 1988.

Bacchus, K. Institute for Educational Development. Progress Report, November 1993 to March 1994. Karachi, 1994.

Bennett, B. The Effectiveness of Staff Development Training Practices: A Meta-analysis. Doctoral Dissertation, University of Oregon, 1987.

Bennett, N. *How Can Schooling Help Improve the Lives of the Poorest? The Need for Radical Reform*, in Henry M. Levin & Marlaine E. Lockheed (eds.), Effective Schools in Developing Countries. London: The Falmer Press, 1993.

Birch, D.R., Lanier, J.E. & Mortimore, P. Report of the Provostial Commission on a Design for an Integrated Institution in Education. University of Toronto, June, 1994, pp.4-5.

Blackwell, R. Recurring Patterns: The History of the Ontario Society for Education through Art. Toronto: Private publication, 1988.

Blackwell, R. *The Visual Arts in General Education in Ontario: Whither and Especially Whence*. The Percy H. Tacon Memorial Lecture, 1988. Journal of the Ontario Society for Education through Art, 1989, 18, pp.17-30.

Blocker, L.S., & Swetnam, L. *The Selection and Evaluation of Cooperating Teachers: A Status Report*, in Teacher Education, V. 30 #3, Winter, 1995.

Bolton, Gavin. Towards a Theory of Drama in Education. London: Longman, 1979, p.61.

Booth, D., & Lundy, C.J. Improvisation: Learning Through Drama. Toronto: Harcourt Brace, 1985.

Booth, D., & Thornley-Hall, C. (eds.). The Talk Curriculum. Markham: Pembroke Publishers, 1991.

Booth, D., & Thornley-Hall, C. (eds.). Classroom Talk. Markham: Pembroke Publishers, 1991.

Booth, D. Story Drama: Reading, Writing, and Roleplaying Across the Curriculum. Markham: Pembroke Publishers, 1994.

Brook, P. The Empty Space. London: Penguin, 1968.

Brookhart, S., & Loadman, W. *School-University Collaboration Across Cultures*. Teaching Education, 4(2), 1992, pp.53-68.

Brookhart, S., & Freeman, D.J. *Characteristics of Entering Teacher Candidates*, in Review of Educational Research, Spring, Vol. 62, No. 1, 1992, pp.37-60.

Brown, A., & Campione, J. *Guided Discovery in a Community of Learners*, in K. McGilly (ed.), Classroom Lessons: Integrating Cognitive Theory and Classroom Practice. Cambridge, MA: MIT Press/Bradford Books, 1994, pp.108-126.

Buntin, E. Our Teacher's Having a Baby. New York: Clarion, 1992
Calmenson, S. The Principal's New Clothes. New York: Scholastic, 1989.
Carnegie Forum on Education and the Economy. A Nation Prepared: Teachers for the 21st Century. New York, 1986.
Clandinin, D.J., Davies, A., Hogan, P. & Kennard, B. (eds.). Learning to Teach, Teaching to Learn: Stories of Collaboration in Teacher Education. New York: Teachers College Press, 1993.
Clark, R. Art Education: a Canadian Perspective. Toronto: Ontario S.E.A., 1994.
Cleary, B. Dear Mr. Henshaw. New York: Morrow, 1984.
Coles, R. The Call of Stories. Boston: Houghton Mifflin, 1989.
Connor, R. Glengarry School Days. Toronto: McClelland & Stewart, 1975.
Cooley, N., & Hitch, E. *The Role of Dynamic Models in Teacher Education,* in Action in Teacher Education, Vol. 15, No. 1, 1993.
Courtney, R. et al. Teacher Education in the Arts. Sharon: Bison Books, 1985.
Courtney, R. The Dramatic Curriculum. New York: Drama Book Specialists, 1980.
Crampton, E. Drama Canada: Trends in Drama in Education During the Past 25 Years. Toronto: Guidance Centre, University of Toronto, 1972.
Cuban, L. A Fundamental Puzzle of School Reform. Phi Delta Kappan, 70(5), 1988, pp.341-44.
Daley, M. Gyn Ecology, The Metaethics of Radical Feminism. Boston: Beacon Press, 1978.
Danzinger, P. The Cat Ate My Gym Suit. New York: Dell, 1974.
Diamond, C.T.P. Teacher Education as Transformation: A Psychological Perspective. Milton Keynes: Open University Press, 1991.
Diamond, C.T.P., & Dixon, B. In Our Own Words: Teacher Stories. Forthcoming.
Drummond, M.J. Learning to See: Assessment through Observation. Markham: Pembroke Publishers, 1994.
Elijah, R. *Professional Lives; Institutional Contexts: Coherence and Contradictions*. Teacher Education Quarterly, Forthcoming.
Ellis, N.E. *Collegiality from the Teacher's Perspective: Social Context for Professional Development*. Action in Teacher Education, Vol. 15, No. 1, 1992-3.
Emerson, J. *Some New Dimensions in the Role of the Art Teacher*. Unpublished Seminar, College of Education, University of Toronto, 1971.
Emerson, J. *The Tangled Web of Art Education in Ontario,* in Art Magazine, 1974, pp.15, 37.
Emerson, J. *Art Education in Ontario: Prospects for the 80s,* in R.N. MacGregor (ed.), Canadian Art Education in the 80s: An Appraisal and Forecast. Edmonton: The Canadian Society for Education through Art, 1980.
Emerson, J. *The Case for Canadian Content,* in R.N. MacGregor (ed.), Readings in Canadian Art Education. Vancouver, B.C. Western Education Development Group, Faculty of Education, University of British Columbia, 1984, pp.167-172.
Emerson, J. *Both Sides Now: Some Reflections on the Design and Delivery of Art Education in Ontario.* The 4th Annual Western Lecture in Art Education. Journal of the O.S.E.A., 23, 1994, pp.15-22.

Erskine-Cullen, E., & Kilcher, A. The Impact of the Mini-Projects on Collaboration. Paper presented at the Canadian Society for Studies in Education Annual Conference, Charlottetown, 1992.
Erskine-Cullen, E., & Sinclair, A.M. Preparing Teachers for Urban Schools: A View from the Field. Paper presented at the Canadian Society for Studies in Education Annual Conference, Montreal, Ontario, 1995.
Faculty of Education. Student Handbook. University of Toronto, 1995.
Faculty of Education. "Choices" (Option) Handbook. University of Toronto, 1995.
Faculty of Education. Annual Report, 1989-1990. Faculty of Education, University of Toronto, 1990.
Faculty of Education, B.Ed. Restructuring Committee Report. Faculty of Education, University of Toronto, 1992.
Faculty of Education, University of Toronto. PJI: Scarborough: Program Handbook, 1994-95. Available upon request from the Elementary Education Department, 1994.
Faculty of Education, University of Toronto. Proposal for a Pilot Project for a Two-year Preservice Teacher Education Program. Faculty of Education, University of Toronto, March 1995.
Fitzhugh, L. Harriet the Spy. New York: Harper & Row, 1964.
Fullan, M. The Role of Leadership in Transforming Colleges of Education, in D. Thiessen (ed.), *The Role of the Dean in Colleges of Education*. Columbus, OH: Urban Network for Improving Teacher Education (UNITE), 1996.
Fullan, M., & Hargreaves, A. What's Worth Fighting For in Your School? Toronto, Ontario: Ontario Public School Teachers' Federation, 1991.
Fullan, M.G., with Stiegelbauer, Suzanne. The New Meaning of Educational Change. Toronto: OISE Press, 1991.
Fullan, M. *The Best Faculty of Education in the Country: A Fable*. Paper presented to the Strategic Planning Committee, University of Toronto, 1991.
Fullan, M. *Leadership for Change*, in K. Leithwood (ed.) International Handbook of Educational Leadership. Kluwer Press, 1995.
Fullan, M., & Miles, M. B. *Getting Reform Right: What Works and What Doesn't*, in Phi Delta Kappan, 73 (10), 1992.
Fullan, M., Connelly, M. & Watson, N. *Teacher Education in Ontario: Current Practice and Options for the Future.* Toronto: Ministry of Education, 1989.
Fullan, M., & Connelly, M. *Linking Classroom and School Improvement*, in Educational Leadership, May 1990, pp. 13-19.
Fuller, F.F., & Brown, O.H. *Becoming a Teacher.* in K. Ryan and K.J. Rhage (eds.), Teacher Education, Part II. The Seventy-fourth Yearbook of the National Society for the Study of Education, 1975.
Goodlad, J.I. A Place Called School. New York: McGraw-Hill, 1984.
Goodlad, J.I. *School-University Partnerships: Rationale and Concepts*, in J.I. Goodlad & Sirotnik, K.A. School-University Partnerships in Action: Concepts, Cases, Concerns. New York: Teachers College Press, 1988.
Goodlad, J.I. Teachers for Our Nation's Schools. San Francisco: Jossey Bass, 1990.
Goodlad, J.I., Soder, R. & Sirotnik, K.A. *Society, Schooling, Teaching and Preparing to Teach*, in The Moral Dimensions of Teaching, San Francisco: Jossey Bass, 1990, pp.296-327.

Goodlad, J., & Soder, R. School-University Partnerships: An Appraisal of an Idea (Occasional Paper No. 15). Seattle: University of Washington, Institute for the Study of Educational Policy, 1992.

Goodlad, J. Educational Renewal. San Francisco: Jossey-Bass, 1994.

Government of Ontario. For the Love of Learning: Report of the Royal Commission on Learning. Toronto: Government of Ontario, 1994.

Gray, B. Collaborating: Finding Common Ground for Multiparty Problems. San Francisco: Jossey-Bass, 1989.

Griffin, G. *Why Use Research in Preservice Teacher Education: A Proposal,* in Journal of Teacher Education, Vol. 35. No. 4, 1993.

Grotowski, J. Towards a Poor Theatre. New York: Simon & Shuster, 1968.

Hadaway, N. & Reinhartz, J. *Circumventing the Funding Issues in Induction,* in Action in Teacher Education, Vol. 14, No. 4, 1992-3.

Hall, G. E., & Hord, S. Facilitating Change. Albany: State Unversity of New York Press, 1987.

Hamilton, V. The Planet of Junior Brown. New York: MacMillan, 1971.

Harman, K. M. *Using Culture to Understand Conflict within a University: Professional versus Academic Values in University Professional Schools in Australia.* Paper presented at the American Educational Research Association Annual Meeting, San Francisco, April, 1989.

Harris, R. C., & Harris, M. F. *Partner Schools: Places to Solve Teacher Education Problems,* in Action in Teacher Education, Vol. 14, No. 4, 1992-93.

Hennessy, C.A., & Booth, D.W. Project in Literacy Attainment: A Partnership: Toronto. Paper presented at CSSE in Calgary, Alberta, 1994.

Hennessy, C.A., & Christy, A. The Child, the Student Teacher and the Coach: Quality Development in a Partnership. Toronto. Paper presented at CSSE in Montreal, Quebec, 1995.

Holmes Group. Tomorrow's Schools: Principles for the Design of Professional Development Schools. East Lansing: Holmes Group, 1990.

Hopkins, W.S. *Clinical Supervision: A Neo-Progressive Approach,* in Teacher Education, V. 30 #3, Winter, 1995.

Howe, J. The Day the Teacher Went Bananas. New York: Viking Kestrel, 1984.

Howey, K.R. The Network of Fifteen. Columbus: Ohio State University, unpublished proposal, 1992.

Hundey, I. Institute for Educational Development, Aga Khan University: FEUT Residency, October 11 to December 10, 1994, 1995.

Jackson, P.W. *Helping Teachers Develop,* in A. Hargreaves & M.G. Fullan (eds.), Understanding Teacher Development. New York: Teachers College Press, 1992.

Johnson, E., & O'Neill, C. Dorothy Heathcote: Collected Writings on Education and Drama. London, UK: Hutchinson & Co., 1984.

Johnston, M. Educators for Collaborative Change. Working Set of Categories. Columbus: Ohio State University, 1995.

Kagan, D. *Implications of Research on Teacher Belief,* in Educational Psychologist, 27 (1), 1992.

Kerr, M.E. Is That You, Miss Blue?. New York: Dell, 1975.

Kilcher, A. Best Practices of Program Options. Toronto: Faculty of Education. Unpublished Manuscript.

Kilcher, A. Professional Development at FEUT: Current Practices, Suggestions, Issues, and Options. Halifax: Paideia Consulting, 1994.

Kilcher, A. Best Practices: Options and Possibilities for Preparing New Teachers. Halifax: Paideia Consulting & FEUT, 1994.

Knowles, J.G., Cole A.L. & Presswood, C.S. Through Preservice Teachers' Eyes: Exploring Field Experiences Through Narrative and Inquiry. Toronto: Maxwell MacMillan, 1994.

Kohn, A. Grading: The Issue is Not How But Why. Ontario Society for Studies in Art, 1995.

Kuzmich, N. *Pilot Project: An Affective Creative Approach to Music Learning,* in Recorder, 15 (2), 1972.

Kuzmich, N. *A More Creative Approach to Teaching Music,* in Reporting Classroom Research, 3 (2), 1974.

Kuzmich, N. *Problem-solving in music learning,* in Recorder, 17 (2), 1975.

Kuzmich, N. *Research, Problem-Solving and Music Education,* in British Journal of Music Education, 4 (3), 1975.

Kuzmich, N. *Canada and China: a Comparison,* in Canadian Music Educator, 37 (1), 1995.

Laing, R.D. Knots. Harmondsworth, England: Penguin Books Ltd., 1971.

Learning Consortium, Annual Report, 1995.

Lee, H. To Kill a Mockingbird. New York: J.B. Lippincott, 1960.

Levine, M. (ed.). Professional Practice Schools: Linking Teacher Education and School Reform. New York: Teachers College Press, 1992.

Little, J. Listen for the Singing. Toronto: Clark Irwin, 1977.

Little, J.W. *The Mentor Phenomenon,* in C. Cazden (ed.), Review of Research in Education. Washington, DC: American Educational Research Association, 1990.

Loucks-Horsley, S. Topics for Change Workshop, Andover: The Network: Unpublished Outline, 1992.

Lundy, C.J., & Booth, D. Interpretation: Working With Scripts. Toronto: Harcourt Brace, 1983.

Martin, R.A. *Field-based Preservice Teacher Education: Reflections on an Experiment.* McGill Journal of Education, 1990.

Martin, R.A., Hunt G.W. & Anderson, D. Partnerships Between Faculties of Education and Schools: Issues; Problems; and Prospects. Paper presented at the Canadian Society for the Study of Education, Charlottetown, P.E.I., 1990.

Martin, R.A., Hennessy, C.A. & Gibson, C. Involving Classroom Teachers in the Delivery of Preservice Teacher Education Programs: Opportunities and Prospects. Paper presented at CSSE in Ottawa, 1993.

Mehta, Y. Valedictory Address, Aga Kahn University Graduation Ceremony, November 1995.

Miles, M.B. 40 Years of Change in Schools: Some Personal Reflections. Address to Division A (Administration), American Educational Research Association meeting, San Francisco: April, 1992.

Neelands, J. Structuring Drama Work: A Handbook of Available Forms in Theatre and Drama. Cambridge: Cambridge University Press, 1990.

Neufield, B. *Professional Practice Schools in Context: New Mixtures of Institutional Authority,* in M. Levine (ed.), Professional Practice Schools:

Linking Teacher Education and School Reform. New York: Teachers College Press, 1992, pp.133-165.
Noddings, N., & Witherell, C. Stories Lives Tell. New York: Teachers College Press, 1991.
O'Hair, M.J., & S.J. Odell, (eds.) Partnerships in Education: Teacher Education Yearbook II. Association of Teacher Educators and Harcourt Brace, 1994.
Ontario Ministry of Education. The Arts in Ontario Schools: a Discussion Paper. Toronto: the Ministry Arts Group, 1984.
Ontario Ministry of Education. Final Report of the Teacher Education Review Steering Committee, Toronto, 1988.
Paterson, K. The Bridge to Terabithia. New York: Crowell, 1977.
Platt, K. The Boy Who Could Make Himself Disappear. New York: Dell, 1968.
Poole, M. *Establishing a Research Culture*, in Higher Education Research and Development News, 1991.
Portman, P.A. *Barriers to Change in Teacher Education,* in Action in Teacher Education, Vol. 15, No. 1, 1992-3.
Ralph, E.G. *Improving Practicum Supervision: A Canadian Experience,* in Action in Teacher Education, Vol. 15, No. 1, 1992-3.
Reed, D., & Simon D. *Preparing Teachers for Urban Schools: Suggestions from Historically Black Institutions,* in Action in Teacher Education, 8(2), 1991, pp. 30-35.
Registrar's Office, Faculty of Education. Data Analysis of Offers to Teacher Candidates. Unpublished Manuscript, 1994.
Report of the Intermediate/Senior Program Review Committee. Faculty of Education, University of Toronto, 1989.
Report of the Provostial Review Committee of the Faculty of Education. University of Toronto, 1987.
Rolheiser, C. Redesigning Teacher Education: Moving Beyond the Classroom. Paper presented at the American Educational Research Association Annual Conference, NewYork, 1996.
Rolheiser-Bennett, C., Bennett, B. & Stevahn, L. Cooperative Learning: Where Heart Meets Mind. Toronto: Educational Connections, 1991.
Ross, J.A. *Professional Development Schools: Prospects for Institutionalization,* in Teaching & Teacher Education, 11(2), 1995, pp.195-201.
Sarason, S. *Two Cultures Meet: The Queens College-Louis Armstrong Middle School Collaboration,* in S. Trubowitz, J. Duncan, W. Fibkins, P. Longo, & S. Sarason (eds.), When a College Works with a Public School. Boston, MA: Institute for Responsive Education, 1984.
Schein, E.H. Organizational Culture and Leadership. San Francisco: Jossey-Bass, 1985, p. 9.
Sichuan, D. Educating the Reflective Practicioner. San Francisco: Jossey-Bass, 1986.
Slade, P. Child Drama. London: University of London Press, 1954.
Stark, S. *Toward an Understanding of the Beginning Teacher Experience: Curricular Insights for Teacher Education,* in Journal of Curriculum and Supervision, Summer, Vol. 6, No. 4, 1991, pp.294-311.
Statement of Institutional Purpose. University of Toronto, 1988.

Stevens, W. Selected Poems. London: Faber, 1953.
Stiegelbauer, S., Woodruff, E., Meyer, K., Hall, J. Cameron, H. & Pireira, D. Educating the FEUTure: Study Groups, Portfolios, and Micro-teaching. Integrating New Approaches to Educating Teachers. Video and Paper Presentation. J/I Downtown Program, Faculty of Education, University of Toronto, 1994.
Stiegelbauer, S.M. Interview with Michael Fullan. Faculty of Education, University of Toronto. Unpublished Manuscript, Jan. 23, 1995.
Stiegelbauer, S.M. Why We Want To Be Teachers: A Report on a Survey of Offers from the Faculty of Education, University of Toronto. Unpublished Manuscript, 1994.
Stiegelbauer, S.M. Teachers as Agents of Societal Improvement, Sample of Offers, Faculty of Education, University of Toronto. Unpublished Manuscript, 1992.
Stiegelbauer, S.M. Why We're Here: Teachers Talk About Their Reasons for Entering the Profession. Paper presented at the American Educational Research Association (AERA) Meetings, San Francisco, 1992.
Stiegelbauer, S.M. *Change has Changed: Implications for Implementation of Assessments from the Organizational Change Literature,* in Ron J. Anson (ed.), Systemic Reform: Perspectives on Personalizing Education, Washington DC: U.S. Office of Educational Research and Improvement, 1994.
Stiegelbauer, S.M. Preservice Strategies for Lifelong Learning: A Pilot Program in Teacher Education. Faculty of Education, University of Toronto. Submitted for Publication.
Stiegelbauer, S.M. *Change has Changed 2: Implications for Implementation of Assessments,* in Michael B. Kane (ed.), Implementing Performance Assessment: Promises, Problems, and Challenges, New Jersey: Lawrence Erlbaum Associates, Inc., 1995.
The World Bank. Pakistan: Education Sector Review, 1988.
Thiessen, D. Images of the Effective Teacher. Policy paper for the Faculty of Education, University of Toronto, 1993.
Thiessen, D. Things to Live By in Preservice Teacher Education. Unpublished Manuscript.
Tietel, L. *The Impact of Professional Development Partnerships on the Preparation of Teachers,* in Teaching Education, 4 (2), 1992, pp.77-85.
UNITE Project (Urban Network to Improve Teacher Education) Information Brochure. Columbus: Project Unite, 1992.
Vaiga, S.R. *Improving Teaching and Learning Through Peer Coaching.* Education, 115 (2), 1994, pp.241-245.
Wagner, B. Dorothy Heathcote: Drama as a Learning Medium. Washington: National Educational Association, 1976.
Watson, N. Learning Consortium: Year 3 Report. The Learning Consortium, Faculty of Education, University of Toronto, 1991.
Way, B. Development Through Drama. London: Longmans, 1967.
Weiner, L. Preparing Teachers for Urban Schools: Lessons from Thirty Years of School Reform. New York: Teachers College Press, 1993.
Weiss, L. My Teacher Sleeps in School. New York: Penguin, 1988.
Wells, G., et al. Changing Schools from Within: Creating Communities of Inquiry. Toronto: OISE Press, 1994.

Wiedmer, T.L. *Instructional Improvement:The Goal of Clinical Supervision,* in Teacher Education, V. 30 #3, Winter, 1995.
Wilder, L.I. These Happy Golden Years. New York: Harper Trophy, 1943.
Wisniewski, R. The Transformation of a College: University of Tennessee College of Education. Knoxville: University of Tennessee. Unpublished Manuscript.
Woodruff, E. Investigating Collaborative Maieutics: An Examination of Peer-assisted Knowledge-building with Face-to-face and Computer Net-worked Communication Media. Unpublished doctoral thesis. Toronto, 1995.
Zeichner, K.M., & Liston, D.P. *Teaching Student Teachers to Reflect,* in Harvard Educational Review, 57, 1987, pp.23-48.